DANTE AND THE I

Nick Havely examines the connections between Dante, the Franciscans and the Papacy as they appear in the *Commedia,* and presents the poem as one concerned with an often dramatic confrontation between authority and idealism in the Church. Havely draws on a wide range of literary, historical and art-historical sources relating to the controversy about Franciscan poverty during the late thirteenth and early fourteenth centuries. He argues that the Spiritual Franciscans' strict interpretation of evangelical poverty provided the poet with a means of addressing the state of the contemporary Papacy and of imagining the renewal of the Church. He also explores the origins and afterlife of the debate about this form of poverty and Dante's contribution to it. This study will appeal to scholars interested in medieval religious and intellectual history, as well as to readers of Dante's poem and other medieval visionary and political writing.

NICK HAVELY is Professor in the Department of English and Related Literature at the University of York. He is the translator of *Chaucer's Boccaccio* (1980, 1992); editor of *The House of Fame* (1994), *Chaucer's Dream Poetry* (1997) and *Dante's Modern Afterlife* (1998); and author of numerous articles on Italian and English medieval literature, including the chapter on 'Literature in Italian, French and English' in volume VI of *The New Cambridge Medieval History* (2000).

CAMBRIDGE STUDIES IN MEDIEVAL LITERATURE

This series of critical books seeks to cover the whole area of literature written in the major medieval languages – the main European vernaculars, and medieval Latin and Greek – during the period c. 1100–1500. Its chief aim is to publish and stimulate fresh scholarship and criticism on medieval literature, special emphasis being placed on understanding major works of poetry, prose, and drama in relation to the contemporary culture and learning which fostered them.

Recent titles in the series

Rita Copeland *Pedagogy, Intellectuals and Dissent in the Later Middle Ages: Lollardy and Ideas of Learning*
Kantik Ghosh *The Wycliffite Heresy: Authority and the Interpretation of Texts*
Mary C. Erler *Women, Reading, and Piety in Late Medieval England*
D. H. Green *The Beginnings of Medieval Romance: Fact and Fiction, 1150–1220*
J. A. Burrow *Gestures and Looks in Medieval Narrative*
Ardis Butterfield *Poetry and Music in Medieval France: From Jean Renart to Guillaume de Machaut*
Emily Steiner *Documentary Culture and the Making of Medieval English Literature*
William Burgwinkle *Sodomy, Masculinity and Law in Medieval Literature*

A complete list of titles in the series can be found at the end of the volume.

Dante and Virgil (left) confront Guido da Montefeltro as Franciscan in the flames (centre), with Pope Boniface VIII enthroned (right).

DANTE AND THE FRANCISCANS

Poverty and the Papacy in the 'Commedia'

NICK HAVELY

CAMBRIDGE
UNIVERSITY PRESS

CAMBRIDGE UNIVERSITY PRESS
Cambridge, New York, Melbourne, Madrid, Cape Town, Singapore, São Paulo, Delhi

Cambridge University Press
The Edinburgh Building, Cambridge CB2 8RU, UK

Published in the United States of America by Cambridge University Press, New York

www.cambridge.org
Information on this title: www.cambridge.org/9780521833059

First published 2004
This digitally printed version 2008

A catalogue record for this publication is available from the British Library

ISBN 978-0-521-83305-9 hardback
ISBN 978-0-521-09904-2 paperback

'. . . nulla pastorali auctoritate abutens, quoniam divitiae mecum non sunt'.

Dante, *Ep.* II.5

'Bakker has . . . contended that his years in prison were his salvation. He re-read all the scriptures and crucially concluded that the so-called "prosperity preaching" of his P[raise] T[he] L[ord] days – wherein he equated dollar-wealth with godliness – was misguided. [. . .] And donations, believe it or not, are rolling in.'

The Independent on Sunday, 15 June 2003

Contents

Illustrations

Acknowledgements

References in all that follows reflect the extent of my indebtedness to other writers on this subject. Particular thanks are due to a number of scholars, friends and colleagues, notably the late Peter Armour, Mark Balfour, John Barnes, Jacques Berthoud, Peter Biller, the late Charles Davis, Carlo Delcorno, Anne Hudson, Fr Stephen Innes, Christopher Kleinhenz, Alastair Minnis, Marjorie Reeves and Corinna Salvadori Lonergan for comments, advice and assistance of various kinds. Since 1991, panellists and audiences at Dante sessions in the Kalamazoo Congress on Medieval Studies have responded generously to my initial papers on this subject. Of these I should name especially Santa Casciani, Caron Cioffi, Rick Emmerson, Christie Fengler-Stephany, Ron Herzman, Chris Kleinhenz (again), Fr Paul LaChance, Dennis Looney, Claudia Rattazzi Papka, Janet Smarr, Bill Stephany, and Barbara Watts. Parts of Chapters 2–4 have appeared as articles in *Dante Studies* (1992 and 1996), *The Journal of the Institute of Romance Studies* (1994) and *Italian Studies* (1997), and I am grateful to the editors of those journals both for their readers' comments on those articles and for permission to reprint some material from them here. Linda Bree's work as Commissioning Editor and Jackie Warren's as Production Editor has been throughout patient, efficient and perceptive, and the copy editing by Dr Rosemary Williams has been both meticulous and scholarly.

Thanks are also due to the Arts and Humanities Research Board, who funded research leave in the autumn of 2000 and thus enabled this book to reach completion. The basic task of research would have been impossible without the assistance of staff in a number of libraries in Britain, Continental Europe and the USA, and, above all, the librarians of the Taylor Institution in Oxford. And persistence in the task would have been difficult without the stimulus of undergraduate and postgraduate students of Dante at the University of York, for whom the book is written.

The cover illustration from Madrid BN MS 10057 is reproduced with the permission of the Ministerio de Educación, Cultura y Deporte; figure 1 (from MS Ricc. 1005) with the permission of the Direzione, Biblioteca Riccardiana, Florence; figures 2 and 3 (from the Bardi Dossal, Santa Croce, Florence and from the panel in San Francesco, Pescia) with the permission of the Prefettura di Firenze (figure 2) and the Ordine Francescano, Pescia (figure 3); and figures 4 and 5 (from MS Banco Rari 39) with permission of the Direzione, Biblioteca Nazionale Centrale, Florence.

Note on citations, translations and manuscript sources

Quotations from the *Commedia* follow the text established by G. Petrocchi in *'La Commedia': secondo l'antica vulgata* (3 vols., Milan, 1966–7), and those from Dante's other works follow the editions mentioned in the Notes and Bibliography. The Vulgate Bible is cited from the *Biblia Vulgata*, ed. A. Colunga and L. Turrado (4th edn, Madrid, 1965), and the translations are from *The New Jerusalem Bible (Standard Edition)*, general editor H. Wansbrough (London, 1985). All other translations, unless otherwise specified, are my own.

MANUSCRIPTS CONSULTED:

Dante: illustrated manuscripts of the Commedia

Florence, Biblioteca Nazionale, MS Banco Rari 39 (microfiche)
Biblioteca Riccardiana, MS 1005 (slides)
London, British Library, Additional MS 19587
Egerton MS 943
Madrid, Biblioteca Nacional, MS 10057 (microfilm)

Giordano of Pisa: sermons

Oxford, Bodleian Library, MS canon. ital. 132

Petrus Iohannis Olivi: Lectura super Mattheum

Oxford, Bodleian Library, MS New College 49
Lectura super Apocalypsim
Rome, Biblioteca Angelica, MS 382 (microfilm)

Sacrum Commercium sancti Francisci cum domina Paupertate

Oxford, Bodleian Library, MS Canon. misc. 263

Servasanto da Faenza: Liber de Virtutibus et Vitiis

Florence, Biblioteca Nazionale, MS Cod. E.6.1046, conventi soppressi

Vaticinia de summis pontificibus

Florence, Biblioteca Riccardiana, MS 1222.2
Oxford, Bodleian Library, MS Douce 88

Abbreviations

AFH	*Archivum Franciscanum Historicum* (Quaracchi).
ALKG	*Archiv für Literatur- und Kirchengeschichte des Mittelalters*, ed. H. Denifle and F. Ehrle (7 vols.) (Berlin, 1885–1900).
BF	*Bullarium Franciscanum*, ed. J. H. Sbaralea and C. Eubel (5 vols.) (Rome, 1759–1898).
BMS	*Illuminated Manuscripts of the Divine Comedy*, ed. P. Brieger, M. Meiss and C. S. Singleton (2 vols.) (New York and London, 1969).
BR	*Dante Alighieri: La Divina Commedia*, ed. U. Bosco and G. Reggio (3 vols.) (Florence, 1979).
Bull.	*Bullettino della Società Dantesca Italiana.*
1 Celano	Thomas of Celano, *Vita prima.*
2 Celano	Thomas of Celano, *Vita secunda.*
CHMPT	*The Cambridge History of Medieval Political Thought, c.350–c.1450*, ed. J. H. Burns (Cambridge, 1988).
CL	*Dante: Commedia*, ed. A. M. Chiavacci Leonardi (3 vols.) (Milan (2nd edn), 1997).
Conv.	Dante, *Convivio.*
DDJb	*Deutsches Dante-Jahrbuch.*
DE	*The Dante Encyclopedia*, ed. R. Lansing (New York and London, 2000).
DS	*Dante Studies.*
DVE	Dante, *De vulgari eloquentia.*
ED	*Enciclopedia dantesca,* dir. U. Bosco, ed. G. Petrocchi (6 vols.) (Rome, 1970–8).
Ep.	Dante, *Epistolae.*

FF	*Fonti francescane: Scritti e biografie di san Francesco d'Assisi; Cronache e altre testimonianze del primo secolo francescano; Scritti e biografie di santa Chiara d'Assisi*, ed. E. Caroli (Padua, 1990).
GDLI	*Grande Dizionario della Lingua Italiana*, ed. S. Battaglia (19 vols. [continuing], Turin, 1961–).
GSLI	*Giornale storico della letteratura italiana.*
Habig	*St Francis of Assisi: Writings and Early Biographies: An English Omnibus of the Sources for the Life of St Francis*, ed. M. A. Habig (Chicago, 1973).
Inf.	Dante, *Inferno.*
JEH	*Journal of Ecclesiastical History.*
Mon.	Dante, *Monarchia.*
Par.	Dante, *Paradiso.*
PL	*Patrologiae Cursus Completus, Series Latina*, ed. J. P. Migne (221 vols.) (Paris, 1844–64).
PMLA	*Publications of the Modern Language Association.*
Purg.	Dante, *Purgatorio.*
SCH	*Studies in Church History.*
S Th	Aquinas, *Summa Theologiae*, Blackfriars Edition (61 vols.) (New York, 1964–76).

Introduction

Soon after the death of Clement V on 20 April 1314, Dante wrote a letter to the Italian cardinals assembled at Avignon to elect the next pope.[1] Accusing them repeatedly of abusing the 'bride of Christ', of leading the chariot of the Church astray, and of failing to act as true pastors, he cited, as the root cause of their betrayal, their Pharisaical greed and their 'marriage' to avarice.[2] Dante speaks here as 'the least of the sheep in Christ's pastures': the authority of his prophetic voice derives, he claims, not from office or power but from 'the grace of God' and even, he ironically implies, from the condition of poverty itself: 'I have no pastoral authority to abuse, since I have no wealth.'[3]

By the time this letter was written poverty had become a recurrent theme in Dante's work. It had featured in some of his early poems, in texts from the first decade of his exile, in the *Convivio* and the *Inferno*, whilst his concerns in the *Commedia* were coming increasingly to focus upon those who had been called 'the poor with Peter' and upon the role of voluntary or 'evangelical' poverty within a vision of renewed religious and ecclesiastical order.[4] As he acknowledges at the beginning of the *Convivio*, Dante's own poverty was due to the misfortune of

[1] On the dating of the letter (*Ep.* II) to the Avignon cardinals – probably May or June 1314 – see Toynbee (ed.) 1966: 124–6, C. Frugoni 1969: 79–80, and Ahern in *DE* 354.

[2] *Ep.* II. 1 and 4–7; see Toynbee (ed.) 1966: 127, 130–5 and 143–5.

[3] 'Nulla pastorali auctoritate abutens quoniam divitiae mecum non sunt', *Ep.* II. 5.

[4] On the distinction between 'pauperes cum Petro', the voluntary or 'holy' poor, and 'pauperes cum Lazaro', the involuntary or 'truly' poor, see for example Mollat 1986: 103–4 and Wolf 2003: throughout (esp. 4, 7, 37 and 85). Wolf's study (*The Poverty of Riches: St Francis of Assisi Reconsidered*), which appeared when this book was very near completion, is a stimulating (if occasionally over-simplified) account of the ironies of Franciscanism endorsing 'a very specific kind of poverty that only Christians of means could effectively embrace' (37).

exile rather than vocational choice. His developing emphasis upon the value of poverty, however, converges with contemporary arguments on the subject, especially in the contributions of the rigorist, or 'Spiritual', Franciscans to the increasingly acrimonious dispute on that subject. The composition of the *Commedia* also coincides chronologically with periods of papal involvement in the controversy about Franciscan poverty: around 1309–12, when Clement V was formally investigating the Franciscan Spirituals; and from 1317 onwards, when John XXII was actively engaged in suppressing them.[5] Voluntary or evangelical poverty, and the tensions within and around the Franciscan Order, were thus significant and urgent issues for Dante and others of his time. Concern about the Franciscans, poverty and their relationship to ecclesiastical authority forms an important part of the *Commedia's* political vision – a subject with which a substantial amount of modern Dante criticism has been concerned.[6]

The present study aims to extend understanding of the *Commedia*'s politics by reading it in relation to Franciscan controversies, particularly those involving poverty and the role of the Papacy. Its objective is neither to identify Dante as a crypto-Spiritual nor to revive the legend of his 'Franciscan vocation'.[7] What will, however, be acknowledged and explored throughout is what several commentators have described as the 'consonance' between the ideas and language of evangelical poverty in the *Commedia* and in contemporary Franciscan writing.[8] The Franciscan traditions and discourses that informed the controversies about poverty will thus be treated here not as a code but as a context for the reading of the poem. By tracing Dante's indebtedness to certain Franciscan traditions (in visual art, drama and poetry), and his appropriation of certain Franciscan discourses as a way of confronting papal authority, the purpose is also to illuminate some further features of the poet's role as lay and vernacular author.

5 The main guides on this controversy are Lambert 1961 (rev. 1998); Leff 1967 (Part 1); and more recently Burr 1989, 1993 (chs. 9–11) and 2001.

6 Particularly significant here has been the work of Davis (1955 and 1984); Ferrante (1984); Armour (1989); and Scott (1996).

7 On this tradition, see Chapter 1 below, p. 32 with n. 85.

8 See Da Campagnola 1971: 293; also CL 2: 932. The Italian term used in both is *consonanza*. For the view that Franciscan poverty 'colors . . . the entire *Commedia*', see Petrocchi 1967: 51–2.

Franciscan politics are of course intricately entwined with Franciscan piety; but since this book's concern is chiefly with the former, it will not lay stress upon orthodox Franciscan mystical writing, important as this may be for the *Commedia*'s broader cultural context.[9] Its approach to Dante's text will, on the other hand, draw upon a variety of sources for the ecclesiastical politics and the Franciscan culture of the period. It will make use of the main prophetic and polemical texts in the protracted dispute about Franciscan poverty, including the writings of Spirituals, such as Petrus Iohannis Olivi and Ubertino da Casale, and papal pronouncements on the subject, such as those by Nicholas III, Clement V and John XXII. It will also take acount of the various media (such as the early Lives of St Francis, the dramatic *Laude,* panel-paintings, manuscript illustrations) through which images of evangelical poverty were disseminated up to, during and beyond Dante's time.[10]

Within such contexts this approach to the *Commedia* attempts to draw together three of the poem's main concerns. They can be briefly defined as Franciscanism, papal power and the vernacular poet's voice. Their drawing together has been chiefly by means of a concept and context which relates all three: that of evangelical poverty and the authority deriving from it. In the *Commedia* and elsewhere (notably the *Convivio* and the *Monarchia*) Dante's writing explores and relates various kinds of authority – that of the Empire, the Papacy, philosophy and the pagan writers, as well as that of Scripture and the poet.[11] Dante's approach to the contentious issue of Franciscan poverty, I shall argue, forms an intrinsic part of this project. As his view of 'pastoral authority' in the letter to the cardinals implies, evangelical poverty has both scriptural and political dimensions, and the process of authorizing it is, as I hope to show, closely bound up with the lengthy process of authorizing the writer's poetic and prophetic voice.[12]

9 For example, on Bonaventura's *Itinerarium* as an analogue for Dante's journey in the *Commedia,* see Freccero 1961; Hagman 1988; and Scrivano 1989.

10 On the Franciscan art of the period, reference will be made particularly to the work of Miller 1961, Stein 1976, Moleta 1983, Stubblebine 1985, C. Frugoni 1988 and 1993, Goffen 1988, and Cook 1989 and 1999.

11 On kinds of authority (epistemological, institutional and poetic) in medieval thought and in Dante's writing, see Ascoli in *DE,* 72–5. On authority, authorship and Dante, see Minnis 1988: 10–12, 116–17, 214–16, and 279 n. 123; also *ED*, vol. 1, 454–60.

12 On this process, see Hawkins 1999: esp. 66–71. For an early Trecento example of the authorizing of the *Commedia* in prophetic and Scriptural terms, see the Prologue to

To speak of 'authorizing' poverty thus implies that the *Commedia* and other Dantean texts are engaged in several related procedures: first, that of recognizing the value of poverty in individual spiritual terms (as in *canzoni* such as 'Tre donne' and 'Doglia mi reca', in *Conv.* 4, *Purg.* 12 and 20, *Par.* 6 and 11 etc.); secondly, that of representing voluntary poverty as the basis of the Church's and the Papacy's institutional authority (as in *Mon.* 3, *Inf.* 19, *Purg.* 9 and 19, *Par.* 9 and 21 etc.); and finally, that of drawing upon the discourses of voluntary and Franciscan poverty to articulate a vision of history, to portray particular apostolic figures (such as St Peter), and to endow the vernacular writer with prophetic status (as in *Ep.* 11, *Inf.* 19, *Purg.* 32, *Par.* 25 and 27 etc.).

These texts convey a variety of attitudes to poverty, yet a certain progression is discernible in works preceding the *Commedia.* The initial stages of that progression are the subject of Chapter 1. Traditional 'negative' views of poverty as disgrace predominate in Dante's earliest writing, such as the exchange of sonnets with Forese Donati; and they even recur in the midst of *Paradiso.*[13] Conversely, several poems of his early years of exile (such as 'Tre donne' and 'Doglia mi reca') glimpse honour and virtue behind the humiliation; whilst the *Convivio* begins to negotiate a route from the shame bred by the 'parching wind' to the value of poverty's 'unrecognized wealth'. Awareness of the traditions of thought about voluntary poverty was probably fostered in Dante by the 'schools of the religious' to which the *Convivio* refers (2.12.7); and his encounters with the Franciscans at Santa Croce would have intensified awareness of the various confrontations between poverty and power and between the Franciscans and the Papacy. This first chapter thus moves from the view of poverty as shame and disgrace to recognition of its value and authority in the eremitical and Franciscan traditions and in the texts of Dante's early exile.[14] The political implications of this process of 'valuing' poverty are also important both for Dante and for the Franciscans; and the chapter concludes by surveying one further

Guido da Pisa's commentary on the *Inferno*, ed. Jenaro-MacLennan 1974: 124–30, and translated in Minnis and Scott 1991: 469–76 (esp. 470 and 473).

[13] See, for example, Cacciaguida's lines on the hardship of exile in *Par.* 17.55–60, and the comments at the beginning of Chapter 1 below, p. 8.

[14] The work resulting from Michel Mollat's research group, *Etudes sur l'histoire de la pauvreté* (Mollat 1974) is contextually relevant to this whole process; so also are the first two chapters of Bronislaw Geremek's *Poverty: A History* (translated into English in 1994).

part of the context: the Franciscans' relationship with the Papacy and the incipient debate about evangelical poverty. The Papacy's role, the debate about evangelical poverty and related discourses of Franciscan culture constitute the main contexts for the reading of the *Commedia* that is undertaken in the following three chapters, each of which addresses relevant episodes, encounters and developments in one of the poem's three *cantiche*.

Hence, in the *Inferno* we find the Dante persona beginning to challenge and to claim authority (especially in canto 19), by speaking out against the 'avarice of high position' that is said to have beset such popes as Nicholas III, Boniface VIII and Clement V.[15] In the *Inferno* the ideals of evangelical poverty and Franciscanism are, like other religious and political values, defined largely by their absence; hence the portrayal of St Francis himself (at the end of canto 27) significantly gives him no voice. Chapter 2 primarily addresses *Inferno*'s recurrent concern with the (broadly defined) 'avarice' of the clergy, giving particular attention to three popes (Nicholas III, Boniface VIII and Clement V) and their Franciscan contexts. It also shows how the emergent Franciscanism here contributes to the confidence of the pilgrim's stance and voice and prepares for his ascent and the extension of his vision in the next *cantica*.

Progress through Dante's Purgatory is on a number of occasions signalled by Franciscan figures, images and allusions; and these are traced in Chapter 3. In *Purgatorio* 12, the citing of the first Beatitude ('Beati pauperes spiritu') carries implications for the whole ascent of the mountain – as does the Franciscan-like habit of the angelic gatekeeper in canto 9. Especially in Purgatory proper (from canto 9 on), souls are envisaged as a restored religious order – a community *in via* which includes the pilgrim as member. The *cantica*'s concerns with poverty, community and authority are intensified, for example, by the portrayal of a Pope (Hadrian V) who repents of avarice, addresses Dante as 'frate' (brother) and urges him to 'rise up'. 'Brotherhood' and the sense of religious community also actively foster the pilgrim's developing vision of the Church's history – a vision which culminates in the apocalyptic scenes of canto 32 – where the 'sense of an ending' converges in some respects with Spiritual Franciscan eschatology, especially that of

[15] For the origin of the term 'avarice of high position', see Chapter 2 below, p. 46 with n. 4.

Petrus Iohannis Olivi's *Lectura super Apocalypsim*. Here and elsewhere *Purgatorio* has structural and thematic parallels with another important Franciscan text, the *Sacrum commercium*; and Chapter 3 will show how both texts engage with the issues of poverty and avarice in comparable ways.

Dante's continuing ascent through the *Paradiso* is accompanied from its early stages by the celebration of poverty and of Franciscan ideals; and Chapter 4 begins by identifying three 'forerunners' of Dante's St Francis (Piccarda, Romieu and Folquet) in cantos 3, 6 and 9. It then shows how, in the 'canto of St Francis' itself (canto 11), Dante draws upon the rich textual and visual traditions of Franciscanism – traditions that for the vernacular poet furnish an important link with the popular culture of his time. *Paradiso* is not, however, solely devoted to celebration. The discrepancy between the perfected circles of Paradise and the wild trajectory of humanity's course generates tension throughout the *cantica*; and the *Commedia* here continues to register the impact of contemporary issues and controversies. Like the *Monarchia* (which may have been composed near the same time), the *Paradiso* concerns itself with the earthly order, the founding principles of the Church and the Papacy's claims to temporal wealth and power. The later stages of Chapter 4 thus investigate the anti-apostolic role of the last pope of Dante's lifetime, John XXII (especially in cantos 18 and 27); and they present the papal persecution of the Spiritual Franciscans (beginning in 1317) as part of the context for the apocalyptic voices and visions towards the end of the *Paradiso*. Voices that concentrate such concerns by challenging the contemporary leadership of the Church include the hermit Peter Damian (canto 21), the apostle Peter (canto 27), and Beatrice (at the end of canto 30). These voices and this challenge are subsumed into the voice of the poet who has to return to earth, as St Peter says, 'because of the burden of mortality' (*Par.* 27. 64).

Many previous accounts of Franciscan influences on and parallels to Dante's work have contributed to this study. Nearly a century ago Felice Tocco (who was to go on to explore the 'question of poverty' more widely in the Trecento) presented a reading of *Purgatorio* 32 that related Dante's apocalyptic vision there explicitly and persuasively to the eschatology of the Spiritual Franciscans' mentor, Petrus Iohannis

Olivi.[16] Later scholars – notably Raoul Manselli and Charles Davis – continued (in the 1950s and onwards) to extend awareness of this polemical context for Dantean prophecy; others have continued to explore the relationship between mendicant and imperial ideas in Dante's reformist vision; and much important work on Dante and Franciscanism has since appeared in Italy, the United States and Britain.[17] In setting out to explore aspects of Franciscanism throughout the *Commedia*, the present work takes account of recent research on Franciscan literature, culture and ideology, and it seeks to give due weight to both the politics and the poetics of poverty in Dante's work.

[16] See Tocco 1902.

[17] See especially Manselli 1959 and 1965a; Davis 1957, 1963 and 1984; and Park 1970. Important recent research can be found in the two collections of essays edited in Mellone (ed.) 1987 and 1992; in Comollo's 1990 study of Dante and religious dissidence; and in the articles and essays by Herzman 1982 and 1992, Moleta 1983, Barański 1994, Mineo 1993 and 1998, and Meekins (*DE* 416–19). For essential recent work on Franciscan poverty in general, see especially: Burr 1981, 1989, 1992, 1993 and 2001; Lambertini 1999 and 2000; and Wolf 2003.

I

From shame to honour: Tuscan and Franciscan poverty

Poverty in medieval society generated a variety of co-existing attitudes and doctrines; and in this period an individual writer's views on the subject can be complex and even inconsistent.[1] Variety and complexity continue to be evident in Dante's mature discourse of poverty. In two cantos of *Paradiso*, for instance, he can both celebrate the imagined austerity of twelfth-century Florence (*Par.* 15.97–132) and deplore the actual hardship of being penniless in Verona (17.55–60). Such diversity is also evident in what we know of his cultural and intellectual milieu during the decade before his exile in 1301/2. In the 1290s he was absorbing the influences of Tuscan burlesque and experimenting with low-style encounters through mockery of his friend Forese's imagined penury. At the same time (according to *Conv.* 2.12) he was frequenting the 'schools of the religious' and becoming aware of the teaching and ideology of Franciscan scholars such as Petrus Iohannis Olivi and Ubertino da Casale.

Tuscan vernacular literature and Franciscan culture and politics in Central Italy are thus the main contexts that will here need to be taken into account when considering how Dante in his early writing – from his sonnets of the 1290s to the *Convivio* and the *canzoni* of the first years of exile – negotiates a wide range of ideas about poverty: as persecutress and bringer of shame, and as source of 'ignota ricchezza', 'unrecognized wealth'.

[1] On 'the great variety of attitudes and doctrines concerning poverty which existed and developed side by side in medieval society' see Geremek 1997: 31; and on further complexities and contradictions in individual attitudes, see Manselli in Mollat 1974: 649.

POVERTY AND SHAME IN TUSCAN POETRY

The notion of involuntary poverty as a moral and social danger, or even as a fate worse than death, is, as Geremek has noted, 'frequent in Italian literature of the fourteenth century'.[2] In rather more detail, Manselli has surveyed Florentine Trecento writing on poverty and has argued for a 'transformation of values' on the subject in the course of the century.[3] Manselli sees this transformation as conditioned partly by socio-economic factors and partly by cultural ones, such as the hostility to the Spiritual Franciscans that is evident in the anonymous *canzone* (perhaps of the 1320s and attributed to Giotto) 'Molti son que' che lodan povertate'.[4] This 'transformation of values', which (for Manselli) is marked particularly by the *canzone*, is perceived to be in sharp contrast to the attitude of Dante, for whom 'poverty is an *ideal* which has to be affirmed and defended, because greed is a vice that poisons the whole world'.[5] As Manselli recognized, such transformations take time to mature, and the attitudes and values that it is convenient for us to categorize are 'not always clear and consistent, even in the same individual'.[6] He did not, however, seek to trace any of the roots of the 'negative' Trecento views on poverty, nor did he consider their possible implications for Dante's developing attitude. The formation and articulation of such views in the work of Tuscan writers of the Duecento will need to be reckoned with, before they are considered in relation to Dante's early work.

Concern about the *poveri vergognosi* (the shamefaced poor) is not hard to find among the poets of this period. For instance, a late Duecento collection of proverbs declares that 'the shamefaced poor man keeps his worth hidden'.[7] The eclipsing of worth is a consequence of poverty that Dante will stress in *Convivio* 1.3, but the subject is also developed in various less solemn ways by other Tuscan writers and even (as we shall see) by Dante himself. The theme seems indeed to be particularly associated with the comic and parodic work of the *giullari* ('jongleurs') of the later

[2] Geremek 1997: 31. [3] Manselli in Mollat 1974: 653.

[4] Manselli in Mollat 1974: 649; Sapegno 1952: 439–42. See also below, p. 14 and n. 24.

[5] Manselli in Mollat 1974: 645. [6] Manselli in Mollat 1974: 649.

[7] 'Povero vergognoso / suo valor tien nascoso'. The lines occur in the 'Proverbi' of 'Garzo', no. 161, in Contini 1960: 2. 307.

Duecento and early Trecento, and perhaps its fullest development in this form is in the burlesque 'Canzone del fi' Aldobrandino'.[8]

Known only by this patronymic and by one manuscript, the writer of this *canzone* stages what could be seen as a comic equivalent of the scenario at the end of Dante's *Epistola* 2 (where Lady Poverty is seen as a 'persecutrix' who, like some romance enchantress, holds her knight in prison). The 'fi' Aldobrandino' represents himself as betrothed to the cadaverous and gouty 'mon[n]a Povertade', whose gloomy gang of personified relatives (Sorrow, Beggary, Longing, Distress etc.) and leaky, comfortless house he describes in some detail; and the scenario takes on an intimately sinister edge as the lady possessively keeps her arms round her lover's neck all the time, runs mad with jealousy if anyone wealthy approaches him, and insists on feeding, dressing and undressing him herself (ll. 61–75). Discourse of involuntary poverty thus converges in this *canzone* with that of vernacular misogyny. Lady Poverty – who had appeared by this time as a romance heroine in the Franciscan *Sacrum Commercium* and was to do so again in *Paradiso* 11 – here becomes a kind of *fabliau* wife – abject in some respects, demonized in others. Her luckless fiancé himself is eventually portrayed in the poem's final stanza as an outcast figure, from whom people flee and hide 'as they would from a rabid dog' (ll. 95–105).[9]

This final stanza and much else in the 'Canzone del fi' Aldobrandino' have some affinities with the wry representations of the penniless and shamefaced lover in the work of the Sienese poet Cecco Angiolieri (c.1260–1312). Lack of *danari*, *fiorini*, *aquilini*, or *lo ritondo* ('the round stuff') is a constant burden in Cecco's sonnets; and the man without money speaks in them of being avoided, ignored and treated like a leper and of slinking around with his head held low, 'more shamefaced than a dog from out of town' ('più vergognoso ch'un can foretano').[10] His complaint-sonnet 'Or udite, signor, s'i ho ragione' plays some further

[8] Ed. Contini 1960: 2. 437–40.

[9] For this part of the scenario in the *canzone*, see ll. 31–60; Contini (1960: 2. 435) places these within the tradition of the *Roman de la Rose*. On the broader traditions of representing Poverty as a woman, see Wolf 2003: 31. Lady Poverty in the Franciscan *Sacrum commercium* describes her repellent and outcast status by citing Job 30: 14: 'abominentur me et fugiunt longe a me, et faciem meam conspuere non verentur'; see Brufani 1990: 164.

[10] Sonnet 76.1–2 ('Quando non ho denar") in Cavalli 1975; and sonnets 87.4 and 92.6 in Lanza 1990.

variations on this theme, as the penniless lover laments his change of status, now that Poverty is his schoolmistress and his lady despises him more than a thief ('mi fa vergogna più ch'a un ladrone', l. 80). It had once been otherwise for Cecco's complainant, as he acknowledges in the sonnet's sestet, but only because of the 'great power and worth that I held in my purse':

> Quand'ei denar, non me solea venire,
> poi ch'avea en borsa la gran degnitate.[11]

Penniless lovers are of course frequently encountered in lyric before and after Cecco and the *giullari*. But the emphasis on the consequent disgrace and loss of status in these poems by Dante's contemporaries is particularly poignant; and one reason for that may be the particularly public nature of Italian urban life, which made lack of social recognition a more immediately and obviously shaming experience.[12]

Dante's own 'lower' style in some of his early *rime* at points evokes his Sienese contemporary, Cecco, as well as the colloquial register of earlier Florentine poets, such as Rustico di Filippo.[13] This is particularly noticeable in the six sonnets of the *tenzone* ('flyting') between him and the friend whom he is later to encounter on the terrace of the gluttons in *Purgatorio*: Forese Donati (d. 1296). The *tenzone* has been dated c. 1293–6, although it could be even earlier than that, as its subject and style suggest.[14] On both sides there clearly seems to be an interest in experimenting with the themes and language of the *giullari*, and this extends here also to the representation of poverty and public disgrace.[15] The roles assigned to each other by the two participants have a certain ironic appropriateness in view of Dante's later experiences and preoccupations as an exile. Dante himself is here represented by Forese as a client of various charitable institutions who is ill placed to talk of anyone else's poverty, and, according to one possible interpretation, as the cowardly son of a usurer.[16]

[11] Ed. Lanza 1990: no. 63, ll. 10–11.
[12] On the public nature of everyday Italian urban life in this period (and its relationship to private experience and personal identity) see Martines 1983: 97–102.
[13] See, for instance, Contini 1970a: 82, and Usher in Brand and Pertile 1996: 6.
[14] On the *tenzone* with Forese, see Stäuble 1995: 151–70. For recent discussion of its authenticity, see Durling in Dante Alighieri 2003: 614–16.
[15] Stäuble 1993: 152–6. [16] Contini 1970a: nos. 27a and 28a.

Dante's caricature of his friend in this exchange is more ruthless; and it is particularly interesting in the present context. In the opening sonnet of the exchange, he imagines Forese's poverty in terms of his wife's physical and sexual privations, and in the third he portrays him as a glutton and spendthrift, heading for the debtors' prison or the thieves' gallows.[17] The sixth of these sonnets responds to Forese's previous picture of Dante in shameful penury, and it returns that taunt with interest.[18] Dante here develops an earlier hint (from the third of his sonnets) about Forese's prospective life of crime into a vivid street scene, in which this shabby desperado confronts the prosperous and apprehensive burghers of Florence:

> 'E già la gente si guarda da lui,
> chi ha borsa a lato, là dov'e' s'appressa,
> dicendo: 'Questi c'ha la faccia fessa,
> è piuvico ladron negli atti sui.'
>
> ['And already people with purses at their belts are looking askance at him as he comes by, saying 'This scarfaced character looks like a notorious thief.'][19]

Dante's adjective *piuvico* (= *pubblico*, l. 8) here emphasizes the stigma deriving from Forese's supposed straits, and it suggests that the poet is also exploring ways of representing poverty as public humiliation that had been mapped out by previous Tuscan writers, such as Cecco Angiolieri and the 'Fi' Aldobrandino'.

Negative representations of poverty were also available to Dante in the French tradition, and especially in the *Roman de la Rose*. Dispute still seems to simmer over the issue of the attribution to Dante himself of *Il Fiore* (summarizing the action of the *Roman* in 232 sonnets), or of the incomplete *Detto d'amore*, which explores some of the themes in a more meditative way.[20] But, whether or not he actually wrote these versions, they both (and especially *Il Fiore*) provide further evidence of writing, or re-writing, about wealth and poverty in his immediate Tuscan milieu.

17 Contini 1970a: nos. 26 and 27.
18 Contini 1970a: nos. 28 and 27a, ll. 12–14.
19 Contini 1970a: no. 28, ll. 5–8.
20 On the attribution of *Il Fiore*, see Contini 1970b and 1973; a somewhat sceptical view of the attribution is taken by Usher in Brand & Pertile 1996: 7 and an emphatically hostile one by Lanza 1991. For a full bibliography, see Rossi 1996: xxix–xxxviii.

Since *Il Fiore* begins at the point where the narrator is smitten by Love, it omits the original's initial portrait of Poverty and Avarice, along with all the other personified figures painted on the wall outside the allegorical garden. Engagement with those subjects occurs at three main stages in the sequence: the encounters with Wealth (*Ricchezza*) in sonnets 71–7, 79, 83 and 85–6; the discourse of False Seeming (*Falsembiante*) in 88–127; and the portrayal of The Old Woman (*La Vecchia*), especially in 152–3, 159–60 and 167–9. *Ricchezza*, in *Il Fiore*, is initially introduced as guarding the route of Extravagant Gifts (*Troppo Donare*), which is the 'fast track' ('via . . . avaccia') to success in love (70.5–14 and 71.1). Pleas from the impoverished Lover are rebuffed by her in terms which prefigure those of Charon's refusal to ferry Dante across the Acheron:

> Quella mi disse: 'Tu se' mio ribello;
> per altra via andrai, ché sarà lasso
> innanzi che n'abatti un sol crinello.'
>
> [And she said to me: 'You're one of my people; you'll have to take a different route, and you'll be worn out before you break down a single one of its battlements.'][21]

Wealth is listed among the God of Love's *baronia* (79, ll. 2) but is not really on his side either, since she eventually refuses to support one whom she considers to be still in thrall to Poverty (83, ll. 5–14); and this leads to a further realignment, with *Amor* swearing vengeance against her and *uomini ricchi*, and declaring himself the lord and ally of *uomini pover'* (85), whilst his *baronia* pledge the active support of 'ladies and maidens' against the wealthy, 'so that the sharpest of them will be fleeced' (86, ll. 5–8). Wealth (presumably the desire for wealth: avarice) is thus idealistically opposed to Love, as it is later to be opposed to nobility in *Convivio* 4.[22]

On the other hand, the figures of *Falsembiante* and *La Vecchia* in their different ways adopt pragmatic attitudes comparable to the 'negative' views of poverty that have been sampled so far. False Seeming's hypocritical attack on the hypocrisy of those who praise poverty taps a vein of

[21] *Il Fiore*, sonnet 76, ll. 12–14; compare *Inf.* 3. 88–92 and see Bassermann in Contini 1965: 768–73.

[22] '[L]e divizie . . . non possono causare nobilitade perché sono vili' ('Riches cannot determine nobility because they are base', *Conv.* 4.10.7).

argument that runs wide and deep in the antifraternal tradition, from Guillaume de Saint-Amour (and the *Roman* itself) onwards to Jean d'Anneux and Richard Fitzralph.[23] As articulated in *Il Fiore*, however, and especially in sonnets 89–90 and 106–9, these views quite clearly form part of a Tuscan vernacular tradition which influenced Dante and later Trecento writers, and to which Dante contributed. For instance, the sonnet 'E' sì vanno lodando la poverta' (*Fiore* 90) could well have provided a starting-point for the anti-Spiritual canzone of the 1320s: 'Molti son que' che lodan povertate'.[24] The ideas and expressions of *Falsembiante* and the canzone also converge at the point where the vices deriving from poverty are described. 'Di peccare è via' ('It is the path to sin'), says the *canzone*,

> facendo spesso a' giudici far fallo,
> e d'onor donna e damigella spoglia,
> e fa far furto forza e villania
> e spesso usar bugia,
> e ciascun priva d'onorato stallo.

> [often making judges go astray; it strips ladies and young women of honour; it leads to theft, violence, base conduct and habitual lying; and it deprives any [who suffer from it] of honourable status.][25]

In his account of these lines, Manselli rightly compares them with the well-known passage from a work by Dante's contemporary, Francesco da Barberino, the *Documenti d'Amore*:

> Fa spessamente poverta fallire
> richeça insuperbire
> dea dunqua luom desire
> aver contento del comune stato
> pero che piu securo e piu laudato.

> [Poverty often leads to disaster and wealth to excessive pride; so one should seek contentment in the middle state, which is safer and more honourable.][26]

[23] This aspect of the antifraternal tradition is traced by Szittya 1986: esp.47–50, 88–9, 126–8, 140–4 and 208–9.

[24] See above, p. 9 and n. 4. For discussion of this canzone, its possible authorship (by Giotto?) and its 'anti-pauperism', see Barnes 1986: 19–22.

[25] Sapegno 1952: 440, ll. 18–23.

[26] Francesco da Barberino, *Documenti d'Amore*, ed. Egidi 1905–27: Part 2, Rule 67.

However, we also need to take into account two things: first, the common source of both passages in Proverbs 30: 8–9; and secondly the fact that *Falsembiante*, following the *Roman* and Guillaume de Saint-Amour, had previously cited and expounded the biblical text and concluded that

> Colui cui povertà tien in dolore,
> convien che ssia ladrone, o muor d'envia,
> o serà falsonier o mentitore.
>
> [One who is afflicted by poverty must need become a thief, or die of envy, or become a forger or a liar.][27]

The Dantean *Il Fiore* thus stands at an intermediary point between the debate about poverty and mendicancy in the *Roman* (and in Guillaume de Saint-Amour) and the subsequent writing on the subject by the Trecento moralists and satirists. Writers like Francesco da Barberino and the author of the anti-Spiritual *canzone* may well have also known the *Roman* in the original, but on such Tuscan readers the epigrammatic summary of its arguments at points like the sestet of *Il Fiore* 109 is also likely to have made an impact.[28]

Falsembiante's views (and those of other figures in *Il Fiore*) are also relevant to Dante's writing about poverty from the 1290s onwards, whether or not we identify Dante as the author of the sequence. As a citizen of one of the biggest towns in Europe (and one that had been stricken by famine early in his own lifetime), he did not, for sure, need to read the *Roman de la Rose* or even Proverbs to know that poverty might lead to theft.[29] Nonetheless, in the *tenzone* with Forese, Dante's fantasy about his friend's spendthrift ways leading him to penury and thence to a life of crime follows a literary style that already existed in Tuscan *borghese* poetry and also characterizes certain passages of *Il Fiore*.

Both *Il Fiore* and another possibly Dantean poem, the *Detto d'Amore*, moreover, touch on some concepts and images of poverty that Dante was to develop later in the *Convivio* and the *Commedia*. The loss or lack

[27] *Il Fiore*, sonnet 109, ll. 12–14.

[28] The single manuscript of *Il Fiore* (MS H 438 in the Bibliothèque de la Faculté de Médecine at Montpellier) is dated by Contini (following E. Cassamassima) to the late thirteenth or early fourteenth century; see Contini 1984: liv–lv.

[29] On food shortages in Italian cities in Dante's time, see Mollat 1986: 158.

of worth experienced by the poor is explicitly and personally recognized by Dante in *Convivio* 1.3.5. Proverbial wisdom on this subject is drawn upon, for example, by *La Vecchia* (The Old Woman) in *Il Fiore* when she emphasizes the worthlessness of the pauper (169, l. 2). More extensive development of similar ideas can be found in the advice that *Ricchezza* gives the lover in the *Detto d'Amore*. At points here *Ricchezza*'s language approaches closely the burlesque style of the 'Canzone del Fi' Aldobrandino'. Thus, she describes Poverty as the maidservant of Mad Extravagance who will even take the socks off anyone who gets involved with her (ll. 318–24 and 353–4); she claims that Poverty has a son called Theft, who will lead the unwary to the gallows and leave them dancing in the wind (ll. 333–42); and she argues that Poverty will cause her victim to lose all respect among friends and family (ll. 349–60). In short, according to the *Detto*, 'Povertat' è . . . / d'ogne dolor la somma', the worst of afflictions (ll. 331–2). Poverty's portrayal here outlines in a burlesque way features of the experience that Dante addresses both in the sardonic *tenzone* with Forese (penury leading to theft) and in *Convivio*'s more deeply felt account of how *la dolorosa povertade* deprives her victim of purpose, status and value.

A somewhat more sober tone is adopted from the start by the *Convivio* in its treatment of poverty. Dante's approach to the subject here is consonant with his later stoical and ascetic treatment of the subject and with the process whereby the very thing that deprives the writer's works of value (*Conv.* 1.3.5) comes itself to be valued (*Conv.* 4.12–13). Midway in the decade between the *tenzone* with Forese and the composition of the *Convivio* comes the beginning of Dante's exile, and there is evidence to suggest a significant shift in the nature of his representation of poverty during these years.

VALUING POVERTY: THE POETRY OF EXILE

> Veramente io sono stato legno sanza vela e sanza governo, portato a diversi porti e foci e liti dal vento secco che vapora la dolorosa povertade; e sono apparito a li occhi a molti . . . nel cospetto de' quali non solo mia persona invilio, ma di minor pregio si fece ogni opera, sì già fatta, come quella che fosse a fare.

> [Indeed, I have been a sail-less, rudderless boat, driven to various ports, harbours and shores by the parching wind that blows from grievous poverty; and I have been exposed to the gaze of many . . . who now consider that not only has my person been diminished but that everything I have done or am yet to do has become of less worth.] (*Conv.* 1.3.5)

'Grievous poverty', as a disorientating and demeaning consequence of exile, forms an important part of Dante's self-image near the opening of the *Convivio.* Similar self-presentation can be found in his letter of about the same time, describing his sudden poverty, caused by exile and characterizing it as a 'savage persecutress' ('effera persecutrix'; *Ep.* 2.7). It prefigures the more specific imagery of deprivation and desiccation through which he later represents the experience of exile: the salt taste of others' bread and the hardness of the trek up and down their stairs (*Par.* 17. 58–60). In placing Dante among those who have come down in the world – those that fourteenth-century Florentine charities would call *poveri vergognosi* – the passage also evokes the horror of exile, impoverishment and loss of status that can also be found in other urban vernacular poets of his region and period.[30]

Exile occasionally features in the poetry of Dante's more immediate circle, the *stilnovisti*: for example in poems by Gianni Alfani (b. 1272/83) and Cino da Pistoia (?1265–1337) as a way of expressing the lady's distance from the lover.[31] Cino is also at several points a little more literal and specific about the causes and effects of his *greve essilio* from Pistoia.[32] And among the sixty-one sonnets attributed to the 'Amico di Dante' in a thirteenth-century manuscript, one seems to focus quite vividly upon the degradation and isolation that result from being poor amongst strangers:

[30] The term *poveri vergognosi* occurs, for example, in Giovanni Villani's *Nuova Cronica* (ed. Porta 1990–1): Bk 11, ch. 163; see also Lesnick 1989: 23 and 25, and Geremek 1997: 24.

[31] Gianni Alfani, *ballate* nos. iv (esp. ll. 10 and 17) and vi (esp. l. 3) in Contini 1960: 2. 610 and 613; and Cino da Pistoia's better-known *canzone* 'La dolce vista e'l bel guardo soave' (esp. ll. 9 and 17–18), Contini 1960: 631. For discussion of 'the troping of the political condition of exile' in Tuscan poetry of this time, see Keen 2000.

[32] Cino, 'La dolce vista', ll. 24–7, in Contini 1960: 2. 631–2, and his sonnets, no. cxix, Contini 1960: 680 and no. cxxx in Contini 1970a: 254.

ed or mi trovo in loco, che malvagio
mi tegno ch'a la gente mi discovra.

[and now I find myself in a place where I seem too contemptible to be seen in public.][33]

In his prose works during exile Dante refers to his condition and its consequences – not only in the *Convivio* and *Epistolae*, as we have seen, but also in *De vulgari eloquentia* (1.6). In his verse the subject is also touched upon at several prominent points before its emergence as a major theme in the *Commedia*. Thus, for example, one of his sonnets addressed to Cino acknowledges the wretchedness of the place where he now is.[34] And the end of his *canzone montanina* ('Amor, da che convien pur ch'io mi doglia') portrays his exclusion from a hostile Florence in terms very close to those used at the opening of *Paradiso* 25.[35]

Amongst the poems that precede Dante's *Commedia*, there are, however, two which are particularly significant from this point of view. These are the two *canzoni* that probably date from early in his exile and may have been destined for commentary in the *Convivio*: 'Tre donne intorno al cor mi son venute' and 'Doglia mi reca ne lo cor ardire'.[36] Of these two, it is the enigmatic and evocative 'Tre donne' which more explicitly addresses the issues of exile and poverty. Like Cino in 'La dolce vista' (which was probably written at about the same time), Dante here refers to the political divisions which have caused his exile.[37] He also portrays the main personified figures of the poem as themselves exiles. The three women (representing aspects of Justice) who gather around the 'home' of Dante's heart (l. 17) are each said to be downcast, weary and 'banished' (*discacciata*, l. 10), and their conduct as they receive the God of Love's prophecy is later seen as exemplary for the banished narrator himself, in lines which have been seen as constituting the most dramatic gesture in the poem.[38]

33 Contini 1960: 2. 755, ll. 7–8.

34 Contini 1970a: 143, ll. 7–8.

35 In lines 76–84 of the *canzone montanina* the terms *crudeltate* and *fuor di sé mi serra* particularly recall *Par.* 25.4.

36 Ed. Contini 1970a: nos 47 and 49.

37 'Tre donne', ll. 101–5; compare Cino, 'La dolce vista', ll. 24–7.

38 Martinez in Cachey 1995: 118.

E io, che ascolto nel parlar divino
consolarsi e dolersi
cosí alti dispersi,
l'essilio che m'è dato, onor mi tegno.

[And I, hearing these noble refugees comforted and grieved by the god's speech, consider the exile imposed on me to be an honour.] (ll. 73–6)

Accepting exile as an 'honour' is consonant with the paradoxical way in which the *canzone* comes to value and celebrate poverty. The figure of universal Justice is portrayed as 'dishevelled and barefoot' ('discinta e scalza', l. 26); she describes herself as poorly clothed and adorned (l. 36); and the God of Love goes on to evoke a state of the world in which other virtues are similarly impoverished (ll. 63–4). The imagery and vocabulary here anticipate the terms in which Dante is to celebrate the austerity of early Florence and the poverty of the Apostles and Franciscans in *Paradiso* 11, 17 and 21.[39] For instance, the adjective *scalza* ('barefoot'), describing the impoverished appearance of Justice (l. 26 of the *canzone*) is relatively rare in Dante's vocabulary, and his usage will need to be considered more fully with regard to images of Franciscan poverty in *Paradiso* 11 (80 and 83) and 12 (131).[40] Moreover, later in *Paradiso scalzo* also describes the Apostles Peter and Paul as they go receiving alms 'da qualunque ostello' (*Par.* 21.127–9) – a scene which perhaps recalls not only Dante's barefoot figure of Justice in the *canzone*, but also the impoverished state of other virtues who are here said to 'go begging' ('mendicando vanno', l. 64).

'Tre donne' may well date from a time when the actual effects of Dante's exile were becoming sharply apparent: when (possibly around 1304) he was also writing of Poverty not as a bride to be embraced but as a

[39] Martinez alludes to the possible connections between the meagre clothing of Drittura in l. 36 and that of Cacciaguida's primitive Florentines (see, for instance, *Par.* 15. 100–2 and 112–17). He goes on to argue that '[t]he same paradox that makes Drittura [universal Justice], as a virtue, "sol di sé donna" ["mistress in and of herself", l. 26]' operates here to exalt poverty in a manner reminiscent of Franciscan values. Indeed Dante's Drittura has much in common with later representation in the *Commedia* of Poverty as the bride of Francis: a figure whose very loathsomeness because poor and outcast triggers a paradoxical language of sexual desire' (Cachey 1995:, 121 and 124 with n. 60).

[40] See below, Chapter 4, pp. 132–9.

'persecutress' (*Ep.* 2.7) and as source of a wind that withers what it blows upon (*Conv.* 1.3.5). As such, this *canzone*'s paradoxical recognitions of the potential value of its impoverished personifications can be seen as playing a particularly significant part in the formation of the poet's more idealistic discourse of poverty. This formative process is also evident (if less obviously) in another moral *canzone* of the early period of Dante's exile.

'Doglia mi reca' is addressed to Bianca Giovanna, who, as daughter of Conte Guido of Poppi, was of a family that gave Dante support in the early years of his banishment from Florence. As Contini points out, it is similar to 'Tre donne' in its metrical and strophic form, but it is considerably longer and much more knotty and discursive in style.[41] It begins on a relatively lofty philosophical level, outlining to its feminine audience the relationship between beauty and virtue, whilst warning of wide-ranging moral criticism to come (ll. 3–6). It finds its focus and idiom, however, only when it descends from the general to the particular ('del tutto / in parte' [ll. 54–5]) and when, in the fourth to the sixth of its seven main stanzas, it addresses the subject of avarice (ll. 64–126).

Representation of avarice is a key feature of Dante's developing discourse of poverty; and from this point of view 'Doglia mi reca' points forward both to the *Convivio* (which Dante may have been beginning to write at the time of composing the *canzone*) and the *Commedia* (for instance, *Inf.* 7 and 19 and *Purg.* 19). Indeed, it has been thought likely that this *canzone* could have been the one that Dante had in mind to comment upon in the projected fifteenth and last treatise of the *Convivio*, when he returned to the subject of *liberalitade* (as promised in *Conv.* 1.8.18).[42] Thus the *canzone* vividly portrays 'l'avaro seguitando avere', the avaricious man in the restless and futile pursuit of possessions, seeking to attain an amount that recedes before him into infinity (ll. 64–73). In doing so, it parallels the endless quest of *l'avaro maladetto* in *Convivio* 3 and 4.[43]

41 Contini 1970a: 182. 42 Contini 1970a: 182.

43 *Conv.* 3.15.9, also 4.12.6–7. On avarice in 'Doglia mi reca', see also Armour 1994: 10 and Boyde 2000: 154–5. Armour notes the echo of the *canzone*'s portrayal of the restless avaricious man (69 and 74–84) in the 'first economic image of the *Commedia*' (*Inf.* 1. 55–8).

Although the main opposition in 'Doglia mi reca' is between avarice and virtue or liberality, in one of its more laconic and enigmatic passages it begins to present a contrast between avaricious wealth and virtuous poverty. Having developed at some length the notion of the avaricious soul as the servant, rather than the master, of wealth, the speaker now becomes yet more dramatic and graphic in gesture and imagery:

> Qui si raddoppia l'onta,
> se ben si guarda là dov'io addito,
> falsi animali, a voi ed altrui crudi,
> che vedete gir nudi
> per colli e per paludi
> omini innanzi cui vizio è fuggito,
> e voi tenete vil fango vestito.
>
> [Here your shame will be redoubled if people follow the direction in which I am pointing, you false creatures, cruel to yourselves and to others – who can see men before whom vice flees going naked across the hills and the marshes, whilst you keep your own dirt dressed up.] (ll. 99–105)

Imagining virtuous souls as nude fell-runners and bogtrotters may seem somewhat bizarre even for this *canzone*, but this modulation of imagery touches on some ideas that have been and are to be of considerable importance in Dante's valuation of poverty. Contrasts between the values of the world and those of the wise – between outward ornament and dress (*vestimenta*) and inner wisdom (*senno*) – are explored in another *canzone* that might also have been destined for commentary in the *Convivio*: 'Poscia ch'Amor del tutto m'ha lasciato' (especially ll. 32–8). Moreover, the dishevelled near-nudity of *Drittura* in the 'Tre donne' – with her 'torn gown' and 'poverty of dress and ornament' – makes a similar point (ll. 27 and 36). And, like 'Tre donne', 'Doglia mi reca' could also be said to be pointing forward to the *Commedia*'s representations of primitive Florentine austerity and evangelical poverty – especially the latter. The virtuous *nudi omini* roaming the hills and marshes in this *canzone* are thus the forerunners of Dante's barefoot Apostles and Franciscans in *Paradiso* 11 and 21 – those of whom it was said that they set out *nudi nudum Christum sequi* ('nakedly to follow the naked Christ').[44] Like the radical Franciscans who resorted to remote mountain hermitages in Tuscany and the Marche rather than the convents of the cities, or indeed like Dante himself as exile *in mezzo l'alpi*, they help to illustrate the paradox that Dante is exploring in the early years of his exile. This paradox is evident in the process whereby what was feared as desiccation and degradation (the *vento secco* of *Conv.* 1) becomes valued as a means of reviving earlier ideals: the 'non ancora intese ricchezze' of the *Convivio* (4.13).[45]

In the fourth treatise of the *Convivio* poverty begins to acquire a high degree of authority and value. Here, in the last treatise of the work, Dante enters into debate with an authoritative figure (the late Emperor Frederick II) on the subject of nobility and inherited wealth, and he proceeds to argue that riches 'cannot be the source of nobility because they are base' ('non possono causare nobilitade perché sono vili', *Conv.* 4.10.7). At the end of this phase of the argument he illustrates the freedom from care that poverty brings, using the example of the encounter between Julius Caesar and Amyclas the fisherman in Lucan's *Bellum Civile*:

> E ciò vuol dire Lucano nel quinto libro, quando commenda la povertà di sicuranza, dicendo: 'Oh sicura facultà de la povera vita! oh stretti abitaculi e masserizie! oh non ancora intese ricchezze de li Iddei! A quali tempii o a quali muri poteo questo avvenire, cioè non temere con alcuno tumulto, bussando la mano di Cesare?
>
> [And this is what Lucan means in his Fifth Book when he commends poverty for its security and says: 'How safe is the poor man's way of life! What humble dwellings and possessions; what as yet unrecognized rich gifts from the Gods! Of what temples or what city-walls could this be said to be the case: that they felt no tremor of alarm when the hand of Caesar summoned?] (*Conv.* 4.13.12)

44 This is a common phrase describing the primitive apostolic life; see Mollat 1986: 112. It was also applied to the early Franciscans by Jacques de Vitry in the *Historia occidentalis* (11. 32. 5).

45 A similar paradox is later apparent in Oderisi da Gubbio's 'obscure' prophecy that Dante's exile will help him to avoid the *confini* of Antepurgatory (*Purg.* 11. 139–41); see also Armour 1983: 72.

Ten years or so later Dante was to return to this particular instance yet more vividly and prominently in the St Francis canto of *Paradiso* (*Par.* 11. 67–9). Meanwhile, here in the *Convivio*, he translates Lucan's text (*Bellum Civile* 5. 527–31) quite closely – particularly when rendering the central paradox of poverty as an unrecognized gift ('munera nondum / intellecta'). The importance of the example and the whole argument in *Convivio* 4 for his thinking on this subject is again indicated in *Paradiso* 11, when he celebrates the evangelical poverty of the earliest Franciscans as *ignota ricchezza*, 'unrecognized wealth' (82).

By the time he wrote the *Convivio* Dante had assimilated a wide range of discourses on poverty and wealth, including those of the 'schools of the religious' which he refers to in *Convivio* 2.12.7.[46] His main classical sources for ideas about wealth and its dangers (apart, of course, from Lucan), are listed by him in *Convivio* 4.12.8 and include Cicero, Horace, Juvenal, Seneca and Boethius.[47] His knowledge of such Latin authors could have derived initially from *florilegia*.[48] It would, however, have been strengthened by the influence of major Florentine writers and teachers, like Brunetto Latini and Remigio de' Girolami, and quite possibly by study at Bologna, which, it has been argued, is the only accessible place where he could have found the resources for the writing of the *Convivio* in 1304 onwards.[49] In the same paragraph he also acknowledges the biblical authorities on wealth and poverty in rather more general terms: 'Solomon and his father' (presumably Proverbs, Ecclesiastes and Psalms) and, even more broadly, *la verace Scrittura* (e.g. Matthew 6: 19–34, Luke 16: 19–31). This stoical and paradoxical view of wealth and poverty – according to which, as Cicero puts it, the *avari* are the real *pauperes* – is, as Dante later shows in *Paradiso* 11, compatible with the Christian traditions on the subject. Lucan's 'unrecognized gift of the Gods', *Convivio*'s 'non ancora intese ricchezze de li Iddei' become

[46] The Franciscan 'school of the religious' at Santa Croce in Florence will be considered in more detail in this chapter, pp. 31–7.

[47] Cicero, *Paradoxa Stoicorum* 1 and 6; Horace, *Satires* 1.1; Juvenal, *Satire* 10, esp. l. 22; Seneca, *Ad Lucilium* 17; Boethius, *Consolatio* 2. pr. 5 and met. 5.

[48] Wieruszowski 1971: 598; Rand 1929: 264.

[49] For the sources of Dante's education in the Latin authors, see Davis 1984: 143, 146–7 and 16, and Wieruszowski 1971: 605, 617–19, 622, and 624 with n. 3. On his association with Bologna, see especially Renucci 1954: 87, Corti 1983: 132, Davis 1984: 9–10, and Scott 1996: 38 with n. 5.

the *ignota ricchezza* recognized and sought by Dante's early Franciscans in *Paradiso* 11.82.[50]

EREMITICAL AND FRANCISCAN POVERTY

There are other important traditions behind the valuing of poverty in the *Convivio* and the *canzoni* of Dante's early exile. As the ascetic figures in those texts suggest, and as Dante's portrayal of the eleventh-century saint Peter Damian (in *Paradiso* 21) will confirm, the association of religious poverty with mountains and other kinds of wilderness reflects an eremitical tradition that stretches back to primitive Christianity, to the Desert Fathers and the Apostles.[51] Dante's Peter Damian contrasts his life as hermit up on the mountain with his reluctant career as cardinal down in Rome (*Par.* 21. 113–26), and the original example of the thin, agile, barefoot Apostles with the modern image of the ponderous, heavy-robed prelates (ll. 127–35) for whom *pastori* ('pastors', l. 131) is plainly an ironic term.

The pastoral hermits of the eleventh and twelfth centuries were notable and dramatic examples of renunciation and voluntary poverty, as the historians of poverty have shown.[52] Of the other religious movements in this period, early Cistercian monasticism is of particular importance in this context, both because of its emphasis on solitude and on strict observance, and because the example and views of Bernard of Clairvaux were to be influential both upon the Italian Franciscans and upon Dante himself.[53] Bernard, as at least one of Dante's Trecento commentators noted, laid considerable stress on voluntary poverty, both positively as a way to salvation and through his critique of monastic (especially Cluniac) opulence and display; and, although he was

[50] The forms taken by clerical discourses of wealth and poverty (patristic, scholastic, monastic and mendicant) within the intellectual and devotional culture of Dante's time will be referenced below (nn. 51–63).

[51] On the early Fathers and poverty, see Mollat 1986: 20–3; and on the relationship between the desert and the city in early Christian culture, see Wolf 2003: 49–52.

[52] For general accounts see Little 1978: ch. 5 ('The New Egypt'); Mollat 1986: 74–81; and Geremek 1997: 32–6.

[53] On Cistercianism and other new monastic orders of the eleventh and twelfth centuries, see Little 1978: ch. 6; and on Bernard and the Italian Franciscans, see Botterill 1994: 31–46.

committed to cenobitic rather than eremitic monasticism, he like other Cistercian writers emphasized the value of solitude in the wilderness.[54] Whether practised in the wilderness or the city, however, voluntary poverty and 'awareness of the connection between poverty and preaching' is very much on the agenda of reformers in Italy and elsewhere between the eleventh century and the thirteenth.[55] The early Christian hermits formed an important part of this tradition; and, as the vocabulary of Peter Damian's speech in *Paradiso* 21 implies, the eremitical ideal he articulates was for Dante a link in the chain that connected the thin, barefoot Apostles ('magri e scalzi', l. 128) with the kind of Franciscan who throws off his shoes ('scalzasi') to chase after St Francis and Lady Poverty (*Par.* 11.79–84).

That such a pursuit – a life of renunciation and observance of the *vita apostolica* – was also compatible with life in the Italian city can be illustrated by the example of the Humiliati of Lombardy in the late twelfth and early thirteenth centuries, as well as by the development of other apostolically minded lay movements, such as the Waldensians and Beguines, in other European cities during the period.[56] Indeed, in the thirteenth century the new orders of friars were from the start most successful in meeting the needs of the urban laity; for 'without the towns', it has been claimed, 'the friars would never have come into existence'.[57]

Nonetheless, the early Franciscans especially appear to have had a somewhat ambivalent attitude towards urban life. St Francis himself, according to Celano, seems to have preferred wood to stone, the cave to the convent, and to have caused everyone including the sick to be evicted from a Franciscan house in Bologna because the whole structure seemed

[54] For Jacopo della Lana's references to Bernard in his commentary on *Inf.* 7 and *Par.* 12, see Botterill 1994: 122–4 and nn. 3–5. For Bernard's own views on voluntary poverty and of failures to observe the monastic ideal, see Botterill 1994: n. 5, and Little 1978: 95 with n. 74.

Bernard even anticipates the pastoral 'sermons in stones' of Shakespeare's Duke Senior when he assures the intellectuals of Paris that 'the woods and rocks will teach you more than any master can'; see *Ep.* 106, in *PL* 182, col. 242, cited and translated in Little 1978: 93 and n. 57. Little also notes 'the formal opposition Bernard makes between city and cloister' in *Ep.* 2, in *PL* 182, col. 86.

[55] Little 1975: 16. [56] Bolton 1975: 57–9; Little 1978: ch. 8.

[57] See Southern 1970: 273–7; and, for Franciscan and Dominican views on the importance of concentrating on cities, Davray 1985: 31.

too permanent.[58] He was constantly drawn to eremitical solitude in the remote mountainous areas of Tuscany and Umbria, yet also impelled to preach to the crowds in the Piazza Maggiore at Bologna.[59] Such ambivalence is of course familiar enough to the twentieth-century reader, but in thus moving between the city and the wilderness, Francis has something in common with Peter Damian before him and Dante later. Perhaps a better way of describing this liminal status is through the comparison that presents Dante as 'poet of the desert . . . much like St Francis in the blurred margin, simultaneously outside the world and in the world'.[60]

When speaking of churches and convents in his *Testament* of 1226, Francis says that the friars should occupy such buildings 'only as strangers and pilgrims' (1 Peter 2: 11), and this sense of their status in the world is closely related to his emphasis on poverty as an essential part of the Rule and of the apostolic life.[61] As the son of a merchant who had renounced his inheritance, he seems to have displayed a violent (or at least vividly dramatized) physical aversion to money.[62] The Franciscan Rules of 1221 and 1223 stress the intregration of poverty into the *vita apostolica* in a way that follows the example of the eremitical and lay movements of the previous two centuries. The strict injunction against handling money and the keen advocacy of begging (especially in the earlier Rule of 1221, ch. 8–9) was however particularly characteristic and became increasingly controversial.[63]

Debate about Franciscan poverty developed intermittently and often intensely through the century before the *Commedia*.[64] This debate will

58 *2 Celano* 56 and 58–9; see also the 1221 *Rule*, ch. 7 and the *Testament* of 1226, in Habig 1973: 68.

59 *1 Celano* 15 and Thomas of Spalato in Boehmer 1904: 106. On St Francis and the wilderness, see Sorrell 1988, Frugoni 1993: ch. 6 and Wolf 2003: 65. See also Chapter 3 below, pp. 91–2 with nn. 13–16, and Chapter 4 below, pp. 139–40 with nn. 39–42. For discussion of Francis preaching and other forms of street-theatre, see Wolf 2003: 80–1.

60 Mazzotta 1979: 111.

61 *Testament* in Habig 1973: 68.

62 *1 Celano* 15 and *2 Celano* 65 and 68.

63 See also the *Rule* of 1223, chs. 4 and 6.

64 Some of its landmarks during Dante's lifetime (such as Nicholas III's declaration in 1279, Clement V's inquiry in 1309–12, and John XXII's pronouncements from 1317 on) will be the subject of later chapters (see especially, Chapter 2, pp. 73–81, and Chapter 4, pp. 159–68 below). For a summary of the main issues discernible in the early Lives of St Francis, see Wolf 2003: 102. More extensive general surveys of the controversy are: Lambert 1961; Leff 1967: vol. 1, chs. 1–2; and Nimmo 1987: 78–210; and there is also a good concise account in *CHMPT*, 631–7.

from now on be a recurrent subject of discussion in this book; and a few of its basic features will thus need to be kept in mind.

First, the Franciscan Order in the thirteenth century (as a highly successful and rapidly expanding organization within the Church) was very much under the eye of papal authority, which meant that the practicality of the ideal of evangelical poverty would be kept under review. The involvement of papal authority had been evident in the roles played by Innocent III, Honorius III and Cardinal Ugolino in the initial establishment of the Order, and it also became apparent through Gregory IX's and Innocent IV's successive interpretations (1230 and 1245) of what was meant by 'possession' and 'use' and in their provisions for the holding of property on the friars' behalf by the 'spiritual friends' who had been mentioned in the 1223 Rule (ch. 4).[65] The institutional importance of the issue is also reflected in the amount of time and energy devoted by subsequent popes to their definitions of and pronouncements upon Franciscan poverty, notably by Nicholas III, Clement V and John XXII.[66]

Secondly, the debate about Franciscan poverty, the validity of mendicancy and the strictness of observance – though much of it was conducted at a highly rarefied intellectual level – came, during the later thirteenth and early fourteenth centuries, to have wider implications and consequences. The question of what those concerned with observing the rule 'spiritually' (*spiritualiter*) were to do is already raised in the Rule of 1223, and observance of strict poverty became increasingly contentious in this context. As Leff argues, 'by 1254 [the beginning of the conflict between mendicants and seculars at the University of Paris] poverty was no longer merely a way of life but the doctrine of spiritual regeneration'.[67] Such a doctrine of regeneration drew in part upon the eschatological work of Joachim of Fiore (c. 1135–1202) and his followers; and there seems to be a connection between some influential Franciscans' apocalyptic thinking during this period and their idealization of voluntary poverty. If the end were at hand, it would be as well to be

[65] For brief accounts of the two bulls, *Quo elongati* (1230) and *Ordinem vestrem* (1245), and on Innocent IV's *Quanto studiosus*, see Moorman 1968: 89–91 and 116–118. For fuller discussion see Lambert 1961: 83–107.

[66] See Lambert 1961: chs. 6 and 8–10.

[67] Leff 1968: 256. On developments in Franciscan ideas on poverty in this early period, see Reeves 1969: ch. 4 and Lambert 1961 and 1998: chs. 4 and 5.

amongst those who were ready for it – namely, those later described by Ubertino da Casale (1259–before 1341) as 'certain new and humble people, who in those last hours would be set apart from all others by virtue of their humility and poverty'.[68] Such connections were also drawn in quite orthodox apocalyptic exegesis, for example that of Bonaventura; but by Ubertino's and Dante's time the debate about strict observance of poverty had intensified within the Order (from 1279 on), and from the 1290s the rigorist ideas of Petrus Iohannis Olivi (1247/8–98) were gaining wider currency and a more radical edge among the Spiritual Franciscans and the laity, especially in Provence and Central Italy, including Tuscany.[69]

Thirdly, both the earlier concerns with strict observance and the later radicalization of rigorist ideas appear to be reflected in a wide range of polemical, devotional and imaginative texts. These include of course the Latin Rule Commentaries and disputations of the rigorist and Spiritual leaders, such as Hugh of Digne, Petrus Iohannis Olivi, Angelo Clareno and Ubertino da Casale, as well as anonymous but influential texts like the *Sacrum commercium Beati Francisci cum Domina Paupertate* (of the second or third quarter of the thirteenth century).[70] Works by several of these writers appear to have achieved wider circulation through the vernacular. The *Sacrum commercium* was translated in the thirteenth or fourteenth centuries; an Italian version of Angelo's *Historia* (completed c. 1325?) was in circulation by 1334; and according to the Inquisitor Bernard Gui and the trial records of the 1320s, the *beguins* of Provence

[68] See Reeves 1969: 175 (on 'the deep connection between the passion of the Spirituals for evangelical poverty and the Joachimist expectation in history') and 207–10; Davis 1984: ch. 3; also Burr 1989: 177–80 and Burr 1993: esp. 95–7, 186–9, 192. The quotation from Ubertino is translated from *Arbor vitae crucifixae* f. ccix r: 'quendam populum novum et humilem in hac novissima hora, qui esset dissimilis in humilitate et paupertate ab omnibus aliis'.

[69] On Bonaventura's apocalyptic exegesis, see Burr 1993: ch. 2 and 43 and 105 On the Spirituals in Provence and Central Italy, see for example: Douie 1932: ch. 7; Manselli 1959; *Cahiers de Fanjeaux* 10 (1975); Von Auw 1979; and Lambert 1992.

[70] Editions: Hugh's Rule commentary by Flood (1979); his *De finibus paupertatis* and *Disputatio* by Sisto (1971): ch. 6; Olivi's *Rule Commentary* by Flood (1972), and his *Quaestio* and *Tractatus* on the *usus pauper* question by Burr (1992); Angelo's *Expositio Regulae* by Oliger (1912), and his *Historia septem tribulationum* by Ehrle in *ALKG* 2 (1886), pp. 106–64 and 256–327; Ubertino's *Arbor vitae crucifixae* in the Venice edition of 1485 (repr. 1961), and for texts of his submissions to the Avignon inquiry of 1309–12, see below, p. 76 n. 118; *Sacrum commercium* by Brufani (1990).

possessed vernacular texts of Olivi's work, including his Apocalypse commentary.[71] By Dante's time, evangelical poverty was also a major theme in Franciscan literature originally composed in the vernacular, and especially in the lyrical, dramatic and satirical ballads, the *laude*, of which the most notable early exponent was a Spiritual Franciscan contemporary of his, Jacopone da Todi (1230/1236–1306).[72]

THE POETRY OF FRANCISCAN POVERTY: JACOPONE DA TODI

Although Jacopone was born some thirty years before Dante, his 'conversion' to Franciscanism did not take place till 1268/9 and his admission to the order followed ten years later.[73] His *laude* are thus likely to have been written late in the century, and some of the most important ones can be assigned to the 1290s or early 1300s, at the time when the conflict between the Spirituals and the Conventuals in the Order was intensifying. They often show the 'theatre of poverty' associated with St Francis himself being performed in brilliantly grotesque and sardonic modes.[74]

Jacopone's rigorist stance is apparent particularly in his ironic and satirical *laude*, such as those addressed to Popes Celestine V and Boniface VIII; more attention will be given to these when we come to Dante's modes of addressing and characterizing popes in *Inferno* 19 and 27.[75] Radicalism is also evident in his complaints about decadence within the Order and the ambition of modern Franciscans for worldly and ecclesiastical preferment.[76] In the great gaol ballad 'Que farai, fra' Iacovone' he moves from the notion of using paternosters to pay his tab at God's tavern (the prison) to that of using such funds to endow friars ambitious for 'horns' (mitres) (ll. 59–70). He then turns to more sombre

[71] See Chapter 2 below, p. 80 with n. 135; and Chapter 4 below, p. 173 with nn. 134–6.

[72] For brief discussion of the early *laude* tradition, see Moleta 1983: 33–7. On the *laude* within the wider context of Franciscan literature, see Fleming 1977: 180–8.

[73] The dates are indicated by his *lauda* written in prison in 1298 or shortly after, 'Que farai, fra' Iacovone', ll. 123–30 in Mancini 1974. For Jacopone's life, see Menestò 1977 and Peck 1980.

[74] On St Francis 'performances', see above, n. 59.

[75] Particularly 'Que farai, Pier da Morrone' and 'O papa Bonifazio, molt'ai iocato al mondo' in Mancini (ed.) 1974: nos. 74 and 83. For further comparisons between Jacopone and Dante, see Chapter 2 below, pp. 60 and 69–70, with nn. 59–61 and 88–93.

[76] E.g. Mancini 1974: nos. 17, 35, 75, 88 and 91.

representations of Franciscan decadence: Lady Poverty as a spurned bride and the Order as a broken sheepfold (ll. 71–90).

When celebrating the original Franciscan ideal, as he does in 'O Francesco, da Deo amato' (Mancini 1974: no. 71), Jacopone exalts Poverty, not only as one of the three vows (ll. 37–8) but also as St Francis's chief advantage in his 'game' with Satan (ll. 21–2). Conversely, the idea of earning money, even to give to the needy, is portrayed as a Satanic temptation, to be rejected in favour of following the true apostolic path ('la via vera') of mendicancy, without scrip or purse and without touching coins (ll. 83–98). Poverty, for Jacopone, is thus imagined as on the one hand the rejection of Avarice, vividly personified amongst the capital sins in a number of the *laude*, and on the other as part of the path of self-denial and self-obliteration (*annullamento*) that leads to his mystically imagined 'Supreme Nothingness' ('Alta nichilitate').[77] These aspects are drawn together concisely and quite soberly in 'O amor de povertate' (Mancini 1974: no. 36). This *lauda* begins by invoking the tradition that goes back at least as far as Juvenal's *vacuus viator* (Satire 10: 22) by representing poverty as tranquillity, as the safe path, and as release from the fear of thieves or tempests (ll. 1–6). It then, like Dante's 'Doglia mi reca', goes on to contrast the liberty of the poor with the subjection of the wealthy (ll. 13–30), mocking the servitude (*vassallaio*) of the *omo avaro*.[78] The path of poverty as part of the mystical *annullamento* of the self is also pointed to later in the poem (especially ll. 75–98); and the earlier contrast between freedom and servitude becomes, in the conclusion, compressed into the paradox whereby Poverty is seen as 'having nothing and desiring nothing, yet possessing everything in the spirit of freedom' (ll. 119–22). In this latter passage, Jacopone is clearly invoking, as he does elsewhere, the apostolic model outlined in 2 Corinthians 6:10, where the 'ministers of God' are seen as 'egentes, multos autem locupletentes: tanquam nihil habentes, et omnia possidentes' ('poor and yet making many people rich; as having nothing, and yet owning everything').

[77] For the personification of Avarice, see Mancini 1974: nos. 6 (ll. 43–5), 30 (ll. 49–96), 59 (ll. 19–22), 77 (ll. 169–70) and 84 (ll. 207–12). The Dionysian *via negativa* is most extensively explored in no. 92 (see esp. ll. 329–52 and 483–4), but see also the final stanzas of no. 51 (ll. 51–68) and no. 36 (discussed below).

[78] '[R]idesse de l'omo avaro, / che sta 'n tanta ansïetate' ('she [Poverty] laughs at the miser who lives in such anxiety'), in Mancini (ed.) 1974, no. 36, lines 13–14.

In 'O amor de povertate' Jacopone thus seems, like Dante in *Convivio* 4.13 and *Paradiso* 11. 82, to develop the paradox of poverty as (to use Dante's term) *ignota ricchezza*.[79] There is no direct evidence that Dante knew either Jacopone or his *laude*.[80] Yet the approaches of the radical Franciscan poet to the definition of wealth and poverty are nonetheless close in time, place and temper to the stoical ascetic stance adopted by Dante in 'Doglia mi reca' and *Convivio* 4. Closer still, however, were probably the resources and teaching available to Dante in late thirteenth-century Florence, at the Franciscan convent and *studium* of Santa Croce.

A SCHOOL OF THE RELIGIOUS: THE IDEA OF POVERTY AT SANTA CROCE

By Dante's time Santa Croce was, physically and culturally, a notable landmark on the Florentine urban scene. It was a dominant presence to the south-east of the old city walls, just as the Dominican convent of Santa Maria Novella was to the north-west.[81] The Franciscans, like the other mendicant orders in Florence (except the Augustinians in Santo Spirito), located themselves in an area of expanding population.[82] The church of Santa Croce was already occupied by them in 1228, and in their new building programme from 1252 onwards they had the support and encouragement of the Papacy and the Commune, as well as the patronage of a number of wealthy and powerful families, especially in the 1290s and the first two decades of the next century.[83] By the end of the thirteenth century, the extent of the Florentine laity's involvement with Franciscanism would have been clearly apparent around this convent. Groups of penitents and tertiaries of both sexes inhabited the neighbouring area, as they did the areas around the convents of the

[79] For documentary references to Jacopone in Dante's time, see Menestò (ed.) 1977: xi–xiv; and on early Umbrian and Tuscan manuscripts of his *laude*, see Sapegno 1926: 189 and Bettarini 1969: 723–7.

[80] For references, see above, nn. 73 and 75.

[81] See the diagrams in Murray 1982: 85.

[82] See Holmes 1986: 56–7 and Murray 1982: 86.

[83] See Goffen 1988: esp. 4–5, 7 and 10, and Davidsohn 1927: vol. 4.3, 29. For more detail on the building of the church and convent, see Paatz and Paatz 1952: vol. 1, esp. pp. 497–500, 505–6 and 510–11. On Franciscan culture at Santa Croce, see Davis 1963 and Manselli 1973.

Dominicans and the Servites.[84] Close association with and instruction of the laity were very much part of the culture of Santa Croce in Dante's time.

The extent of Dante's own formal association with the convent remains unknown. The claim that he was actually a Franciscan novice in his youth appears first in the late Trecento commentary (c. 1385–95) by Francesco da Buti, when he is glossing the 'fine and remarkable fiction' of the cord that the pilgrim throws into the abyss (*Inf.* 16.106–23); it may have been invented for this hermeneutic purpose, and was understandably adopted by later poetry-loving Minorites.[85] But if, as seems reasonable, we take Dante's broad claim to have frequented 'the schools of the religious and the disputations of those who teach philosophy' (*Conv.* 2.12.7) to include the *studium* of Santa Croce – which was (as Barnes has pointed out) less than half a mile from where he lived – then there is a fair amount of firm evidence about what, in the 1290s, he would have encountered there and what this might have contributed to his understanding of religious poverty.[86]

During the late thirteenth century the Santa Croce *studium*, like the Dominican one at Santa Maria Novella, was an important school in its Order's educational hierarchy.[87] Its library contained, among manuscripts written around 1300 or earlier, relatively few classical texts (although Virgil and Boethius seem to have been represented).[88] Amongst the works that were probably either in the collection at this time or copied in the Santa Croce scriptorium during the thirteenth century, there are some that are clearly relevant to the traditions of thought that are being outlined here. For instance, in his account of the transmission of St Bernard's work in medieval Italy, Botterill notes that, although

84 See Davis 1984: 147–8 and n. 39; Holmes 1986: 61–2; and on the *pinzochere* (the female devotees) see Davidsohn 1900–8: vol. 4, 487, Manselli 1973: 327, and Papi 1996: esp. 91–2.

85 See Buti, ed. Giannini 1858–62: vol. 1, 438–9; and the repetition of the claim in his comment on *Purg.* 30. 41–2, in vol. 2, 735. For discussion of the tradition, see Gardner 1926: 70–1; also Davis 1984: 152, and the summary of opinions (mostly sceptical) in *ED* 2, 208a (Pazzaglia here points out that Franciscan tertiaries wore a leather belt, not a cord). On the associations between Dante, the culture of Santa Croce and Olivi's ideas, see Manselli 1973: 332–4.

86 Barnes 1986: 6.

87 Davis 1984: 151 and 155–6.

88 '[I]ts main strength', according to Davis, 'was in traditional and scholastic theology . . . and also the logical works of Porphyry, Boethius and Aristotle and various texts of canon law' (Davis 1963: 399; see also Davis 1984: 148–51).

there appear only two works of Bernardine interest that can be assigned to the Santa Croce library itself, all of Bernard's major texts are included in the manuscripts attributed to the scriptorium.[89] It is very likely that Santa Croce would also have given Dante his first acquaintance with the work of Bonaventura.[90] Copies of the latter's commentary on Book 4 of Peter Lombard's *Sentences* are listed as 'for the use of' Fra Bono da Legnaria (active in the 1290s) and Fra Enrico de' Cerchi (who donated books to the library in 1285), and Dante might have had access to a text of the *Legenda maior* here.[91] Also of interest in the catalogue (and reserved 'for the use of' Fra Jacobus de Trisanctis, active in the 1290s) is a collection of sermons by the Apulian Franciscan Luca of Bitonto (d. 1241), who, amongst other things, ironically makes the spirit of avarice (like Jacopone's Satan tempting St Francis) urge 'the heart of man' to accumulate wealth 'so that you may have something to pass on to your children and something to dole out as charity to the poor'.[92] Beyond the *studium*'s collection of books, Dante would probably also have been able to see images of St Francis's renunciation and evangelical poverty in the church itself – for instance in the mid-thirteenth-century Bardi Dossal; and he would presumably have heard the theme developed by any number of the convent's preachers.[93] Of these preachers and teachers, two (Olivi and Ubertino) are obviously central to the story of Dante and Franciscan poverty, and they will be considered shortly. There are others, however, who are less familiar but are also of major significance in the Florentine Franciscan scene.[94] Amongst them, particular mention should be made of Servasanto da Faenza, who entered the Order at Bologna between 1244 and 1260 and was active as a writer and preacher at Santa Croce in the second half of the century.[95]

Servasanto is known to have composed a number of penitential and encyclopaedic works, and of these the most popular appears to have been

[89] Botterill 1994: 58 and 60; see also Davis 1963: 406, item 33, and 407, item 36.

[90] Davis 1984: 153–4. [91] See Davis 1963: 409 (with item 46), and 411.

[92] Davis 1963: 408, item 44; see also Murray 1982: 87 and (for the passage quoted) 91 n. 3: 'ut habeas quid filiis tuis dimites, quid pauperibus pro dando tribuas'.

[93] On the Bardi Dossal, see Goffen 1988: 29–30, and Frugoni 1988: esp. 7–9 and 41–8; see also below, Chapter 4, pp. 135–7 with nn. 33–6 and Appendix II.

[94] For some of these see Davis 1984: 152.

[95] The basic study of Servasanto and his work is by Oliger 1924; see also D'Avray 1995 and Delcorno 1996: 57–8.

a collection of moralized examples for the use of preachers: the *Liber de exemplis naturalibus*, of which nineteen manuscripts survive.[96] Another major treatise, surviving in two manuscripts (one of them from Santa Croce) is his *Liber de virtutibus et vitiis*. This latter work is of particular interest: it was written towards the end of the thirteenth century and shows how a major Franciscan preacher and instructor of preachers in Dante's time and place addresses the ethics of finance and usury and the relationships between the rich and the poor. Thus the fourth *distinctio* of the *Liber* concerns itself with the nature of charity, and the twelfth deals with 'avarice, usury, robbery, prodigality and the remedies for these', whilst the eleventh is devoted to 'the virtue of poverty and examples inspiring the love of poverty'.[97] Reference is made throughout not only to Augustine, Bernard and Seneca, but also to the acts of St Francis in the *Legenda maior* and to wealth and poverty in Florence and Tuscany.[98] For instance, in the fourth chapter of *distinctio* 11 (on 'the love of poverty') the argument that 'the poor are often cheerful when the wealthy are gloomy' is illustrated by the example of St Francis renouncing his worldly possessions and clothing and going off singing into the wilderness.[99] Possible connections between Servasanto's examples and Dante's imagery have been suggested, but of the Franciscans at Santa Croce's 'school of the religious' in the last decade or so of the century, there were two who especially influenced the shaping of the *Commedia*'s ideas on evangelical poverty.[100] These are two figures who have briefly been mentioned before in the context of Franciscan ideas on poverty: Petrus Iohannis Olivi and Ubertino da Casale.[101]

Olivi's and Ubertino's approaches to the subject of poverty are both narrower and broader than those of Franciscan preachers like Servasanto. They are narrower in the sense that they are concerned intellectually and (especially in Ubertino's case) politically with *usus pauper*, 'restricted

96 Oliger 1924: 156–62. 97 Oliger 1924:, 175–6, 177.

98 Oliger 1924:, 177 and 182. With reference perhaps to Dante's anonymous Florentine suicide in *Inferno* 13 (143–52), it is interesting to note that Servasanto illustrates his argument about the cares of wealth by mentioning the numbers of Florentines 'who have lost their money and hanged themselves' (Dist. 4, c. 38, f. 50va).

99 BNF Ms Conventi soppressi E. 6. 1046, f. 99rb: 'Exemplum de beato Francisco qui coram episcopo denudatus incedens per deserta securus voce gallica decantabat.'

100 On Servasanto and Dante, see Delcorno 1996: 57.

101 For basic information about Olivi and Ubertino, see Douie 1932, chs. 4 and 5. See also Manselli 1973, Burr 1989 and 1993 and Potestà 1980.

use', as an essential feature of the evangelical perfection embodied in the Franciscan Order. They are broader in the sense that they saw this perfection as necessary to the spiritual leadership that would be found during the 'last days' in that group who, as Ubertino put it, 'would be set apart from all others by virtue of their humility and poverty'.[102] They were both in Florence in the late 1280s: Ubertino from 1285 to 1289 and Olivi for a shorter period (1287–9).[103] Although Dante in *Convivio* 2.12.7 implies that he began to frequent the 'schools of the religious' only after 1290 (the year of Beatrice's death), it is conceivable that he might have done so earlier, and virtually certain that he would have heard something about Olivi's and Ubertino's ideas at Santa Croce during the early 1290s, a time when the divisions between Spirituals and Conventuals were intensifying and when the Spiritual movement looked set to achieve some degree of support and recognition.[104]

We do not know what specific aspects of evangelical poverty Olivi or Ubertino actually addressed during their years at Santa Croce. Olivi, the elder of the two, had begun to engage with the issue in the mid-1270s and had written on it, in questions eight and nine of his *Questions on Evangelical Perfection*, shortly before Nicholas III's declaration on Franciscan poverty in *Exiit qui seminat* (August 1279).[105] His most important work on the subject, the *Tractatus de usu paupere*, dates from between 1279 and 1283, and it methodically asserts the importance of 'restricted use' as an essential part of the Franciscan vow.[106] A range of his opinions had been examined by a commission of the Order at Avignon in 1283, and this had resulted in his colleagues' somewhat confused condemnation of his ideas on *usus pauper*.[107] Although his writings were subsequently banned, he was able sucessfully to defend himself at the

[102] See above, p. 28 with n. 68.

[103] See Douie 1932: 89–90 and 123–4; also Burr 1989: 172 and Potestà 1980: 22. Ubertino may also have revisited Florence in 1298–1302; see Mineo in Mellone (ed.) 1992: 231–2, and Chapter 4 below, p. 151 with n. 70.

[104] See Moorman 1968: 193–5, and Burr 1989: 107–8.

[105] On the chronology of Olivi's work on poverty see Burr 1989: ch. 2, esp. 43–51. A recent review of research on Olivi is by Flood 2000: 111–19.

[106] See Burr 1989: 49 and 57. For editions of both question 9 of the *Questions on Evangelical Perfection* and the *Tractatus*, see Burr (ed.) 1992. Discussion of the relationship between Olivi's doctrine of *usus pauper* and ideas about the use of money in his economic treatises is in Lambertini 1999: 193–205.

[107] See Burr 1989: ch. 4.

Chapter meeting of 1287, and was in consequence appointed lector at the Santa Croce *studium*.[108] He thus came to this school of the religious as a rehabilitated figure whose apocalyptic thought and ideas on poverty were already beginning to fuel a further and more acrimonious phase in the dispute about Franciscan ideals and their practice.[109]

Ubertino da Casale was to be an energetic participant in that phase of the debate and an active propagator and defender of Olivi's ideas, especially during the inquiry at Avignon in 1309–12. He had entered the Franciscan Order in 1273 and studied at Paris from 1274 to 1283.[110] His convergence with Olivi in Florence in the latter part of his four-year residence (1285–9) took place at a relatively early stage in a long and turbulent career which included a probable second spell in Florence; preaching in Tuscany and Umbria; enforced retirement at La Verna (1305); and diplomatic tasks on behalf of the papal legate in central Italy (1307–8), as well as a leading role in the Avignon inquiry (1309–12) and some prominence in the public eye at least up until 1325 and possibly even 1328.[111] Ubertino's views on evangelical poverty are in texts which date from c. 1305 (the *Arbor vitae crucifixae*), 1310–11 (the submissions to the Avignon inquiry) and 1322 (responses on the question to John XXII).[112] His active preaching career in central Italy, however, began much earlier than that, and, as Davis argues, his most ambitious work, the *Arbor vitae*, although not completed till 1305, was probably compiled from earlier works, some of which may have been known to Dante.[113]

The careers and writings of both Olivi and Ubertino are important not only because of their opinions on the issue of poverty, but also because of their negotiations with and views on papal authority. As we have seen, Olivi's main treatises on *usus pauper* were written around the time

108 Burr 1989:, 107.

109 Burr 1989:, 107–8 and 172–83. See also Burr 1993: 66–7. On the continuing influence of Olivi upon Santa Croce and Italian Franciscanism during the fourteenth and fifteenth centuries, see Manselli 1973: 336–42.

110 See Potestà 1980: 22.

111 Ubertino's possible second spell in Florence is mentioned by Mineo 1993: 561. On his career from c. 1300 to 1328, see Potestà 1980: 22–4; and on the mystery of his final years, see Burr 2001: 277. For his later views (in 1322) on the poverty question, see Davis 1981: 1–56, and Burr 2001: 267–75.

112 For the dating of Ubertino's six Avignon submissions, see below, Chapter 2, p. 76 with n. 118, and Potestà 1980: 181–2.

113 Davis 1984: 153 with n. 100.

of Nicholas III's *declaratio* on Franciscan poverty in *Exiit qui seminat* (1279), and he is known to have contributed an opinion (on the Rule and the ownership of property) to the commission advising the pope at that time.[114] Ubertino had the ear not only of Cardinal Napoleone Orsini but also (to some degree) of Clement V and, later, even John XXII. To varying degrees – Ubertino far more explicitly than Olivi – they both identified the monsters of the Apocalypse with corrupt ecclesiastical authority, and even (in Ubertino's case) with specific popes.[115] In their various ways, Olivi and Ubertino, like Dante and Jacopone, fell foul of Boniface VIII's assertions of papal power and authority during his pontificate (1294–1303).[116] Ubertino and Dante were also (literally or figuratively) to confront both Clement V and John XXII. All of these popes will be encountered or addressed by Dante in the *Commedia*, but before proceeding to them we should consider, as the final part of our context here, the background to such confrontations with papal power.

THE FRANCISCANS AND THE PAPACY

In one sense, the Franciscans had helped to buttress papal authority in the thirteenth century. From their foundation under Innocent III they had served a useful purpose for the Papacy. Like the other mendicant Orders, they were seen as a means of channelling and controlling reformist energies that over the previous two centuries had taken various orthodox and unorthodox forms.[117] Franciscans, like Dominicans, were actively involved in the battle against heresy, and in Dante's Florence, for example, the Franciscan convent of Santa Croce was not only home to a 'school of the religious' but also the headquarters of the Tuscan Inquisition.[118] On the other hand, controversies within and around the Franciscan Order – particularly concerning property and the strict

[114] See Burr 1989: 39 and nn. 5–6.

[115] For Olivi's views, see Burr 1993: esp. 94–5; and for Ubertino's identification of Boniface VIII and Benedict XI as beasts of the Apocalypse, see Ubertino da Casale, 1485, repr. 1961 Bk 5, ch. 8, 459–70.

[116] See Burr 1989: 112–26.

[117] On the far-sightedness of Innocent III's strategy see Ullmann 1974: 218. Wolf (2003: 91) argues that 'from the perspective of his [Francis's] papal supporters, poverty played an ancillary role to the primarily pastoral one that they envisioned for the new order'.

[118] See Davies 1984: 148 with n. 40. Dante would have been aware of Santa Croce's role as (in Davis's words) 'a citadel of orthodoxy': in 1283 Farinata degli Uberti (who appears in

observance of the Rule – were, over the course of the century, a recurrent problem for the Papacy. The question of property and use of material resources was both highly controversial and obviously crucial to the effectiveness of the Order as an organization within the Church, and it was addressed, reviewed and revised by a number of popes, from Gregory IX through Innocent IV, Nicholas III and Clement V to John XXII.[119]

For Franciscan relationships with papal authority, the role of the Order's official Cardinal Protectors was of importance at a number of points, both early in the century and in Dante's time.[120] Early on, Innocent III's nephew, Cardinal Ugolino da Segni, had been the Order's first Protector (from 1220 to 1227) and had been instrumental in shaping it as an effective preaching organization, often in the face of opposition from St Francis himself.[121] In 1227 Ugolino succeeded to the Papacy as Gregory IX; and his Bull *Quo elongati* of 1230 sanctioned the Franciscan use of material resources that 'do not exceed the standard of poverty' and allowed the use of a *nuntius* to administer donations.[122] Ugolino's nephew Rainaldo da Segni became Cardinal Protector in 1227 and continued to exercise this office when he, too, succeeded to the Papacy (as Alexander IV, 1254–61). A similar progression (from Protector to Pope) was followed by Giovanni Gaetano Orsini, who as Protector (1263–77) considerably increased the Order's power and influence. As Pope Nicholas III (1277–80), he not only (as we shall see) earned a prime place among the simonists in Dante's *Inferno*, but also issued one of the most important declarations on Franciscan poverty (*Exiit qui seminat* of 14 August 1279).[123] Nicholas kept the Protectorship of the Franciscans in the family, too, handing it over to his nephew Matteo on what seems

the circle of heretics in *Inf.* 10) was condemned for heresy by the Franciscan inquisitors there; see also Holmes 1986: 31 and n. 17.

119 See n. 64 to this chapter, above.

120 On the role of the Cardinal Protectors in this period, see Thompson 1972.

121 See especially: 1 *Celano* 73–4, 99–101; 2 *Celano* 25, 58, 63; Bonaventura, *Legenda maior* 5 and 7; the *Legenda trium sociorum*, chs. 61–7; the *Legend of Perugia*, chs. 61, 82 and 92; and the *Speculum perfectionis*, chs. 6, 21, 23, 43, 65, 67 and 68; also Moorman 1968: 46–57.

122 *Quo elongati* (28 Sept. 1230), in *BF* 1: 69; see also Lambert 1998: 83–93, Moorman 1968: 90–1 and Burr 1989: 61 and 99–100.

123 On Orsini as Cardinal Protector, see Sternfeld 1905; and on Nicholas III and *Exiit*, see below, Chapter 2, pp. 51, 56, 73, 78.

to have been a highly emotional occasion, and during what has been called 'the high point of papal connections with the Franciscans'.[124]

By Dante's time Franciscans had themselves become involved in the government of the Church at high levels through appointment as bishops, archbishops and cardinals; and one, Jerome of Ascoli, had advanced from being Minister General of the Order (1274–9) to becoming the first Franciscan Pope, Nicholas IV (1288–92).[125] Jerome was an effective politician and efficient Minister General, but was not much concerned with issues of evangelical poverty or strict observance; as Burr puts it, 'he is distinguished from Boniface VIII by the degree of his favouritism toward the order, not by any superior sensitivity to its original aims'.[126] The Minister General through most of Nicholas IV's pontificate, Raymond Gaufridi (Geoffroi), was on the other hand sympathetic to the rigorists in the Order. Relationships between the two were uneasy from the point of Raymond's election in 1289, and in 1290 the Pope was instructing the Minister General to investigate friars in Provence who 'seemed to introduce schism . . . considering themselves to be more spiritual (*spiritualiores*) than the others'.[127]

The early 1290s – the time when Dante may have been frequenting the Franciscan *studium* at Santa Croce – were alternately exciting and depressing years for the Spirituals and their sympathizers. After an interregnum of twenty-seven months following the death of Nicholas IV, the hermit Pier da Morrone was elected (on 5 July 1294) as Pope Celestine V, and it seemed that the Spirituals might now expect support for their cause from the very top of the hierarchy.[128] The then Minister General, Raymond Gaufridi, along with more radical spirits, such as Jacopone da Todi, Angelo Clareno and Conrad of Offida, looked to Celestine to provide a lead, and he did so, after a fashion, by allowing a group of Spirituals from the Marche to form a breakaway order called 'the Poor

[124] Holmes 1986: 50. For more details of this succession from uncle to nephew, and its significance for Nicholas III's relationship with the Franciscan Order, see also below, Chapter 2, pp. 50–1 with nn. 22–3.

[125] The process appears to have begun in the 1240s, with the first known appointment of a Franciscan bishop dating from 1244; see Moorman 1968: 296–7.

[126] Burr 1989: 127 and n. 86. On Nicholas IV's actions as pope concerning the Order, see Moorman 1968: 217 and Ullmann 1974: 263.

[127] *Chronica XXIV Generalium Ordinis Fratrum Minorum* in *Analecta Franciscana* 3 (1897): 420–22, cited and translated in Burr 1989: 108.

[128] On Celestine in general, see Petrocchi 1967: 42–3 and Herde 1981.

Hermits of Pope Celestine', under the leadership of Peter of Macerata (Brother Liberato) and the protection of Cardinal Napoleone Orsini.[129] However, that moment of official recognition lasted no longer than the five-month pontificate itself; and Celestine failed to meet the *paragone*, the challenge set out by Jacopone in the *lauda* he had addressed to the new Pope.[130] The identification of Celestine with Dante's 'ombra di colui / che fece per viltà il gran rifiuto' ('the shade of him who through cowardice made the great renunciation', *Inf.* 3.59–60) is plausible in several ways and may perhaps be reinforced by a parallel with Jacopone's *lauda*. The *lauda* puts before the Pope a positive example and image of moral determination:

> Quanno l'omo vertüoso
> è posto en loco tempestoso,
>
> sempre 'l trovi vigoroso
> a portar ritto el confalone
>
> [When the courageous man is put in a stormy place, you will always find him keen to hold the standard high] (ll. 31–4)

– whilst the restless 'standard' (*'nsegna*) which Dante's cowardly souls (led by 'Celestine') are ironically condemned to chase in *Inferno* 3 (52–7) has much the same significance as Jacopone's *confalone*. For, whether or not Dante regarded Celestine's abdication as a betrayal of the Spirituals, he would surely have seen it (in view of what followed) as the failure of the Papacy to seize its moment of opportunity for renewal.

Although, with the resignation of Celestine, the Spiritual Franciscans lost favour at the Curia, they still maintained some footholds of influence. Several Orsini and Colonna cardinals acted as friends at the papal court (or as allies outside it) during the pontificates of Boniface VIII, Clement V and John XXII. The Colonna cardinals challenging Boniface in 1297 were supported by a number of dissident Franciscans, the most notable being Jacopone himself; whilst during the early fourteenth century Napoleone Orsini employed and protected Ubertino da Casale over a long period, and Giacomo Colonna assisted both Ubertino and

[129] See Angelo Clareno, *Historia septem tribulationem*, in *ALKG* 2. 308–9. On Napoleone Orsini as protector of the 'Poor Hermits of Pope Celestine', see Douie 1932: 55, Moorman 1968: 195–6, and Burr 1989: 112–13.

[130] Mancini 1974: no. 74.

the leader of the Spirituals in the Marche, Angelo Clareno.[131] Such dissident Franciscans' criticisms of and collisions with papal authority took a variety of forms from the 1290s on. The Spirituals by their very nature could hardly be said to constitute a coherent, ideologically unified movement, but were, as Burr puts it, 'at their most organized . . . a loose coalition of like-minded individuals'.[132] This can be illustrated, for example, by their reactions to the abdication of Celestine and the accession of Boniface (in December 1294). At this juncture some Spirituals (like Angelo Clareno and Liberato) went into exile; some (like Jacopone) aligned themselves with Boniface's political opponents and suffered the consequences; and some (like Conrad of Offida) were eventually reconciled with the Order and the Papacy. Olivi, the intellectual mentor of the Spirituals, on the other hand, argued vehemently with those who denied the validity of Celestine's resignation and (as he saw it) threatened the integrity of the Franciscan Rule.[133]

Later, in the first quarter of the fourteenth century, as we shall see, the careers of the leading Italian Spirituals, Ubertino da Casale and Angelo Clareno, reflect a varied range of attitudes towards papal authority. Ubertino in the *Arbor vitae* (completed 1305) denounces the two most recent popes (Boniface VIII and Benedict XI) as apocalyptic beasts and accuses Nicholas III of hanging a millstone around the belly of the Franciscan Order, in the form of the interpretation of poverty in *Exiit qui seminat*.[134] On the other hand – and in a more public forum (Clement V's inquiry of 1309–12) – Ubertino referred more respectfully to *Exiit* and he retained the support not only of Napoleone Orsini (Nicholas III's nephew) but also of Clement V, who incorporated a number of his arguments into the bull *Exivi de paradiso* (6 May 1312), and later of John XXII, who arranged for his transfer into the Benedictine

[131] On the Colonna cardinals as allies of the Spirituals against Boniface, see Boase 1933: ch. 6. On Napoleone Orsini as patron of Ubertino da Casale, see Willemson 1927: ch. 3, Douie 1932: 126–31, and Potestà 1980: 23. For information about Giacomo Colonna as supporter of the Spirituals and of Ubertino and Angelo Clareno, see Douie 1932: 17 and 61–2, Potestà 1980: 23 and Potestà 1990: 8 and 34–5.

[132] Burr 1989: 124.

[133] See Olivi's *Epistola ad Conradum de Offida*, dated 14 September 1295, ed. Oliger in *AFH* 11 (1918): 366–73, and especially pp. 369–70, on the obedience due from Franciscans to the *auctoritas* of the Church and the Papacy. For a concise account of the letter and its context, see Burr 1989: 112–24.

[134] See below, Chapter 2, p. 78 with n. 128.

Order in 1317 and solicited his opinion on the poverty question in 1322.[135] Angelo Clareno, the chronicler of the Italian Spirituals and their tribulations, despite his own direct experience of imprisonment and exile, reflects in his letters an unresolved conflict between respect for established authority in the Church and insistence on strict observance of both the Rule and the more contentious Testament of St Francis.[136]

The contrast between the abdication of the saintly Celestine and the energetic worldliness of the lawyer Boniface, who succeeded him, led some at this time to question the long-accepted emphasis on the importance of the office rather than the person of the Pope. For, by this time, as Ullmann argues, the 'crucial papal distinction between office and person was . . . beginning to be reversed. What began to matter was the personality of the pope, was whether he was a morally "good" or "bad" pope'.[137] This shift of emphasis is reflected in an extreme form in the anonymous but widely diffused series of Franciscan prophecies about popes called the *Vaticinia de summis pontificibus*.[138] It is also evident in the reported ideas of the Spirituals' followers in Provence and Italy who had taken Olivi's interpretation of the *meretrix magna* of Revelation 17 to apply to the Papacy and who were also said, for instance, to believe that an angel had 'deprived the Lord Pope Nicholas III of his papal authority on account of his sins and vested it in certain friars and their followers who lived in the spirit of apostolic poverty'.[139] And later, following John XXII's attack on the basis of the Franciscan doctrine of apostolic poverty (*Cum inter nonnullos*, 12 November 1323) and his subsequent breach with the then Minister General, Michael of Cesena, both Spirituals and 'Michaelists' (like William of Ockham) were quite ready to affirm that this pope was not a Catholic.[140] Dissident views of this sort

[135] On Ubertino's later career, see above, n. 111. For the document transferring him into the Benedictine Order, see below, Chapter 4, p. 165 and n. 111. For discussion of Ubertino's treatise on *altissima paupertas*, written for John XXII, see Davis 1981 (with edition of the text on pp. 43–56), and Burr 2001: 267–75.

[136] See especially *Epistole*, ed. Von Auw 1980: no. 7; the comments on this in Potestà 1990: 104; and the discussion of Angelo's position in Burr 1989: 123.

[137] Ullmann 1974: 270; see also ibid., 257–8 and 261.

[138] For further discussion of the *Vaticinia* and its possible origins, see below, Chapter 2, p. 52 with nn. 30–32.

[139] See Chapter 2, p. 79 with n. 130.

[140] For these later views, including the assertion by the *fraticelli* that 'dom. papa Johannes non est papa', see the Epilogue below, p. 181, n. 2

implicitly contrast the apostolic authority of the Franciscans (and most often the Spirituals) with the abuses of papal power. As such they form an important element in the late thirteenth- and early fourteenth-century context within which Dante came to value and authorize poverty.

Thus, as the *Convivio* and the two great *canzoni* of Dante's early exile suggest, by the time he began the *Commedia* a number of cultural and political influences had combined to stimulate in his thinking a recognition of poverty as potentially authoritative. He had, first of all, inherited a vernacular tradition of poetry in which poverty was in various ways a common topic. Secondly, at Santa Croce during the decade or so before his exile, he had access to both radical and orthodox Franciscan ideas on the subject. And thirdly, events involving the Spiritual Franciscans and the Papacy had, during that same decade, brought evangelical poverty to the fore as an urgent political issue.

In the texts of Dante's early exile the language and allusions through which the value of poverty is conveyed prefigure those through which it will be represented in the *Commedia*. Poverty as virtue cannot however be defined without reference to its opposite vice. Dante's concern with avarice and its associations with power is evident before the *Commedia* – most notably in 'Doglia mi reca' and the *Convivio*. And, as we shall see, the effects of avarice in the Church and Papacy are encountered, identified and deplored at several levels during the ensuing journey through the *Inferno*.

2

Inferno: avarice and authority

Povertà is a word that is never heard in Dante's *Inferno*, but *avarizia* and related terms certainly are. Throughout the *cantica* greed is located both in cities such as Florence, Siena and Bologna and at the highest level of the Church; and Peter Armour has pointed out that '[o]f the twenty or so punishments in the *Inferno*, ten deal in some way with wealth-related sins and the corrupting effects of money in society'.[1] Early on, in cantos 1–7, there is developing awareness of the convergence between avarice and clerical authority; and the association is emphasized by Virgil in canto 7 (46–8). Later, in *Inferno* 19, greed is acknowledged by Pope Nicholas III as the impulse which drove him down into his present 'purse' in the rock of Malebolge (71–2); and avarice is at the heart of the speech that Dante's pilgrim addresses to him and other 'pastors' (90–117). That reproachful 'song' has as its burden the 'gold and silver' that the Apostles rejected and modern 'pastors' idolize (94–6, 112–14), and it takes an apocalyptic view of a world coming to grief because of papal greed:

> ché la vostra avarizia il mondo attrista
> (2.104)

In canto 19 the pilgrim's heightened status is conveyed through mendicant imagery and language; through the position he adopts 'standing like a friar' beside the inverted Pope (*Inf.* 19.49); and (most importantly) through his appropriation of Spiritual Franciscan apocalyptic exegesis in the denunciation itself (90–117). Later on the pilgrim's

[1] Armour 1994: 14. For further discussion of 'wealth-related sins' in the *Inferno* (from the she-wolf in canto 1 to Judas in canto 34), see pp. 14–19 of Armour's article; and for the argument that avarice is the sin most addressed in the *Commedia* as a whole, see Mezzadroli's article on 'Virtues and Vices' in *DE* 866–71 (especially 870). The relationship between avarice and poverty in the *Commedia* is also discussed by Boyde 2000: ch. 7.

quasi-mendicant role is more explicitly suggested through the comparison of Virgil and Dante, moving silently and alone through Malebolge, to a pair of Franciscans on the road: 'come frati minor vanno per via' (*Inf.* 23.1–3). Subsequently, in *Inferno* 27, the story of an encounter between an actual friar, now in Hell, and a pope destined soon to go there draws together some of the main issues concerning Franciscanism, the Papacy and worldly power. The relationship between Guido da Montefeltro (the soldier and politician who became a Franciscan) and Boniface VIII at the end of that canto focuses upon the extent of the Pope's spiritual authority and upon his desire to extend his temporal power. Boniface's 'fever of pride' can be seen as what an earlier pope, Gregory the Great, had called 'avarice of high position'; and the form it takes in the *Commedia* can be compared with the portrayal of this pope's *pessima avarizia* in the work of his Franciscan rigorist critic, Jacopone da Todi.[2]

Clement V (1305–14) was to follow Boniface on earth as in Dante's Hell; and he is the third of the papal 'pastors' to whom the pilgrim's accusations in *Inferno* 19 apply. As a figure 'from out of the west' and a 'pastor without principle', Clement thus completes the threefold descending pattern (Nicholas, Boniface, Clement) that conveys the degradation of papal authority in the canto. As the first of the Avignon popes he was associated, as we shall see, with a fatal compromising of papal authority. His dealings with the Spiritual Franciscans at the Avignon inquiry of 1309–12 were not themselves among his *più laida opra*, but they form an important context for Dante's appropriation of Spiritual apocalyptic discourse when imagining and addressing the Papacy in this canto. For these reasons – and because the *Inferno* may have been revised at a late stage to accommodate him – Clement and his dealings with the Franciscans will require closer attention.

Franciscan discourse in the *Inferno* thus develops through the condemnation of clerical avarice and is brought to bear more broadly upon the contexts and relationships of three popes. Of these three, Boniface VIII as he appears in *Inferno* 27 is most explicitly contrasted with St Francis, who makes a silent appearance at the end of that canto. But the degradation of papal authority represented by all three also contrasts with the Franciscan features of the pilgrim's increasingly confident

[2] For Gregory the Great's assertion, see *XL Homiliarum in evangelia libri duo* 1.16 in *PL* 76, col. 1136, quoted and translated in Little 1971: 20.

stance and voice. The contrast thus prepares for the Franciscan features of Dante's ascent and vision in the *Purgatorio* and for the eventual celebration of Franciscan apostolic idealism in the *Paradiso*.

As the pilgrim's apocalyptic speech to Nicholas III in *Inferno* 19 reminds us, however, there is a long way to go. The *avarizia* of which such popes stand accused is far removed from apostolic or Franciscan idealism and it is deeply rooted in the imagined world of the *Inferno*. Initially, then, we need to consider some of the ways in which this *cantica* has begun to define and dramatize the nature of and relationships between avarice and papal authority.

AVARICE AND AUTHORITY: CANTOS 1–7

Avarizia for Dante usually means more than simply desire for money, although it often includes that. As he would have known, in the long medieval tradition of characterizing and classifying this sin there are a number of definitions which significantly widen its range. Augustine saw it as the sin of Lucifer: the love of power.[3] Gregory the Great argued that 'Avarice has to do not only with money but high position; it is rightly called avarice when prestige is sought beyond measure.'[4] Aquinas, to whose analysis of sin Dante's general classification (e.g., in *Purg.* 16.91–2) is particularly indebted, sees it as consisting very broadly 'in appetitu cuiuslibet exterioris rei' ('in the appetite for any kind of external thing').[5] In such wider senses *avaritia* seems to overlap with *cupiditas*, and for many medieval writers the terms seem to have been interchangeable. Hence what is said by St Paul about 'love of money' (Greek *philargyria*, translated by Jerome as *cupiditas*) as 'the root of all evil' (1 Timothy 6: 10) complements, for example, Augustine's view of avarice as the chief obstacle to the root of all virtues, *caritas*.[6] The concept of *cupiditas* or *avaritia* as the source of evils and obstacle to the exercise of virtue seems to be dramatized at the start of *Inferno* by Dante's confrontation with the most vicious of the beasts that block the path of his ascent (*Inf.* 1.49–60

[3] Augustine, *De genesi ad litteram* 11: 15 in *CSEL* 28: 347–8.

[4] For the source in Gregory, see note 2 above. CL 2. 551 also cites Hugh of St Victor, *De fructibus* 8, on similar lines.

[5] Aquinas, *S Th* 2.2.118, quoted in Bonora, *ED* 2. 463.

[6] Augustine, *De diversis quaestionibus octogintatribus*, cited in *ED* 1, 463b. For evidence of the distinction between *avaritia* and *cupiditas*, see Little 1971: 18 with n. 12.

and 94–111). The voracious and insatiable she-wolf, let loose upon the world by the envy of Lucifer and destined to be destroyed only by the enigmatic *veltro*, is, in the opinion of many commentators, identifiable with *cupiditas*. The latter is seen here to be the origin of evils for Italy, the Church and the world. The particular association of avarice/cupidity with Florence and the Papacy is thus reinforced by later comparisons of both to wolves.[7]

We are made aware of the spiritual authority of the Papacy at several points during the first three cantos of the *Inferno*: through the description of either Purgatory or Paradise as 'la porta di san Pietro' at the end of canto 1 (135); through the reference in canto 2 to Aeneas preparing in Rome a place for St Peter and his successors and for the wearing of the 'papal mantle' (24 and 27); and, probably, through the oblique allusion to Celestine V and the *viltà* of his abdication in canto 3.[8] It is in canto 7 of the *Inferno*, however, that avarice converges explicitly and directly with the clergy and the Papacy. Here, at the start of the descent to the fourth circle of Hell, Dante and Virgil encounter the figure of Plutus who is first of all described as 'il gran nemico' ('the great enemy', *Inf.* 6.115). Like Virgil's initial reference to him as 'maladetto lupo' ('accursed wolf', *Inf.* 7.8), this description associates him with the major obstacle and enemy of *Inferno*'s first canto, the she-wolf, and with *cupiditas* as 'the root of all evil'.

Plutus' initial utterance, 'Pape Satàn, pape Satàn, aleppe', is an enigma that, for at least the last two centuries, has attracted a great deal of scholarly ingenuity. There seems to be a degree of consensus among recent commentators that it forms some kind of invocation to Satan and expresses a degree both of shock and of threat towards Dante and Virgil.[9] In this respect Plutus' attitude is similar to the mixture of

[7] The ambiguity of the *veltro* in *Inf.* 1. 101–11 reflects both parallels and differences between Dante's prophetic vision and that of the Spirituals. As an ascetic enemy of avarice (born 'tra feltro e feltro'), the figure has certain Franciscan connotations; on the other hand, as the redeemer of 'quella umile Italia' for which both Latins and Trojans died, it clearly carries imperial connotations (for further arguments on these aspects, see Mineo 1998: 30–1). For discussion of its full range of significances, see Kaske 1961, Davis in *ED* 5. 908–12, and Cassell in *DE* 851–4. On the Florentines as avaricious 'wolves' (*lupi*), see *Purg.* 14.49–51 and 59, *Par.* 25.6 and Havely 1986: 105–6; and on the same metaphor for the Papacy and the 'pastors' of the Church, see *Par.* 9. 127–32 and 27.55–7.

[8] *Inf.* 3.58–60. On Celestine, see Chapter 1 above, pp. 38–9 with nn. 128–9.

[9] See, for example, Caccia in *ED* 4. 281a–b and BR 1. 106.

dismay and hostility shown by those who warn Satan of the descent of Christ in the Gospel of Nicodemus or (later) in the plays of the Harrowing of Hell.[10] The interpretation of the words themselves that was proposed by Guerri in 1908 continues to command a good deal of support. According to this, *pape* is a Latin interjection (deriving from Greek *papai*) and *aleppe* (from *aleph/alpha*) means 'the first', therefore 'God'; hence Plutus is saying something like: 'Ah Satan, Satan, [our] God'.[11] There is an attractive alternative rendering (proposed by Porena and developed by Marti), according to which Plutus, the guardian of the circle which already contains popes and cardinals, is warning of the advent of Dante, the chief 'enemy' or 'adversary' (*satan*) of the present Pope (Boniface VIII).[12] In this particularly grotesque and at points satirical canto – which is comparable stylistically to some of the scenes in Malebolge – its most grotesque single figure may thus be playing upon several meanings of the repeated word *pape*.[13]

The connection between Plutus and the avaricious clerics under his rule was noted first of all by Guido da Pisa (c. 1328) when describing him as 'tamquam episcopum avarorum' ('like the bishop of the avaricious'), and several of the illustrated manuscripts reinforce the point by providing him not only with moneybags but also a crozier and mitre.[14] The subsequent portrayal of the souls of the avaricious and the prodigal surging against each other, like the 'waves of cupidity' that Dante mentions in *Paradiso* and *Monarchia*, comes to focus primarily upon the former, and of these the only group actually identified are 'clerics' (*cherci*, 38–9 and 46–8).[15] In response to Dante's question about them, Virgil further specifies that some of them were popes and cardinals, and he ironically uses the language of power and authority to describe their proneness to avarice:

10 See the 'Acts of Pilate' in James 1924: 124–5.

11 See Guerri 1908. His interpretation is largely accepted by, for instance, Vallone 1965: 8–9; Caccia in *ED* 4: 281a; BR 1: 106. *Aleppe* could also perhaps signify 'alas'; CL 1: 233 cites evidence for the use of *aleph* as 'interiectio dolentis'.

12 For this emphasis on the Papacy, see Porena 1947: ll. 73–4 and B. M. Marti 1952.

13 See M. Marti 1957: 11.

14 Guido da Pisa, *Expositiones et Glose super Comediam Dantis*, ed. Cioffari 1974: 136–7; and (for the illustrations of Plutus as 'bishop') see BMS 1: 124 and 2: 104.

15 For the comparison of the clashing souls to waves see ll. 22–4 here; and for the 'waves of cupidity' compare *Par.* 27.121–3 and *Mon.* 3.16.11.

Questi fuor cherci, che non han coperchio
  piloso al capo, e papi e cardinali
  in cui usa avarizia il suo *soperchio*.

[These who have no covering of hair upon their scalps were clerics, popes and cardinals, over whom avarice *reigns supreme* (my italics).] (*Inf.* 7.46–8)

The association of the clergy, Rome and the papal court with avarice had long been a commonplace of ecclesiastical satire. In the twelfth century, for instance, the occupation of St Peter's house by money-changers, the Pope's adoration of 'St Cupidity', and the power of 'Mistress Purse' at Rome had been noted by John of Salisbury, Walter Map and others.[16] This part of *Inferno*, however, seems to combine the influences of such traditional antisacerdotal satire with some of Dante's more urgent developing concerns about the nature of avarice and power. These concerns had begun to take shape in the uncompleted *Convivio*, particularly in its attention to the nature of and desire for wealth in part 4, and (earlier) in its representation of *religiosi* along with lawyers and physicians studying not for the sake of wisdom but for wealth and status (*Conv.* 3.11.10). They are also apparent in the contrast between wealth and poverty in the *canzone* of exile, 'Doglia mi reca', a poem whose themes and harsh interrogatory style have in several ways been compared to those of *Inferno* 7.[17]

Inferno 7 is a canto in which, although no single person or episode predominates, Dante appears to be identifying avarice and cupidity predominantly in terms of the higher clergy. Lines 46–8 are, as Vallone points out, the *Commedia*'s first general allusion to popes and cardinals; and since the fault of greed for temporal power is presented as widespread through this class, there seems to be no need for names.[18] As with the only other pope who may have been glimpsed so far (Celestine V in canto 3), Dante is at this stage looking at these clerical figures from some distance and interpreting them by way of Virgil. By the time he

[16] These twelfth-century sources of anti-curial satire are cited in Little 1971: 22.

[17] On 'Doglia mi reca', see Chapter 1 above, pp. 20–2; and for comparison with *Inf.* 7, see M. Marti 1957: 9–10 and 13, and BR 1: 103.

[18] Vallone 1960: 16. Anastasius II will subsequently be proclaimed as a heretic in *Inf.* 11. 7–9; on Pier delle Vigne (*Inf.* 13) as symbol of the self-destructiveness of the Papacy, see Ferrante 1984: 107–8.

reaches the circle of the simonists in Malebolge, however, he will be much closer to the persons concerned. He will then hear names named and will start to speak for himself.

STANDING LIKE A FRIAR: CANTO 19

By the time Dante reaches the *bolgia* of the simonists a number of papal figures have already appeared or been mentioned. As well as the (possible) shade of Celestine V (*Inf.* 3.59–60) and the anonymous popes of canto 7 (47–8), an early pope has been entombed among the heretics (11.7–9), and there have been several allusions to the various actions of the soon-to-be damned Boniface VIII (6.69, 15.112–13, and 18.29). However, the first pope to be directly encountered and addressed by Dante's pilgrim is Nicholas III, upended with feet aflame in the rock of the third bolgia. The portrayal of Nicholas has been described as a 'Franciscan tragedy', comparable to that of Guido da Montefeltro later on, and emphasis on the Franciscanism of the episode is, in my view, certainly justified; but both the Franciscan and the 'tragic' features of the episode require reassessment in the light of the canto's language, allusions and contexts.[19]

Nicholas was undoubtedly an important figure in the early history of Franciscanism. He had been closely associated with and concerned about the Order during his brief pontificate (25 November 1277–22 August 1280). His father, Matteo, was a friend of St Francis and belonged to a Franciscan tertiary order, whilst he himself is said to have been introduced to the saint early in life.[20] In 1263, as Cardinal Giovanni Gaetano Orsini, he was (apparently at the request of the Order's Chapter General) made Protector of the Franciscans, in which role he proved highly effective, presiding over an increase in the Order's significance and influence during the next two decades.[21] On the occasion at which, in 1279, he appointed his nephew, Matteo, to succeed him as Cardinal Protector, he is said to have described the Order in highly emotive terms, as 'melius quod habemus . . . cordis nostri desiderium, pupillam

[19] Gardner 1926: 79.

[20] See Sternfeld 1905: 2; also Demski 1903: 7, 17–18 and 315 n. 3, and Thomson 1972.

[21] Sternfeld 1905: 35–7.

oculorum nostrorum' ('the best thing we have . . . our heart's desire, the apple of our eye').[22] The Franciscan chronicle which quotes this speech mentions appreciatively the amount of time that Nicholas and his advisers spent on the drafting of the bull *Exiit qui seminat* (14 August 1279), which was intended to be the definitive interpretation of the Order's Rule; and it also notes the grief of the Order at his death a year or so later.[23]

Nicholas and the Orsini family continued to have close associations with the Franciscans in several ways during Dante's time. He may have had some influence upon the early phase of the fresco programme in the Upper Church at Assisi, where Cimabue's paintings in the cross-vault (1278–80) bore the Orsini coat of arms; and the Orsini family continued to have a close association with Assisi and the Franciscan Order during Dante's lifetime.[24] One of his nephews, Napoleone Orsini (d. 1342), was to be an important ally of the Spiritual Franciscans at the papal curia, and Dante mentions him by name in his letter to the Avignon cardinals in 1314.[25] Yet another of Nicholas's nephews, Matteo, as we have seen, succeeded him as Cardinal Protector and continued to act in that capacity until 1306.[26]

Why then, if Nicholas III and his family had such a close and seemingly honourable relationship with the Franciscan Order, does Dante choose to consign him to the holes of Malebolge as the harbinger of Boniface VIII and the first pope to speak and be spoken to in Hell? Why is he made so emphatically to embody papal *cupiditas*, as the modern Simon Magus and as the inverted figure upon whom Dante the

[22] The scene is reported in the *Chronica XXIV Generalium Ordinis Fratrum Minorum*, in *Analecta Franciscana* III 1897: 367–9.

[23] Ibid., 369 and 371.

[24] On Nicholas III and the Assisi paintings, see Belting 1977: esp. 88–94 and Lunghi (tr. Evans) 1996: 28. A chapel in the Lower Church at Assisi is the burial place of one of Nicholas's nephews, Gian Gaetano Orsini (d. 1292/4). Its fresco programme (the life and miracles of St Nicholas of Bari) was a mark of honour to Nicholas III on the part of another nephew who commissioned the project, Cardinal Napoleone Orsini; see Stubblebine 1985: 121–5 and Lunghi (tr. Evans) 1996: 102–5.

[25] For references to the role of Napoleone Orsini in the election of Clement V and the Avignon inquiry of 1309–12, and as addressee of Dante's *Epistola* II, see nn. 108, 157 and 160–1 of this chapter.

[26] See Moorman 1968: 179 and 295.

pilgrim focuses his contempt for the avarice of modern 'pastors' and his lament for the consequences of Constantine's Donation (ll. 90–117)? And why also should the poet – hostile as he was to French ambitions in Europe – be so vehement here against a pope who had long been leader of the anti-French party in the Curia?[27] Dante may well have been concerned about Nicholas's political ambitions and strategies in Tuscany and the Romagna; yet, as many commentators conclude, he was probably more influenced by this pope's reputation for nepotism.[28] Allegations of the latter kind can be found in several contemporary chroniclers, including Salimbene and Villani; they are alluded to in *Inferno* 19, when Nicholas acknowledges his eagerness to advance the 'bear-cubs' (*orsatti*) of the Orsini family (ll. 70–2); and they are related to ones that dissident Franciscans were also levelling against this pope.[29]

By the time of the *Commedia*'s composition, certain groups within the Order were energetically condemning Nicholas III; and the influence of radical Franciscan prophecy can be seen behind Dante's choice of him as the first in the line of contemporary corrupt pontiffs. In particular, it is thought that Dante could have been aware of the pseudo-Joachimist *Vaticinia de summis pontificibus*, a sequence of fifteen brief prophecies about popes which begins with a denunciation of Nicholas III. According to Herbert Grundmann, this text originated among a group of Spiritual Franciscans led by Angelo Clareno in Perugia during the summer of 1304.[30] Grundmann's attribution has been questioned on several occasions, and two authorities on the subject have recently located the origins of the *Vaticinia* variously in England or (perhaps more plausibly) in Catalonia or southern France.[31] In any case, the text, wherever it may have sprung from, was widely disseminated and became indeed a 'best-seller of the later middle ages'.[32] Moreover, the *Vaticinia* clearly associates Nicholas's own pontificate with the *principium malorum* ('the onset of evils'), and it labels the Orsini pope with the

[27] Foster 1969: 56. [28] Foster 1969: 56.

[29] For Salimbene, see *MGH* 1905–13: vol. 32, 170; for Villani, see Villani 1990–1: vol. 1. 494–6. See also Martin of Poland in *MGH* 1896: vol. 30.1, 711; and, for a modern assessment of Nicholas's 'nepotism', Demski 1903: 325–7.

[30] Grundmann 1932: 235 and 250–2; also Grundmann 1977: 14 (with n. 48) and 32. See also Douie 1932: 39 (n. 5); Reeves 1969: 193–4; and Potestà 1989: 120–2.

[31] See Lerner in *MGH Scriptores* 1988: vol. 33.5, 611–35 and Reeves 1992.

[32] Reeves 1992: 156.

words 'Genus nequam ursa catulos pascens' ('an evil sort of she-bear feeding her cubs').[33] The coincidence that Dante in *Inferno* 19 presents Nicholas as the first in his own succession of corrupt popes and refers explicitly to his advancement of the 'bear-cubs' (*orsatti*, l. 71) is plainly too strong to be overlooked.

Some broader features of radical Franciscan rhetoric have also been discerned behind the imagery of *Inferno* 19 and the pilgrim's address to the pope. The vision of the contemporary Papacy as Revelation's Whore of Babylon (106–11) has been linked with the apocalyptic exegesis of a Franciscan who had taught at Santa Croce in Dante's time: Petrus Iohannis Olivi.[34] Charles Davis has argued that Dante applied this image to papal Rome in a way that differs not only from Revelation (17: 18) but also from most commentators on the Apocalypse (such as Richard of St Victor, Joachim of Fiore and Ubertino da Casale), and that conversely his ideas and their ordering in this passage show close resemblances with those of Olivi.[35]

Bearing such contexts in mind, we can see that certain features of this canto reinforce both the Franciscan dimensions of Nicholas III's Dantean history and damnation and the more positively 'Franciscan' role of the pilgrim who 'stands like a friar' beside the inverted pope. Such features can be defined in terms of apostolic allusions (inverted and otherwise); political and apocalyptic vocabulary; and what might be called the wisdom of Dante's folly.

Inferno 19 is punctuated throughout with ironic inversions. The *pietra* (l. 14) in which the pope is planted head-first is itself, as the pun on *Petrus /Pietro* implies, an inverted Rock of the Church.[36] The flames playing upon the upturned soles of the pope's feet (ll. 25–30) have been thought to represent an ironic inversion of the Pentecost and the apostolic spirit, a spirit which the Franciscans themselves are known to have invoked by holding their chapters at Pentecost.[37] Following these apostolic allusions, the word 'friar' (*frate*) itself appears (l. 49) for the very first time in the poem. *Frate* in the *Commedia* can mean either 'friar' or 'brother',

[33] The verbal correspondence between the *Vaticinia* and the words of Dante's Nicholas III in *Inf.* 19. 70–1 is noted by Davis 1984: 59–60. The Florence manuscript of the *Vaticinia* (Riccardiana 1222.2) shows Nicholas III accompanied by a bear with four cubs (f. 1r).

[34] On Olivi, see Chapter 1 above, pp. 34–6 with nn. 101–9.

[35] Davis 1957: 226–7. [36] Herzman and Stephany 1978: 42

[37] Foster 1969: 54–5; Herzman and Stephany 1978: 40–1.

and we shall return later to the wider implications of that usage.[38] 'Friar' is, however, the predominant, and often ironic, meaning of the word in the *Inferno*, and its use here reflects both upon the pope's distance from the apostolic ideal and the pilgrim's gradual progression towards it. The comparison of the pilgrim to a Franciscan friar has already been suggested by the reference to the *corda* he wears (*Inf.* 16. 106) and will become more explicit in *Inferno* 23. 3, where he and Virgil are said to walk behind one another like Franciscans on the road ('come frati minor vanno per via'). In this context the Dante persona could be said to achieve a degree of both ironic and actual authority, standing 'like a friar' as confessor to the humiliated pope. A similar effect may also be generated by Dante the pilgrim's subsequent 'promotion' (through Nicholas's mistaking of identities in ll. 52–7) from friar to pope – and no less a pope, indeed, than Boniface VIII. The Franciscan apostolic theme is thus developed in a dourly comic way that is consonant with the canto's overall tone. It also reinforces the notion of a new or renewed hierarchy of authority: an alternative to that which has been corrupted by Nicholas and the simonists. This begins to be suggested by the contrast between two of the pilgrim's early speeches: one of them (ll. 37–9) affirming trust in and obedience to the poetic father, Virgil; the other (ll. 46–8) drawing attention to the grotesque condition of the delinquent papal father, 'planted there like a pole' ('come pal commessa', l. 47). Further consequences for the Dante persona derive from this reversal. It has been noted by Herzman and Stephany that the 'confession' by the pope eventually brings not absolution but 'the stinging rebuke of Dante . . . [who], acting once again in a priestly fashion, chooses to bind rather than loose (Matt. 16: 19)'; and the attitude of this authoritative, friar-like pilgrim towards the avaricious pope can also be seen as comparable to the posture adopted in Dante's letter to the Avignon cardinals and at the opening of Book 3 of the *Monarchia*.[39] The contemporary political context within which these contrasts and confrontations are locatable includes both a wider dispute and some specific assertions: the

[38] For Dante's use of the term *frate* in the *Commedia*, see Chapters 3 and 4 below, pp. 98–104 and 128–9; and on the word's contemporary semantic range see Onder's article in *ED* 3. 50.

[39] Herzman and Stephany 1978: 55. Also on the consequences of Nicholas's 'confession', see Emmerson and Herzman 1992: 125. On Dante's stance in the letter to the cardinals and *Mon.* 3, see this chapter below pp. 83–5 with nn. 154–61 and Chapter 4 below, pp. 154–9.

developing conflict between the Spiritual Franciscans and the Papacy; the circulation of the *Vaticinia de summis pontificibus*; and the belief current among certain Franciscan dissidents that Nicholas III's papal authority had been revoked by an angel and 'vested in certain friars and their followers who lived in the spirit of apostolic poverty'.[40]

There are also political contexts for several other features of the canto's vocabulary and imagery. For instance, the *borsa* ('purse' or 'pouch') in which Dante's Nicholas III now knows himself to be confined has a certain grimly appropriate reflexivity. He underlines the point through the uncomfortable zeugmatic construction of the line in which he acknowledges this condition and what caused it:

> che sù l'avere e qui me misi in *borsa*.
>
> [that I put wealth up there and myself down here in a *purse*.] (l. 72)

Nicholas's use of the word *borsa* here not only embodies his alleged simony and avarice in a palpable form, but also recalls one of the central images of the debate about Franciscan poverty: the Apostles' purse. The problem of squaring the evidence of Christ's and the Apostles' use of money (for instance Luke 22: 36, John 13: 29 and Acts 4: 34–7) with Christ's injunction not to possess gold, silver or money, or carry a purse (Matthew 10: 10, Mark 6: 8, Luke 9: 3) was one that opponents of strict Franciscan poverty would eagerly exploit.[41] St Francis's own Rule of 1221 obviously alludes to the Gospel injunctions concerning the *pera* and *pecunia*, such as that in Luke 9: 3.[42] Subsequently, at least four of the early lives of St Francis describe an occasion on which he is said to have responded immediately and dramatically to the reading of this part of the instructions to the Apostles.[43] But how to reconcile this basic apostolic prescript with the evidence that Christ and the Apostles

[40] See this chapter below, p. 79 and n. 130.

[41] On the problem of Christ's purse or 'bag' for the Franciscans (and the use of scriptural evidence by their opponents), see Davis 1990: 250–2 and Wolf 2003: 92. In 1321–3 the Dominican Hervaeus Natalis prepared for John XXII the *Liber de paupertate Christi et apostolorum*, which attacks the Franciscan position on evangelical poverty and refers throughout to Christ's purse and to its implications for the Church. See Hervaeus Natalis (tr. Jones) 1999: esp. 23–4, 73–4, 96–7, and 108–14, with (for the responses of Franciscan cardinals and bishops) 121–47.

[42] Section 14 of the 1221 Rule.

[43] See *1 Celano* 1.9; *Legenda maior* 3.1; *Legenda minor* 2.1; and *Legenda trium sociorum* 25.

did possess purses (*loculos*, John 13: 29) was a question with which later Franciscans, such as Bonaventura (in the *Apologia pauperum*), were recurrently concerned.[44] Following Bonaventura, Petrus Iohannis Olivi addressed the problem at several points in the ninth of his *Quaestiones de perfectione evangelica* (shortly before 1279), and he explicitly took issue with Aquinas on the subject in his *Postilla* (or *Lectura*) *super Matthaeum* (late 1279/early 1280).[45] Nicholas's clarification of the Franciscan Rule in *Exiit qui seminat* (14 August 1279) adopts a number of legal and exegetical arguments from Bonaventure's *Apologia pauperum*, and it also follows him in its resolution of the problem of Christ's purse.[46] Like Bonaventure, *Exiit* distinguishes between the counsel of perfection (abandoning the purse and the possession of money) and concessions to imperfection (the use of the bag entrusted to Judas), and this distinction on the part of *dominus Nicholaus* and his bull was acknowledged shortly afterwards by Olivi in the second of his major works on Franciscan poverty, the *Tractatus de usu paupere*.[47]

The acknowledgement by Dante's Nicholas III of how he has filled both an earthly and an infernal 'purse' may thus invoke an exegetical tradition to which Nicholas himself had contributed, whilst grimly underlining his personal failure to fulfil the apostolic counsel of perfection. His use of the word *borsa* here does not of course indicate assent on Dante's part to any particular radical Franciscan agenda on poverty, such as Ubertino da Casale had more recently adopted in the *Arbor vitae crucifixae* (c. 1305).[48] It does, on the other hand, suggest that Dante was responding to a debate about Franciscan poverty that was developing and intensifying during the years in which the *Inferno* was being written,

44 See for instance the *Apologia* in Bonaventura 1882–1902: vol. 8, pp. 236, 237, 284–6 and chapter 10.

45 For references to the *loculi* in the *Quaestio*, see Burr (ed.) 1992: 7–8, 29–30, 46 and 51–2; and for the argument against Aquinas in the Matthew Commentary, see Burr 1989: 48 and n. 36. On Olivi, see Chapter 1 above, pp. 34–6 with nn. 100–8.

46 See the text of *Exiit* in Gay (ed.) 1898–1916: no. 564, p. 234; and for discussion see Lambert 1961 (repr. 1998): 143–4 with n. 3.

47 The *Tractatus*, according to Burr 1989: 49, was written 'after October 1279 and probably before Easter 1283'. Its comment on Nicholas's interpretation of the *loculi* problem, in relation to the larger issue of *usus pauper*, is in lines 902–9, in Burr 1992: 117.

48 Ubertino, like some other Spirituals, even regarded *Exiit qui seminat* as dangerously compromising Franciscan ideals (see *Arbor vitae*, p. 432a), although he paid public tribute to its good intentions at the Avignon inquiry of 1309–12 (see this chapter below, p. 78 with n. 127).

and that he is here deploying some of the vocabulary associated with that debate, in order to extend the *cantica*'s political perspective. The effect in this particular instance is to increase the sense of an erstwhile Cardinal Protector's distance from the Franciscan ideal and thus further devalue Nicholas III's authority.

Political vocabulary and imagery are given a yet wider historical application in the subsequent speech through which the pilgrim inveighs against 'pastors' such as Nicholas himself, Boniface VIII and the first Avignon pope, Clement V, whose 'avarice is bringing the world to grief' (ll. 90–117). This speech – to which the pope is allowed no word of reply – begins with three ironic allusions: to the disregard for money in the calling to the Apostolate of Peter (Matthew 4: 18–22 and 16: 24); to the election of Matthias to replace Judas as apostle (Acts 1: 15–26); and to the influence of money upon Nicholas's policy as pope (ll. 90–9). The authority of evangelical poverty is thus contrasted with the compromised authority of the simoniac pope, and the model of early Christian idealism is set against the image of a modern papacy that has become venally political. In this context the pilgrim's subsequent gesture of 'reverence' for the pontifical keys ('le somme chiavi') – a symbol that had been brandished so frequently by contemporary popes and papal apologists – seems a somewhat perfunctory acknowledgement.[49]

The apocalyptic terms in which such 'pastors' are then condemned by Dante's pilgrim (ll. 106–17) also converge with those of Spiritual Franciscan polemic. Several modern commentators have shown that this passage's identification of such pastors with the 'meretri[x] magn[a] quae sedet super aquas multas' is particularly close to the apocalyptic exegesis of such Franciscans as Olivi, Ubertino and their followers.[50] Dante will return to this image – and its application to the Papacy – in both *Purgatorio* and *Paradiso*, and on those occasions, too, the Spiritual Franciscan imagining of the contemporary *ecclesia carnalis* (the 'carnal Church') will be invoked.[51] There is no need to assume that the poem is hereby adopting a specific ideological agenda, but the marked Franciscan

[49] On the interpretation of the symbolism of the papal keys by political theorists of Dante's time and earlier, see Chapter 4 below, p. 156 and n. 86.

[50] See Davis 1957: 29, and 1984: 59; also Manselli 1965: 124–5 and nn. 41–2; Manselli 1975: 185–6; BR 1: 289 (note on l. 106); and Davis in Mandelbaum *et al.* (eds.) 1998: 269–72.

[51] See *Purg.* 32.148–60 and *Par.* 27.58–60, and Chapters 3 and 4, pp. 115–17 and 171–3 below.

tenor of the passage, like other features of the canto's imagery and vocabulary, serves to reinforce the process whereby the pilgrim appears to be acquiring prophetic authority through challenging that of a pope.[52] Hence, in his address to Nicholas here, the Dante persona accuses him (perhaps in a parody of Luke 1: 52–3) of treading the worthy underfoot and exalting the unworthy ('calcando i buoni e sollevando i pravi', l. 105). This prompts Virgil – the voice of Empire and the ideals of Rome – into symbolic action. Virgil has been silent and unnoticed all the while since he urged Dante to correct Nicholas's mistaken identification of him with Boniface (ll. 61–2); but now – as if in response to this, and to confer validity upon the pilgrim's *parole vere* – he gathers the pilgrim up and ascends with him to the summit of the bridge from which the vision's next revelation will be made (ll. 121–33). Once again, as at the start of this canto, the actions of the poetic 'father' contrast sharply with the example of the papal one.[53]

In his final speech or 'song' to Nicholas III the pilgrim appears to acknowledge not only the authority of poverty but also (and especially on his own part) the wisdom of folly. His arrogation of authority to speak to a pope in terms such as these could, he implies, be seen as comparable to the audacity of the fool:

> Io non so s'i' mi fui qui troppo folle (l. 88)

This stance has a precedent in the Franciscan embrace of the role of *pazzus*, *stultus* or *idiota*. In the early lives of St Francis and the chronicles of the Order there are frequent descriptions of the saint and his followers as fools or madmen. Several of the biographies, for instance, reproduce Thomas of Celano's story of the newly converted Francis being pelted with mud and stones by his fellow citizens, who regard him as 'insanum ac dementem'.[54] Significantly, it is the most important of the unofficial lives of St Francis, the *Legenda trium sociorum* (dating from 1246, but probably assembled and completed in Dante's time by dissident friars) that seems most to emphasize the 'folly' of the saint and

[52] On this process, see Musa 1974: 53–7.

[53] See *Inf.* 19. 37–9 against 46–8. A similar view of Virgil's action, as 'the intended embrace of authority', is taken by Hawkins 1999: 33.

[54] *1 Celano* 11; see also *Legenda maior* 2.2, *Legenda minor* 1.6, *Legenda trium sociorum* 6.17.

his followers.[55] An important unofficial compilation of Dante's time, the *Speculum perfectionis*, describes a dramatic assertion of such 'folly' late in St Francis's career. At the meeting of the Order called 'the Chapter of the Mats' or 'the Chapter of Five Thousand Friars', a number of 'educated and learned friars' are said to have asked the 'Cardinal of Ostia' to advise Francis to accept their guidance, quoting the precedent of previous religious Rules.[56] On hearing this, Francis is then said to have taken the cardinal by the hand, led him before the assembled friars and bitterly denounced any attempt to revise his original apostolic principles of 'simplicity and humility'. To support his position in the face of the 'learned' friars, he is said to have added that

> dixit Dominus michi quod uolebat quod ego essem unus *novus pazzus* in mundo; et noluit nos ducere Deus per aliam uiam quam per istam scientiam . . .
>
> [the Lord said to me that he wished me to be a new-born (or 'new kind of') fool in the world. God did not want to lead us by any other way than this kind of learning . . .][57]

The original Franciscan 'fool' here confronts the two earthly authorities, his learned colleagues and the cardinal, whilst claiming for himself the authority of divine inspiration. Such a confrontation has features in common with the scene in which the pilgrim addresses the pope in *Inferno* 19, and it may well have been known to Dante, since it appears or is referred to in several contemporary Franciscan sources.[58] During Dante's own time the stance of 'fool of God' had also been adopted by

55 *Legenda trium sociorum*, chs. 2.4, 6.17, 7.21, and 9.34–5. On the dating and composition of the *Legenda*, see Desbonnets in Habig 1973: 877–9. For further discussion of 'Franciscan folly' and its relationship to biblical and Christian traditions, see Saward 1980: 84–9 with nn. 14–32.

56 The 'Chapter of the Mats' took place either in 1219 or 1221, and depending on which date is right, the cardinal of Ostia at the time would have been either Ugolino (subsequently Gregory IX), or Capocci; see Caroli in *FF*, 1376, n. 69.

57 *Speculum perfectionis*, ch. 68; see Brooke 1970: 288–9, Habig 1973: 1196–7, and Moorman 1968: 54–5.

58 These include Spiritual Franciscan sources such as Ubertino da Casale, *Arbor vitae* 5.7, and Angelo Clareno, *Historia septem tribulationum* 2.3. See also *Leggenda antica perugina* 114, and *Verba sancti Francisci* 5.

the Spiritual Franciscan Jacopone da Todi.[59] A number of Jacopone's *laude* represent divine love as a kind of madness.[60] In particular, the 'madness' of Christ's love (which leads to the Incarnation and the Crucifixion) evokes in several of his poems a similar kind of passionate folly on the part of the apostolic Christian. Thus one of Jacopone's *laude* shows how the act of a God who is considered 'foolish' ('stolto') and 'maddened by love' ('empazzato de l'amore') generates a similar 'madness' ('pazzia') in humanity; and another claims it to be the highest wisdom and learning to become one 'who acts the fool for Christ' ('chi pro Cristo va empazzato').[61]

Dante's somewhat disingenuous concern about whether his persona's address to the pope might be considered 'foolish' or 'rash' is of a piece with his rather perfunctory recognition of papal authority.[62] It also recalls how, at several points earlier in the *Inferno*, similar terms have been used to describe the audacity of the whole journey. In the well-known passage at the start of *Inferno* 2 where Dante (again disingenuously) denies any resemblance between his visionary enterprise and those of Aeneas and St Paul, he tells Virgil that he fears 'the venture may be foolhardy' ('che la venuta non sia *folle*', l. 35); and this is also how the guardians of Dis later regard his journey (*Inf.* 8.91). On both occasions it may well be that the use of the term reflects at one level the limitations of human powers and the need for divine grace.[63] Yet also implicit here, and in *Inferno* 19, is the paradoxical recognition that what, in the eyes of the pusillanimous and corrupt, may seem to be 'folly' is, in terms of the poem's developing vision, the highest wisdom. The paradox of the

59 On Jacopone, see Chapter 1 above, pp. 29–31.

60 See, for example Mancini 1974: nos 16.6 and 41.2.

61 See Mancini 1974: nos. 48.7 and 29–34, and 87.7. Compare also nos. 44. 71–3 (on God's madness); 79. 57–64 (on the *stoltia* of the Incarnation), and 89. 33, 161, 179 and 229 (on the madness of the Christian soul). Behind these Franciscan stances, and behind the 'folly' of Dante's persona in *Inferno* 19, lie the Pauline notions of God's 'folly' (*stultitia*) contrasted with human 'wisdom' (1 Corinthians 1:18–27), and of being a 'fool for Christ's sake' (1 Corinthians 3:18 and 4:10). Throughout 2 Corinthians 11 (and in 12:11) Paul's ironic adoption of the fool's role is clearly designed for confrontational purposes (to expose the pretended 'wisdom' of the Corinthians' compromises) and ultimately to buttress his divinely appointed mission and authority (*potestas*), as the epistle's conclusion shows (13:10). The Pauline stance thus provides an apostolic precedent for the kinds of subversive 'guerrilla theatre' that were subsequently enacted by St Francis, Jacopone and the pilgrim of *Inferno* 19.

62 *Inf.* 19. 100–3.

63 Thus BR 1: 20; see also Bosco 1966: 55–7.

'wisdom of folly' seems to have been revived with particular vigour in Dante's time. Siegfried Wenzel has suggested that the 'spiritual upgrading of the domestic fool' by the Franciscans could be related to changes in social structure and attitudes to authority (especially that of the higher clergy) in this period; and primitive Franciscanism itself appears to have involved certain reversals of values.[64] It is also, in *Inferno* 19, consonant with other sardonic and grotesque features and inversions that are evident throughout the canto.

The recurrent inversions of *Inferno* 19 thus have some strikingly positive effects, and their pattern reinforces a developing Franciscan discourse in the *Inferno*. The canto not only stresses the distortion of the apostolic mission through the cupidity of popes such as Nicholas, Boniface and Clement; it also yields prophetic authority to the still somewhat ignorant pilgrim who not only 'stands like a friar' but also speaks at points like a certain kind of Franciscan, and even sings a kind of Jacoponian *lauda* to accompany the impotent dance of the pontiff's flailing legs. The whole episode can therefore be seen not as a 'Franciscan *tragedy*' (*pace* Gardner), but rather as the satirical statement of what is to become a major theme in Dante's comedy – a theme that will continue to develop, with variations, in *Inferno* 27.

FAILED FRANCISCAN AND PAPAL PHARISEE: CANTO 27

There are several similarities of tone, imagery and theme between the encounters and exchanges in *Inferno* 19 and those in *Inferno* 27. In both, the central clerical figures (Nicholas and Guido) are addressed in harshly ironic terms and are entrapped and tormented by flame.[65] In both the images, issues and history of papal authority and Franciscan idealism interact (through, for example, the keys and the purse in *Inferno* 19 and the keys and the cord in *Inferno* 27). And in both Boniface VIII is represented as a major political player. There are, however, also some

[64] See Wenzel in Benson and Wenzel 1982: 227–31 and 239. On reversals of values in early Franciscanism, see Manselli 1975: 174.

[65] In several of the manuscripts the illustrators emphasize the point in Guido's case by not only placing him inside a flame but also dressing him in a friar's habit; see BMS 2: 274a and 275c (this may also reflect the play upon the word *vestito* in *Inf.* 27. 129). For different treatments of the flames in relation to the simonists' legs and enclosures, see ibid., 215a and c, 216b, 217a–c, 219a, 220b, 221 and 222 a–b.

significant differences between the two cantos, even in their portrayal of relationships between the Papacy and the Franciscans. For instance, the Franciscan dimensions in Guido's drama of damnation are much more explicit. We hear him speaking *as a friar* and confronting the authority of the pope; and we are shown the final conflict over his soul between the ruthlessly logical devil and the silent, powerless figure of St Francis, who is mentioned by name here (l. 112) for the first time in the *Commedia*.

Within this scenario, Dante's persona and voice are less prominent and more modulated than in *Inferno* 19. Unlike the pilgrim confronting Nicholas III, the figure here is not compared to a friar, nor does he aggressively adopt the role of Franciscan 'fool' or prophet. Indeed, there appear to be no explicit signs on his part or Virgil's of response to Guido's unfolding plight. His presence is strongly marked only in the first half of the canto. His speech (in reply to Guido's question) about the state of the Romagna (ll. 37–53) may perhaps be comparable in its historical sweep to the pilgrim's condemnation of the decadence of modern 'pastors' in *Inferno* 19, but stylistically it has rather more in common with outbursts like those of Guido del Duca in *Purgatorio* 14 or Cacciaguida in *Paradiso* 16. His description of the Romagna's chronic instability (ll. 51 and 54) and the discrepancy between the outward appearance of peace and the instinct for war 'in the hearts of its tyrants' (ll. 37–9) reflects the division in the identity of Guido himself (as the warrior-politician whose inner nature had been merely disguised by the Franciscan habit).[66] To expose this inner nature, the pilgrim addresses Guido as a somewhat devious confessor, encouraging him to think of how his name and fame may 'stand firm' ('tegna fronte'), whilst at the same time letting him believe that he is speaking off the record (ll. 55–66). As a confessor who holds out false promises and generates trust in outward signs and appearances, the pilgrim could thus be said in some ways to anticipate the Boniface of Guido's narrative (ll. 101 and 108–9). Of course, the Dante persona is only ironically comparable to his chief papal enemy Boniface here; his deviousness towards Guido is designed ultimately to reveal the truth. Yet we are now very deep in the circles of fraud, and this canto is fraught with distrust and uncertainty for all concerned.

[66] On the political state of the Romagna at this time, see Larner 1965: 1–98. For Dante's earlier assessment of Guido's conversion see *Conv.* 4.28.8.

One form of uncertainty involves the part that is played in this complex scenario by the pope himself. For, if Guido is telling the truth about how Boniface had encompassed his 'fall', why is the latter destined only for the eighth circle and not the ninth?[67] Of course, it is important that Guido himself should be regarded as ultimately resposible for his own damnation, but the pope's role as a proximate cause is so powerfully portrayed as to make the issues rather more complex than some interpreters have allowed.[68] Historically, Boniface appears to have been taking advantage of a challenge to his authority and the very legitimacy of his accession from the Colonna cardinals, in order to consolidate the fortunes of his own dynasty; and it has been seriously questioned whether he ever solicited or used Guido's services at all.[69] Yet Dante's Boniface is an almost Luciferian figure who comprehensively illustrates what a much earlier pope (Gregory I) had called 'the avarice of high position'.[70] He is given only six lines of direct speech in the whole canto (ll. 100–5), but these two *terzine* convey a concentrated and increasingly confident assertion of papal ambition and power. Boniface's aspiration to rule both in this world and the next is simply but strikingly conveyed by the juxtaposition of *terra* ('earth') and *ciel* ('heaven') in two adjacent lines (ll. 102–3). He then flourishes the traditional image of the papal keys (l. 104) with a conviction that had been somewhat lacking in the pilgrim's earlier depiction of Nicholas III's authority.[71] He concludes by expressing contempt for his predecessor Celestine V's lack of will to wield these emblems of sovereignty (l. 105). This last remark could also be construed as a veiled warning to Guido about the dangers of opposing this pope's will, since it was widely believed that Boniface had not only engineered Celestine's resignation but had done away with him as

[67] See *Inf.* 19.52–4 and *Par.* 30.148.

[68] For example, Baldi (in Mellone (ed.) 1987: 147 and n. 21) rather too readily dismisses the question of responsibility raised by Sanguineti (1961: 271–80) as 'priva di senso'.

[69] See Boase 1933: ch. 6, esp. 170 and on the 'fable' of Guido's involvement, 179–80. Dante's source for the story is probably the *Historie* of Riccobaldo of Ferrara, written in Padua c. 1308–13; see Boase 1933: 179 and Davis 1984: 89–92, esp. n. 56. Baldi (in Mellone 1987: 134) rejects this hypothesis on somewhat questionable grounds (Renucci's dating of *Inf.* 8–27 to 1306–7).

[70] *XL Homiliarum in evangelia libri duo* in *PL* 76, col. 1136.

[71] On the use of this image by papal theorists, see Chapter 4 below, p. 156 with n. 86; and for its recurrence in *Inf.* 19.101, see this chapter above, p. 57 with n. 49.

well.[72] Threats as well as promises are part of the pope's repertoire, as Guido acknowledges when he mentions the unspecified forms of 'heavy pressure' ('argomenti gravi') that speeded his assent and his 'fall'.[73]

In fact, the scene that Guido represents as crucial to an individual destiny is also redolent of the more extreme claims about papal power that were made by Boniface and his apologists. Thus, in describing the pope as *principe* ('prince, ruler', l. 85), rather than 'priest' (as earlier, l. 70), Guido may be already highlighting his temporal ambitions.[74] In an odd reversal of roles, which likewise reinforces Boniface's pretensions, the pope figures not as the ecclesiastical recipient of the famous Donation (Pope Sylvester I) but as its secular dispenser, Constantine; and his fever for power is compared with the Emperor's leprosy (ll. 94–7).[75] His claim in his speech to be able to control access to Heaven and to absolve Guido 'in advance' ('finor', l. 101) approaches the kind of wildly extravagant claim that Dante will cite as absurd when, in the *Monarchia*, he defines the limits to the power of Peter's keys.[76] And at the very end of this scene in Guido's narrative, Boniface is elevated once again to a Satanic eminence through the old politician's claim that fraudulent counsel will enable him 'to triumph in the high seat' ('triunfar ne l'alto seggio', l. 111), like Isaiah's Lucifer (Isaiah 14: 13–14).

Guido is not, however, simply the victim of Boniface and his will to power. Indeed, the two of them, the failed Franciscan and the 'prince of the new Pharisees', fully deserve each other. There are, it is true, elements of the tragic and the pathetic in the drama of Guido's fall.[77] Nonetheless,

[72] The accusation that Boniface murdered Celestine was made in the second Colonna manifesto of 16 May 1297. See Denifle 1889: 515–16 and Boase 1933: 172 and 176.

[73] Baldi (in Mellone 1987: 135) plausibly suggests that the threat of excommunication is heavily implied here and in ll. 103–4.

[74] In *Monarchia* the term *princeps* will be used almost exclusively of secular rulers: see, for example *Mon.* 3.1.5, 3.14.1, 3.16.11 and 16.

[75] On the significance of this role-reversal in *Inf.* 27. 94–6, see also Ferrrante 1984: 97–8.

[76] In *Mon.* 3.8.7 Dante argues that, if 'Whatsoever thou shalt bind' were interpreted in an absolute sense, 'He [Peter] could . . . absolve me without my having repented, which even God himself could not do' (tr. Shaw 1996: 76–7). This of course lends further authority to the devil's logic in *Inf.* 28.118–20.

[77] Guido's concern for the peace of his *dolce terra* (ll. 25–8) is almost Francesca-like in its pathos; his use of the seafaring metaphor (ll. 79–81) poignantly recalls the more successful existential journey with which Dante had associated him in *Convivio* 4.28; and his use of the verb *rendersi* to describe his decision to enter the Franciscan order (l. 84) echoes what the same chapter of the earlier work had evocatively said about the 'noble soul' in old

his story and his relationship to the cunning pope and the astute devil can also be seen as a grim comedy of connivance, deception and outwitting. His indignant description of Boniface as 'prince of the new Pharisees' (l. 85) is itself more than a little ironic in the circumstances, and not wholly in the way that he seems to intend. For 'Pharisee', in the sense of 'observer of religious forms rather than substance', had been used pejoratively since the time of Guillaume de Saint Amour, and subsequently in the verse of Rutebeuf and Jean de Meun, to describe the alleged hypocrisy of the friars themselves.[78] Dante, as reader (and possibly translator) of the *Roman de la Rose*, would have been familiar with this feature of the antifraternal tradition. In this 'fraternal' sense, then, Guido is himself a 'Pharisee', since he acknowledges that his belief and conversion were not *intero* (l. 69), and he frankly admits to foxy behaviour, cunning and deception (ll. 74–8).

An outward and visible sign of Guido's Franciscanism is the cord (*corda* or *capestro*, referred to in ll. 67–8 and 92–3), and this image has perhaps even more resonance both within and outside the *Commedia* than that of Nicholas III's *borsa* in *Inferno* 19. The cord was a distinctive feature of Franciscan dress, mentioned in Francis's Rules of 1221 and 1223, as well as in his *Testament* of 1226; and by the later thirteenth century it had yielded the familiar term by which Guido identifies the Order and himself: *cordigliero* (l. 67).[79] The Dante persona twice treats the cord as part of a rite of passage in the course of his journey: in *Inferno* 16 (106–114), where it may suggest integrity; and in *Purgatorio* 1 (94–5 and 133–6), where it seems to signify humility. In both cases, and particularly the second, the ritual appears to reinforce the pilgrim's purposes in a way that contrasts with Guido's hesitant and ultimately inadequate commitment. In a number of the early Lives of St Francis, the

age. For the voyage metaphor, applied to both Guido and Lancelot, see *Conv.* 4.28.7–8. For the verb *rendersi*, see 4.28.7: '*Rendesi* dunque a Dio la nobile anima in questa etade etc.'. On the relationship between *Inf.* 27 and *Conv.* 4.28 see also Moleta 1983: 83–6.

78 One of Guillaume's most widely disseminated works was the sermon *De Pharisaeo et publicano* (August 1256); see Szittya 1986: 34–41 and 115–18. For Rutebeuf's poems, including 'Du pharisien ou C'est d'hypocrisie', see Faral and Bastin 1959–60; and for Jean de Meun on the friars as Pharisees, see *Roman de la Rose*, ed. Langlois 1914–24: ll. 11605–36. Dante himself obliquely signals the relationship between friars and Pharisees in *Inf.* 23, where he brings together as *gente dipinta* (the hypocrites) both *frati* (109) and *Farisei* (116).

79 See *GDLI s.v. cordigliere* (where Dante's use is listed as the first) and *ED*, 2, 208b.

adoption of a cord rather than a belt forms part of a ritual of commitment to the apostolic mission.[80] It is also often mentioned as one of the visible signs of apostolic poverty; and the Saint's own cord is in several sources endowed with talismanic status as the source of miraculous cures.[81] These are the elements of Franciscan tradition that Guido invokes when describing his encounter, as a Franciscan, with a pope who had no regard for the ideals of his own office and priesthood

> . . . né in me quel capestro
> che solea fare i suoi cinti più macri.
>
> [nor in me for that cord which used to make those who wore it grow more lean.] (ll. 92–3)

The emblems of Franciscan poverty and integrity that Guido and Boniface are about to betray are here contrasted with the arrogance and power of the pope, who is described in this same context as a 'prince' (l. 85), 'like Constantine' (l. 94) and afflicted by a 'fever of pride' (l. 97).[82] One of the very early illustrated manuscripts of the *Commedia* reflects this contrast. Florence Riccardiana 1005 was produced in Bologna in the second quarter of the fourteenth century and contains the vernacular commentary of Jacopo della Lana. Its illustrations are confined throughout to historiated initials for the opening of each canto and the start of its commentary. On this occasion (see fig. 1) Lana's first sentence opens with the dispute over the dying Franciscan's soul (St Francis flying down from the right and the devil climbing up on the left); whilst the initial 'G' of the text itself shows Guido as a tonsured friar making his fatal submission to the regal Boniface.[83] The illustrations here concisely convey the canto's sardonic asssociation between the corruption of the papal office and that of Franciscan ideals. A yet more ambitious grouping is

80 See Bonaventura, *Legenda maior* 3.1 and *Legenda minor* 2.1; and *Legenda trium sociorum* 25.

81 For the cord as a sign of poverty, see *Legenda maior* 7.1, *Legenda minor* 3.5, *Speculum perfectionis* 3, and Jacques de Vitry, *Historia occidentalis* 2, ch. 32.2.

82 The reference to becoming 'lean' (*macri*) may also be significant here: the early Apostles will be described as *magri* in *Paradiso* 21. 128.

83 Riccardiana 1005 (containing *Inf.* and *Purg.*) is part of the same manuscript as Milan BN Braidense A. G. XII.2 (which contains *Par.*). Its copyist was Maestro Galvano of Bologna (d. 1347) whose name appears on f. 100r of the latter. On its importance as an early text of the *Commedia* and its unusual illustrative layout, see D'Arcais 1978.

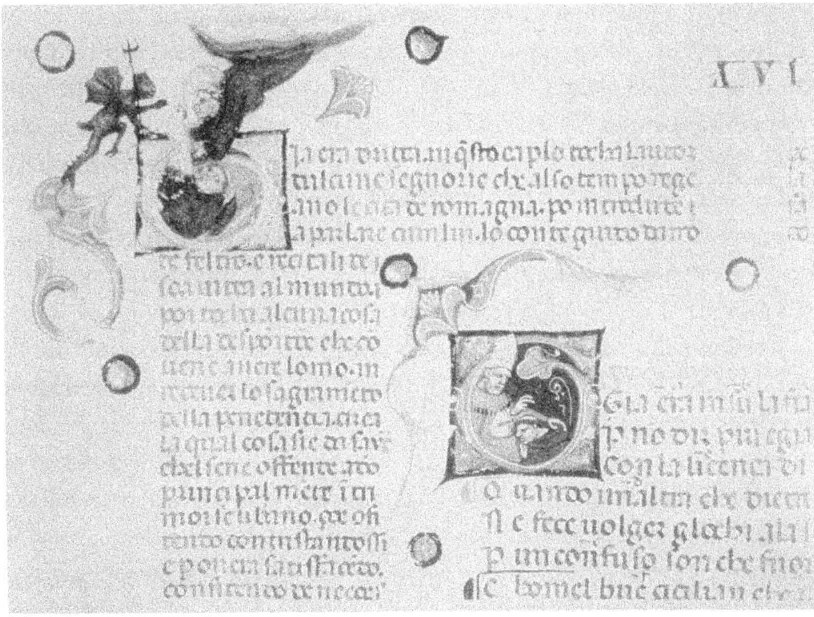

Figure 1. St Francis and the devil in dispute over the soul of Guido da Montefeltro (upper left); Boniface VIII absolves Guido (centre).

ventured by a later Italian artist: the mid-fifteenth-century illustrator of Madrid BN 10057 (see frontispiece). In one of this manuscript's many drawings, Guido appears as the man in the middle, with the Franciscan cord visible around his waist and arms devotionally crossed in the midst of the flame. On his left the figure of Boniface is proudly enthroned, and on his right stand the two poets. The identical admonitory gestures of the pope on one side and Virgil on the other accentuate the grim struggle between political pressure and religious idealism that constitutes this particular drama of damnation.

The same drama culminates in the struggle between the saint himself and the devil over Guido's soul (ll. 112–23). St Francis here, attempting in vain to redeem the dead friar, is a voiceless and powerless figure; and he has to be reminded by the devil, speaking with the residual wisdom of the fallen angel, of the simple but fatal contradiction that vitiates Guido's apparent penitence and piety. There may be a number of possible reasons for Francis's silence at this point. Despite his highly vocal presence in the early Lives and his prominence in Dante's hagiography, he is never made to speak in *Paradiso*; and here, in a situation where the power of speech is abused (by Boniface, Guido and the devil) to deceive or damn, it may also be even more fitting for the saint to remain silent. Francis's defeat by the devil at the end of this canto may also reflect what some would have seen (back in the 1290s) as the stifling of Franciscan idealism by the figure who has been seen in this scenario as the devil's ally: Boniface.[84] There are varying interpretations of the historical Boniface's motives and strategies towards the rigorist Franciscans, such as Angelo Clareno and the Poor Hermits of Pope Celestine.[85] The Boniface of *Inferno* 27, however, with his contempt for the 'cord' and his 'avarice of high position', is clearly recognizable as an entrenched and avowed enemy to Franciscan ideals.

The final struggle over Guido's soul has been compared not only to the corresponding conflict between angel and devil over his son Bonconte

[84] On the stylistic relationship between Boniface's speech and that of the devil and the common purpose of their different kinds of logic, see Baldi in Mellone 1987: 139. Baldi also (142) draws attention to the description of the devil as 'un d'i neri cherubini' and sees the confrontation between St Francis and the devil in terms of a conflict between ('seraphic') charity and ('cherubic') logic, comparing *Par.* 11. 37–9.

[85] See, for instance, Boase 1933: 167–9 and Burr 1989: 112–26.

(*Purg.* 5. 103–29), but also to the popular tradition of such deathbed scenarios and the genre known as the *contrasto*.[86] This genre, which can be found in medieval Latin as well as in the vernaculars, often involves encounters between devils and saints as well as devils and angels, and when it takes the form of disputes over the souls of the dying the conflict can, of course, be resolved either way.[87] Franciscan writing of Dante's time also develops such features of the genre in ways that are directly comparable with the *contrasto* at the end of *Inferno* 27, and once again, contemporary evidence can be found in the work of the turbulent Spiritual Franciscan Jacopone da Todi.[88] Jacopone, with his characteristic impulse towards dramatization, incorporates forms of *contrasto*, or (as he sometimes calls it) *entenz[as]one*, into a number of his poems.[89] In one of his *laude* to St Francis, for instance, he stages an extensive confrontation between the saint and the 'Enemy' (*lo Nimico*) which develops into a battle of words and, in contrast to *Inferno* 27, concludes with the devil being utterly routed.[90] Several of Jacopone's poems come even closer to the themes of Guido's narrative in *Inferno* 27 by representing the human soul as it confronts diabolical temptation, death, judgement and the otherworld.[91] Amongst Jacopone's *laude*, perhaps the most striking parallel to the drama of *Inferno* 27 can be found in the *contrasto* 'O Iesù Cristo pietoso' (Mancini, ed., no. 63). Here the human soul, cornered by death, appeals for mercy to God, but the devil intervenes to demand his rights (ll. 21–8), and subpoenas the soul's guardian angel to testify against it. In the light of the evidence the devil's demand for strict justice ('rasone', ll. 24, 84, 95) prevails; the time for repentance is said to be past (ll. 109–10), and a gang of fork-wielding demons finally appears on the scene to sing cheerful songs of welcome as the guilty soul is pitched into the flames (ll. 133–48). The combination of grim humour and legal punctiliousness (characteristic of many medieval devils) is a notable feature of the soul's 'enemy' in both Jacopone's and Dante's *contrasti*, whose scenarios also both run the complete gamut from Heaven to Hell.

[86] See, for instance, BR 1: 395 and Baldi in Mellone 1987: 140–1.

[87] See Gurevich 1990: 186–7.

[88] On Jacopone, see chapter 1 above pp. 29–31, and this chapter above, p. 60 with nn. 59–61.

[89] For the term *entenz[as]one* in Jacopone's verse, see Mancini 1974: nos. 7.1, 57.1 and 63.22. On this aspect of his writing, see also Ageno 1953: xv–xvi.

[90] Mancini 1974: no. 71, esp. 67–162.

[91] Mancini 1974: nos. 42, 54, 56, 62, 63 and 88.

Jacopone also parallels the Dante of *Inferno* 27 in the way he elsewhere stages sardonic dramas of failed Franciscan commitment, notably in the address to the soul of the departed 'Frate Rinaldo', and in 'Assai m'esforzo a guadagnare', where a friar confesses to being led astray by false goods.[92] Moreover, as is well known, he confronted in verse the pope who had imprisoned him – most notably in the savagely satirical 'O papa Bonifazio, molt'ài iocato al mondo'.[93] In this latter poem Jacopone envisages the pope's own reluctant departure from a world where he has rapaciously heaped up wealth (ll. 12–14), achieved dominance through trickery ('astuzie', l. 31), set up his throne like Lucifer (the parallel is explicit in ll. 47 and 51) and suppressed true religion (l. 55). And the 'thirst of avarice' with which Jacopone's Boniface is afflicted (l. 63) corresponds closely to the appetite that is said to drive Dante's Boniface in *Inferno* 19. 55–7. Since, as *Inferno* 27 shows, Dante knew of Boniface's conflict with the Colonna family and the fall of the fortress of Palestrina in 1298, he may well have known about Jacopone as a signatory to the first of the Colonna manifestoes, as a prisoner after the defeat, and as a fellow-victim and critic of papal *Realpolitik*.[94]

There is one further phase in this infernal pattern of encounters with papal politics and authority. For, just as the Franciscan *Vaticinia* portrayed a succession of evil popes, so Dante, through Nicholas III, imagined a sequence of decline in which Boniface was to be succeeded by a ruler guilty of 'yet worse deeds' ('più laida opra'). To complete the sequence of Dante's infernal *vaticinia*, then, we need to return to *Inferno* 19; to the pope who, in Dante's view, is destined to follow Boniface down to Hell and who transferred papal authority westwards to Avignon: Clement V.

DANTE'S CLEMENT V

The previous section of this chapter showed how features of language and allusion in *Inferno* 19 reinforce the Franciscan dimensions of the canto. Deployment of certain kinds of political and apocalyptic

92 Mancini 1974: nos. 75 and 88. 93 Mancini 1974: no. 83.

94 Jacopone is named (along with two other Franciscans) as a witness to the first Colonna manifesto against Boniface (10 May 1297); see Denifle 1889: 495 and 514, and Boase 1933: 171.

vocabulary does not, of course, imply acceptance on Dante's part of any particular Franciscan agenda. Such features do, however, seem to mark a response in the text to a debate in and about the Franciscan Order that was intensifying and undergoing several crises during the first two decades of the fourteenth century, precisely the years in which the *Commedia* itself was taking shape. They thus extend the political perspective of the poem, and the pilgrim's discourse can be seen to converge with the two major Spiritual Franciscan themes of poverty and apocalyptic prophecy. Franciscan discourse thus becomes, here and later in the *Commedia*, a way of both addressing and assuming authority – a way of talking to popes and locating the Papacy in history.

Clement V (1305–14) does not figure in the *Commedia* as frequently as Boniface VIII or as vividly as Nicholas III. Yet, as the first of the Avignon popes, the ally of the French monarchy and the supporter, but subsequently the adversary, of Henry VII, he had a unique importance for Dante and the *Commedia*. He is mentioned three times in *Paradiso* and is the subject of Beatrice's very last words in the poem (*Par*. 30.142–8); and Dante probably revised *Inferno* 19 soon after his death, in order to include him as one of the corrupt 'pastors' of the Church.

In *Inferno* 19 Nicholas III – who is 'planted like a pole' in Dante's Malebolge and due to be driven down further into the fissures of the rock by the advent of Boniface VIII – prophesies that Boniface will not stay long with his 'flaming feet' above the surface, since

> . . . dopo lui verrà di più laida opra,
> di ver' ponente, un pastor sanza legge,
> tal che convien che lui e me ricuopra.[95]
>
> [. . . after him will come from out of the west a pastor without principle, guilty of yet worse deeds, who is due to be placed on top of both him and me.]

This pastor is Clement, and the threefold descending sequence (Nicholas, Boniface, Clement) puts him at the end of the process of papal degradation in this canto and in the *Inferno*. His identification with Jason, the hellenizing High Priest of 2 Maccabees (4: 7–26) who bought his office with promises of huge amounts of silver, also associates

[95] *Inferno* 19. 82–4.

him closely with the avaricious 'pastors' who are the subject of the pilgrim's subsequent visionary diatribe (ll. 90–117). The whole episode also forms part of the first occasion in the *Inferno* on which contemporary popes are precisely identified, and the references to Clement's origins and pontificate constitute the *Commedia*'s first allusion to the Avignon Papacy.[96] The repeated patterns of inversion and descent in *Inferno* 19 and the description of this particular pope as a 'pastor without principle' ('sanza legge') coming from the west ('di ver' ponente') thus reinforce the poem's concern with what, in the view of Dante and others, was a fatal transfer of papal authority.[97]

The date of *Inferno* 19's composition is impossible to ascertain precisely, but there is a strong possibility that it may have been revised after the death of Clement V in April 1314, since it refers quite specifically (in ll. 79–81) to Nicholas having to wait longer for Boniface to appear (from 1280 till 1303) than Boniface will have to wait for Clement (from 1303 till 1314).[98] The decade before 1314 was one in which Dante's attitude towards the Papacy and papal authority was undergoing significant changes. The transfer of its seat of government to France, beginning with Clement's election in 1305, was of marked consequence and concern to Italians – and during 1310–13 Dante was also urgently concerned about Clement's handling of Henry VII's attempt to assert imperial authority in Italy, and about the process by which the Gascon pope, having initially supported Henry (as a counterbalance to the power of France) then 'betrayed' him in the face of opposition from Robert of Anjou.[99] It was during this same period, too, that the relationship between the Franciscans and the Papacy reached one of its periodic crises.

[96] Earlier references to popes are indirect (*Inf.* 3. 58–60 and 6. 69), generalized (*Inf.* 7, 47), or to a much earlier figure (the heretical Anastasius II in *Inf.* 11. 8–9).

[97] Clement V (Bertrand de Got) was of a noble Gascon family and at the time of his election was Archbishop of Bordeaux; see Mollat 1949: 28. For further references to the Avignon 'captivity' in the *Commedia*, see, for instance, *Purgatorio* 20. 85–96 and 32.142–60, and *Paradiso* 27. 40–60; and, on the rationale of the move westwards, see Renouard (tr. Bethell) 1970: 32–5.

[98] The dating of *Inf.* 19 is discussed by Gorra 1917: 211–17. On the question of the canto's revision, see: Petrocchi 1957: 658, 667; Vasina 1982: 177; Davis 1984: 56 (n. 47), 58 (n. 52) and 83; and BR 1: 286–7 (n. on l. 81).

[99] On the effects upon Italy of the Papacy's move to Avignon see Holmes 1986: 182–5. For Clement's attitude towards Henry VII's Italian expedition, see Mollat 1949: 309–29 and Barraclough 1968: 143. The accusation of betrayal comes from Dante's Cacciaguida in *Par.* 17.82.

THE FRANCISCANS AND THE PAPAL INQUIRY OF 1309–12

The occasion that focused Franciscan attention on Avignon was the process leading up to the fifteenth general council of the Church, the Council of Vienne (1311–12). The Council itself was chiefly concerned to ward off Philip IV's attack on the doctrines of Boniface VIII by sacrificing the Templars and their wealth to him, and it was thus, as one historian has concluded, 'not an edifying assembly'.[100] Dante certainly knew about this feature of the Council's dealings, since in *Purgatorio* 20 (ll. 91–3) he explicitly refers to the suppression of the Templars as an instance of Philip IV's insatiable avarice. The Council of Vienne was, however, also concerned with proposals for ecclesiastical reform, and, as part of this more edifying agenda, attempted to resolve the bitter and long-standing dispute between the Spirituals and the Community over the observance of the Franciscan Rule.[101] The outcome of the latter process was the bull *Exivi de Paradiso*.[102] *Exivi*, issued by Clement on 6 May 1312, took full account of the Spirituals' complaints about relaxations and transgressions within the Order, especially with regard to buildings, clothing, church ornaments and money. On the other hand, it refused either to accept the Spirituals' view of *usus pauper* (restricted use of material resources) as a binding part of the Franciscan vow beyond what is specifically demanded in the Rule, or to let them secede from the Order and practise their own more rigorous interpretation of evangelical poverty. From the Spiritual Franciscan point of view, therefore, this papal decision was (to quote Leff's concise formulation) 'favourable to them . . . in detail' but 'against them in substance'.[103] *Exivi de Paradiso*, like Nicholas III's *Exiit qui seminat*, was thus yet another compromise settlement of the controversy about the interpretation of the Franciscan Rule, and it was to be supplanted by John XXII's much more radical solution in the early 1320s. Its decision on points of obligation in the Rule, however, proved extremely durable; and as Cardinal Giacomo Colonna (one of the allies of the Spirituals) pointed out a few years later, it had received a very substantial amount of attention during almost

[100] See Gorra 1917: 200–2; Ullmann 1974: 241 and 280–2; and Barraclough 1968: 138. For more detailed accounts of Clement's motives and procedure at this stage of the Templar case, see Barber 1978: ch. 9 (esp. 224–5) and Menache 1998: 235–46.

[101] Barraclough 1968: 138–39.

[102] For the full text of *Exivi*, see *BF* 5, no. 195, 80a–86a.

[103] Leff 1967: 155.

three years of official inquiry by a papal commission of investigation, from September 1309 until March or April 1312.[104]

Four questions were initially proposed for investigation by the inquiry: first, the possible connection between the Franciscans' followers and the supposed heresy of the Free Spirit; secondly, the observance of the Franciscan Rule; thirdly, the orthodoxy of Olivi's writings and teachings; and fourthly, the persecution of the Spirituals.[105] In the event, however, debate centred mainly on the second and third of these questions. The inquiry's dealings with these two main issues – the observance of the Rule and the doctrines of Olivi – have been held to represent 'the high watermark of the doctrinal struggle between the two parties' in the Franciscan Order.[106]

A number of eminent figures were involved. The pope's auditors who reported back to him were two successive pairs of cardinals: De Capella and Jorz up to 1310, and then Fredoli (an ally of the Spirituals) and Ruffati (Clement's nephew). The defenders of the Franciscan 'Community' against the Spirituals included the Minister General, Gonsalvo of Valboa; the English Provincial, Richard of Conyngton; the future Minister General, Alexander of Alexandria; and the jurist Bonagrazia of Bergamo – as well as the Order's procurator at the Curia, Raymond of Fronsac, who was later to provide a catalogue or summary of the proceedings.[107] Supporters of the Spirituals, in Avignon and elsewhere, included Robert of Naples (who in the summer of 1309 had written to the General of the Order requiring him to intervene to protect them); the pope's

[104] Cardinal Giacomo Colonna asserted in a letter to the Provost of Maguelonne that 'non meminimus iam dudum aliquod negotium cum maiori vel tanta maturitate a Romana Curia emanasse' ('I cannot recall for ages any business emerging from the Roman Curia after greater or even equal consideration'); see Mellone 1987: 50–1 (n. 213) and Oliger 1923: 351–2. The history of this investigation has been very fully narrated by Müller 1934: 236–386, and more recently by Burr 2001: chs. 5 and 6. Most of the relevant arguments presented can be found in the documents edited by Ehrle in *ALKG* 1886: 355–416 and 1887: 1–195. Briefer accounts in English are: Lambert 1961 (repr. 1998): ch. 8; Leff 1967: 139–57; and Nimmo 1987: 119–34. Both sides in the dispute – the Spirituals and the Community – had agreed to an inquiry, but it was instituted as, in part, a response to a complaint from the Spirituals about persecution in Provence; see Ehrle, *ALKG* 1887: 18, and Müller 1934: 252–54.

[105] See *ALKG* 1886: 361 and 1887: 51, 142–44.

[106] Leff 1967: 141.

[107] For Raymond's summary, see *ALKG* 1887: 1–32. For Conyngton's contribution to the debate, his *Tractatus de paupertate*, see *AFH* 1930: 1–11; and for Alexander's *Circa materiam de usu paupere*, see *AFH* 1917: 116–22.

physician, the ubiquitous Arnoldus of Villanova; the two Colonna cardinals (Giacomo and Pietro); and Cardinal Napoleone Orsini.[108] Angelo of Clareno, chronicler of the persecution of the Spirituals and their leader in the March of Ancona, is known to have been in Avignon (under the protection of the Colonna cardinals) during the later stages of the inquiry.[109] A former Minister General, the Provençal Raymond Gaufridi (Geoffroi), who had been deposed by Boniface VIII in 1295, was active on the Spirituals' behalf during the early months of the inquiry, until his death in April 1310; and nearly all the actual representatives of the Spirituals were, like Gaufridi, from Provence.[110] The dominant presence in the party, however, and the moving spirit in the inquiry as a whole, was an Italian who is mentioned by name in the *Commedia* and whose work Dante could have known or known about: Ubertino da Casale.

Ubertino's path may well have crossed or come near to crossing Dante's at several points in their respective careers and wanderings in the twenty years or so before the Avignon inquiry. For instance, after studying in Paris, it seems that Ubertino spent about four years in Florence, from 1285 to 1289, perhaps as lector in the *studium* at Santa Croce, thus overlapping with the period of Olivi's lectorship (1287–9).[111] After his period of retirement at La Verna, when (around 1305) he completed the *Arbor vitae crucifixae*, he entered into public life again as chaplain to and diplomatic negotiator for Cardinal Napoleone Orsini, the papal legate in central Italy.[112] Indeed, his activities in Italy shortly before the Avignon inquiry relate quite closely to some of Dante's political concerns. In the later part of 1307 Ubertino was involved, as Napoleone's agent, in the process of detaching first Siena, then Montepulciano and San Gimignano from the Florentine League, and he was also the cardinal's

108 See generally, Müller 1934: 251–54; more recently on Arnoldus, see Lee, Reeves and Silano 1989: ch. 3, 44–45, and Burr 2001: 111–12.

109 See the later parts of Angelo's *Historia septem tribulationum*, ed. Ehrle in *ALKG* 1886: 125–49, 287–327, and his *Epistola excusatoria* of 1317, ed. Ehrle in *ALKG* 1885: 521–33; also Douie 1932: ch. 3, and Daniel 1973: 89–98.

110 On the Provençal Spirituals at the Avignon inquiry, see Péano 1975: 55–6.

111 See Douie 1932: 121–24, and Potestà 1980: 22. On Ubertino's career, see also Chapter 1 above, p. 36 with nn. 110–13.

112 On the composition and dissemination of the *Arbor vitae*, see Charles Davis's introduction to the facsimile of the 1485 edition, Davis 1961: iii–v; on Ubertino's re-entry into public life, see Douie 1932: 126–27, and Potestà 1980: 23.

representative at the League's conference at Fucecchio (near Montecatini) in November 1307, when reconciliation and the recall of the Florentine exiles were on the agenda.[113] He appears to have remained in Italy during Napoleone's mission to Henry VII in Germany but is known to have been in Avignon, along with the Orsini cardinal, by the beginning of the inquiry in September 1309.[114]

The inquiry's precise terms of reference are not extant and can be reconstructed only from the writings of those involved – for instance, Raymond of Fronsac's later summary (dated late summer, 1318).[115] It began its proceedings at Malaucène, where Clement was residing at the priory of Groseau, and it followed him to Avignon in late November 1309.[116] The two opposing parties at the inquiry only rarely appeared together at hearings, and the debate seems to have taken the form of a 'pamphlet war' from which the cardinals charged with the commission compiled excerpts for their report to the pope.[117]

Ubertino's contributions to the debate were crucial to the Spirituals' case. They survive in the form of six submissions, which appeared over a period of nearly two years (from the beginning of 1310 to August 1311) and appear to have dictated the course of the debate.[118] The second and third of these are the tracts known by their opening phrases as *Rotulus iste* and *Decretalis etiam*, both of which Ubertino submitted to the commission in late 1310. These contained specific charges about relaxations and abuses in the Order's observance of the Rule which were accepted and reproduced not only by the papal auditors in their

[113] On Napoleone's expedition and Ubertino's diplomatic role, see Willemsen 1927: ch. 3, and esp. 47–48. See also Compagni (ed. Luzzato) 1968: Bk 3, chs. 15 and 17–18.

[114] Müller 1934: 254 with n. 95; Douie 1932: 127–28; Potestà 1980: 23.

[115] See Ehrle, *ALKG* 1887: 1–32.

[116] See Müller 1934: 255 with n. 102; and more recently Burr 2001: 113.

[117] Müller 1934: 261. Burr (2001: 113) on the other hand, compares Clement to 'a modern conference organizer . . . issu[ing] a call for papers'.

[118] These are, in order of composition: *Sanctitas vestra* of early 1310 (ed. Ehrle, *ALKG* 1887: 48–89); *Rotulus iste*, later in 1310 (ed. Ehrle, *ALKG* 1887: 89–130); *Decretalis etiam* of the same date (ed. Ehrle, *ALKG* 1887: 130–35; *Sanctitati apostolicae* of June 1311 (ed. Ehrle, *ALKG* 1886: 374–416); *Declaratio fratris Ubertini de Casali et sociorum eius contra falsitates* of August 1311 (ed. Ehrle, *ALKG* 1887: 160–95); and *Super tribus sceleribus*, also of August 1311, ed. Heysse in *AFH*, 1917: 103–74. A concise summary of the exchanges is in Potestà 1980: 180–1. Ubertino's account, in *Rotulus iste* and *Decretalis etiam*, of transgressions in the Order's observance of the Rule seems even to have influenced some features of the papal declaration in *Exivi de Paradiso*; see Ehrle, *ALKG* 1887: 89–90.

report but eventually also in the parts of *Exivi* that favoured the Spiritual cause.[119] The convolutions and tactics of the debate need not be traced in detail here, but two of its main features are worth emphasizing.

First, the cogency of Ubertino's arguments on the subject of Franciscan poverty and the current state of the Order were clearly recognized by his opponents and by the papal authorities; and the importance of his role as spokesman would have been obvious to anyone who knew that the inquiry was going on. A specific example of such recognition is the word that Dante's Bonaventura later uses (in *Par.* 12.126) to describe Ubertino's attitude to the Franciscan Rule: 'coarta' ('restricts'). Dante's Italian verb derives directly from the group of terms defining the stance that Ubertino was seen to be adopting at the Avignon inquiry: *ar[c]tus, artitudo* and *artare. Ar[c]tus* ('restricted') was commonly used as an adjective to gloss the key term in the Spirituals' vocabulary of evangelical poverty, *usus pauper*; and it serves this purpose in *Exivi de paradiso*, in the report of the papal commission and in Ubertino's own contributions to the inquiry.[120] The term itself and the related noun (*artitudo*) and the verb (*artare*) had been used by the historical Bonaventura himself in the *Apologia pauperum*, and they were taken up by the intellectual mentor of Ubertino and the Spiritual Franciscan movement, Petrus Iohannis Olivi, in two of his most important works on evangelical poverty, the *Quaestiones* and the *Tractatus.*[121]

Secondly, a number of specific ideas and issues debated by Ubertino and others in the course of the inquiry correspond to ones explored in *Inferno* 19 and elsewhere in the *Commedia.*[122] One of the most obvious of these concerns the reputation and authority of a previous pope, Nicholas III. Several contemporary chroniclers, as well as Dante in

[119] On the cardinals' report, see Fussenegger 1957: 145–77; and on the correspondences especially between *Rotulus iste* and *Exivi de paradiso*, see Lambert 1998: 211–12, and Mellone 1987: 51 and n. 216.

[120] For the phrase 'arctos usus seu pauperes' in *Exivi*, see *BF* 5, 85a; and for the equivalent term in the commission's report see Fussenegger 1957: 174–5. For examples of Ubertino's use of the word *arctus* in relation to the observance of poverty, see chapter 4 below, pp. 152–3 with n. 75.

[121] See *Apologia* in Bonaventura, 1898–1902: 8. 272–3 and 323; and Burr (ed.) 1992: 34 (ll. 1049, 1057 and 1060), 98 (ll. 282 and 290), 99 (l. 308), 103 (l. 463), and 113 (ll. 792 and 799).

[122] For concise accounts in English of the arguments at the inquiry, see the references to Lambert, Leff and Nimmo, above, n. 113.

Inferno 19 and the radical authors of the *Vaticinia de summis pontificibus*, regarded Nicholas as a simonist and nepotist, a feeder of the Orsini 'bear cubs'.[123] His name is also frequently invoked by both parties at the Avignon inquiry, but their attitude towards him is uniformly respectful.[124] The reasons for this are not hard to find. Nicholas's main declaration on Franciscan poverty, the bull *Exiit qui seminat*, provided some common ground for the disputants, since it was based largely on the moderate doctrine of St Bonaventure's *Apologia pauperum* and was accepted by Olivi as an authoritative declaration.[125] It also laid the foundation for the compromise settlement put forward at the end of the inquiry, in the bull *Exivi de Paradiso*; indeed, Clement refers early in the text of the bull to the glossing of the Franciscan rule by 'praedecessor noster'.[126]

Ubertino, in his first submission to the inquiry, repeatedly and somewhat uneasily stressed his respect for the good intentions of the 'declaracio domini Nicholai' (i.e. *Exiit*).[127] He was clearly constrained by the tactical requirements of the occasion, as well as by the fact that his own protector and employer, Napoleone Orsini, was Nicholas III's nephew. Five years or so earlier, however (and in a very different context), he had been markedly less circumspect – describing *Exiit qui seminat* in Book v of the *Arbor vitae*, along with other 'declarationes et dilatationes', as 'a millstone tied to the belly of the [Franciscan] Order'.[128] Luckily for him, his opponents on the Community side appear to have been unaware of the *Arbor vitae*; for, had they known of it, they would undoubtedly have used this passage and others to query his earnest protestations of loyalty

[123] See Villani (ed. Porta) 1990–1: vol. i. 494–6. For the chronicler's views of Nicholas's nepotism, see this chapter above, n. 29.

[124] See, for example, *ALKG* 1887: 54, 59, 76, and 89 (Ubertino); and pp. 142, 143, 145, 147, 151, and 154 (Raymond of Fronsac and Bonagrazia of Bergamo).

[125] On St Bonaventure and *Exiit*, see Lambert 1998: 151–3 and Leff 1967: i. 97–100. On Olivi's attitude, see Burr 1989: 39, 61–63, 74, and 99–101.

[126] *BF* 5, 81b. Clement here follows Nicholas III's lead in declaring that Franciscans are pledged by their vows to observe in the Rule solely those 'consilia evangelica, quae in ipsa regula preceptorie vel inhibitorie seu sub verbis aequipollentis exprimuntur' – repeating Nicholas in *Exiit*, *BF* 5, col. 1112 (also Olivi, *Tractatus* in Burr 1992: 115, ll. 844–66). See also Müller 1934: 314; Lambert 1998: 213–14; Leff 1967: 155–56; and Nimmo 1987: 122–3.

[127] See n. 37 above, and Nimmo 1987: 107–8. On Ubertino's tactics with regard to Nicholas III's authority and on his reading of *Exiit*, see also Burr 2001: 131–4.

[128] *Arbor vitae crucifixae*, Book v, 432a.

and respect.[129] At a later stage in the debate, they were ready, on far less solid evidence, to impute to Olivi (and by implication Ubertino) responsibility for the belief circulating among some followers of the Spirituals that an angel had apocalyptically 'deprived the lord Pope Nicholas III of his papal authority on account of his sins and vested it in certain friars and their followers who lived in the spirit of evangelical poverty'.[130] Ubertino in his reply vigorously rebutted the charge, denying that there was anything in Olivi's writings to support it.[131] The question of Nicholas's authority, however, clearly involved even larger issues for him – as it did for Dante's pilgrim in *Inferno* 19.

The Dante persona of *Inferno* 19 identifies the 'Evangelist's' vision of the Whore of Babylon, sitting upon many waters and consorting with kings (Revelation 17), explicitly with the sequence of papal decadence (the avarice and corruption of 'voi pastor') that he has himself just witnessed. Dante here differs from most commentators on the Apocalypse (including Ubertino), but closely resembles Olivi.[132] Olivi's doctrines had already been the subject of investigation and censure by the Community during his own lifetime.[133] After his death in 1298 his tomb at Narbonne (one of the strongholds of the Spirituals in Provence) had become the centre of a cult which was to last up to and beyond the removal of Olivi's body in 1318.[134] The more radical ideas of the Provençal Spirituals and their followers, the Beguins, were, they are alleged to have said, derived from Olivi's *Lectura* or *Postilla super Apocalypsim*, which (according to the Inquisitor Bernard Gui) 'they have both

[129] On Ubertino and papal authority, see also Chapter 1 above, pp. 41–2 with nn. 134–5. Book v of the *Arbor* also contains abusive references to Boniface VIII, Benedict XI and Clement himself (447a–448b) – and Leff 1967 (1. 152, n. 8) argues that, had the *Arbor* been known to the Community, it would have been used in Bonagrazia of Bergamo's indictment of Ubertino in 1317 and at Ubertino's trial in 1325. There are, as far as I can see, no grounds for Sophia Menache's assertion that the Avignon commissions 'received for their consideration the *Arbor vitae crucifixae*' (thus Menache 1998: 295 and n. 109). If they had done so, they would certainly have been less ready to accept the arguments of Ubertino's other submissions. On the restricted circulation of the *Arbor vitae*, see Davis 1961: iii; Potestà 1980: 18–21; and Mineo 1993: 577.

[130] *ALKG* 1886: 371 (my translation). For earlier instances of this kind of belief (in the 1290s) see Burr 1989, 112–24.

[131] *ALKG* 1886: 410–11. [132] Davis 1957: 226–7. [133] See Burr 1989: 88–111.

[134] See esp. Leff 1967: 1. 195–230; and (on the various accounts of the removal of Olivi's body) Burr 2001: 211–12.

in Latin and also in vernacular translation'.[135] The Inquisitor's evidence derives from the persecution of the Spirituals and their followers at a later stage, during the first few years of John XXII's pontificate (from 1317 to the early 1320s); but Olivi's doctrines and their effects were already a major bone of contention at the Avignon inquiry. Allegations similar to Gui's had also been put before the inquiry by the Community's spokesmen in March 1311, when they accused Olivi of having uttered 'false and fantastic prophecies concerning the Church . . . especially in his *Postilla* on the Apocalypse where he calls the Church a great whore'.[136] The Community's spokesmen closely and explicitly link such doctrines with the Spirituals' alleged belief in the angelic revocation of Nicholas III's authority.[137] In his reply to the Community (the *Sanctitati apostolicae*) in June 1311, Ubertino adroitly disposed of this charge by citing chapter and verse of the *Postilla* and Olivi's own explanation of it, in order to claim that – far from identifying the whole Church with the *meretrix magna* of Revelation 17 – Olivi had stressed the 'universal authority' of the Roman Church. He also argued that Olivi's crucial distinction was between the *ecclesia electorum* and the *ecclesia reproborum*.[138] Thus Ubertino in 1311 presents Olivi's apocalyptic doctrines in a way that aligns them quite closely with the contrasts (between St Peter, as the Primitive Church, and the popes, as the contemporary corrupt Church) that Dante dramatizes in *Inferno* 19. 90–117.

There are some further specific convergences between Ubertino's language at Avignon and that of Dante in *Inferno* 19, involving several of the central images of evangelical poverty. For instance, as the previous chapter suggested, the ironic equation, in *Inferno* 19. 72, of the *borsa* of the Pope's worldly wealth with that of Malebolge evokes the debate about the apostolic purse in which many Franciscans and Nicholas III himself had engaged.[139] The imagery of the purse is deployed by Ubertino to similar satirical effect when, for example, he describes opulent Franciscan

135 Mollat 1926: I. 110–12. On the work itself, see Manselli 1955 and Lerner 1994. On Olivi's apocalyptic doctrines and their subsequent condemnation, see Burr 1993: chs. 9–11. For further discussion of the beliefs and persecution of Olivi's followers, see Chapter 4, pp. 172–5, below.

136 *ALKG* 1887: 370 (my translation).

137 *ALKG* 1887: 371.

138 *ALKG* 1887: 407–9. On the scope that Olivi's *Lectura super Apocalypsim* allows for such a dissident reading, see Chapter 3 below, pp. 115–16 with nn. 88–90.

139 On the 'purse' or 'bag' see this chapter above, p. 55 and n. 41.

prelates riding into town for a Chapter meeting along with their *bursarii* – and, like other participants in the debate about poverty, he and Dante both focus sharply upon the imagery of Franciscan clothing and possessions.[140]

Dante may not have known the specific details of Ubertino's submissions, although manuscripts of them appear to have circulated in Italy.[141] Nonetheless, he demonstrably knew quite early on about one of the main actions of Clement's Council of Vienne (the suppression of the Templars), since, as we have seen, he refers to this in *Purgatorio* 20.[142] Moreover – as the recurrence of similar ideas in *Inferno* 19 and the later reference to Ubertino's rigorism in *Paradiso* 12 suggest – he is very likely to have been aware of the central issues of the Avignon inquiry, as well as the main thrust of Ubertino's arguments. His attention was anyway, as we shall see, in part focused upon Clement's shifting tactics during Henry VII's campaign in Italy (1310–13), a period which includes the later proceedings of the inquiry; and his letters of this time are urgently concerned with the Papacy's role and authority.[143]

DECLINE IN THE WEST: DANTE, AVIGNON AND ASSISI

It has been argued that the 'apocalyptic religious radicalism' that characterized Dante's later political thought was 'connected with his reaction to the change of papal policy by Clement V [in 1312]' and that the process by which this happened remains 'perhaps the most mysterious part of his

140 *ALKG* 1887: 121–2. For other references by Ubertino to the abuse of *bursarii*, see *ALKG* 1887: 71, 104. For Ubertino's remarks about Franciscan clothing (esp. footwear), see, for example, the *Decretalis etiam* (*ALKG* 1887: 130–5) and the *Sanctitati apostolicae* (esp. 185, lines 31–2); and compare, for instance, Dante's use of *scalzarsi* and *scalzo* in *Paradiso* 11. 79–87; 12. 130–32; and 21. 128.

141 According to Ehrle, several of the manuscripts in which the submissions to the inquiry survive are in Northern Italy. The main or sole witness for four of the six documents is Padua Cathedral Library MS A. 60, and two are also found in Biblioteca Laurenziana in Florence; see Ehrle, *ALKG* 1886: 326, and 1887: 50, 91, and 162. For the fifth (*Super tribus sceleribus*), Heysse used the Florence Laurenziana MS, with Ravenna (Biblioteca classense) 298; see *AFH* 1917: 114–15.

142 On Dante's awareness of the suppression of the Templars see this chapter above, p. 73.

143 See *Ep.* 5. 10 (Toynbee 1966: 57 and 62) and *Ep.* 7. 7 (Toynbee 1966: 99 and 104), both of which allude to Clement's initial authorization of Henry's venture. See also Mineo in Mellone 1992: 229 and Cosmo in *Giornale dantesco* 8 (1900): 181.

spiritual biography'.[144] This mystery deepens when we consider *Inferno* 19's representation of Clement as 'di più laida opra' than Boniface VIII and as a 'pastor sanza legge'. Dante's contemporary, the chronicler Dino Compagni, had also characterized Clement as a simonist and as one among a number of 'evil pastors', and Villani was to list a number of lurid accusations.[145] In Dante's eyes, the 'evil deeds' of this particular pastor are likely to have included the appointment of nine French cardinals (five of them relatives) at the beginning of the pontificate in 1305; and the term *laida opra* in its immediate context clearly refers in some way to the pope's dealings with Philip IV (ll. 85–7).[146] If we accept a late dating (after 1314) for the account of Clement in *Inferno* 19, then the phrase could also be seen as alluding to the Papacy's concessions to French power that culminated in the suppression of the Templars, to which Dante refers in *Purgatorio* 20.[147] It may thus also refer to what in Dante's view was an even baser act: Clement's 'betrayal' of Henry VII between March and May of 1312 – an action for which he is condemned by both Cacciaguida and Beatrice in *Paradiso*.[148]

Although Clement's issuing of *Exivi de Paradiso* and its compromise settlement of the Franciscan dispute coincided almost exactly with the moment of his 'betrayal' of Henry VII (in the spring of 1312), it is nonetheless highly unlikely that Dante would have regarded the bull itself as a *laida opra*. It is known that the reaction of the Tuscan Spirituals to *Exivi* was rapid and unfavourable, and that conflicts between them and the Community continued there, as well as in Sicily, Provence and Catalonia.[149] However, as we have seen, *Exivi* conceded a number

[144] Holmes 1980: 37.

[145] See Compagni, ed. Luzzato 1968: Bk 3, ch. 22, and Villani, ed. Porta 1990–1: 2.197–8.

[146] Mollat 1926: 31 and 33; Renouard (tr. Bethell) 1970: 20. For a vividly imaginative account of Clement's agreement with Philip, see Villani, ed. Porta 1990–1: 2.160–1.

[147] On the question of the possible revision of *Inferno* 19, see this chapter above, p. 72 with n. 98.

[148] See *Par.* 17.82 and 30. 133–48. For a concise account of Henry's venture and Clement's role, see Holmes 1986: 189–92; and on Dante's reactions to the papal, French and Angevin alliance, see Vasina 1982: 180–3.

[149] The Tuscan Spirituals had taken matters into their own hands even before the issuing of *Exivi*; see Douie 1932: 15–6, and Ini 1973: 312–316. On the aftermath of *Exivi* in Tuscany, see Ini 1973: 316–21; on the Tuscan Spirituals in Sicily, see Finke 1908: 661–70. The wider conflict between Spirituals and Community following *Exivi* is discussed by Lambert 1961: ch. 9 and Burr 2001: ch. 7.

of specific points to Ubertino's arguments about the observance of the Rule, and Clement here and in other ways adopted, as far as possible, a conciliatory policy towards the Spirituals.[150] From the standpoint of (say) Dante's Bonaventura, pronouncing upon the Franciscan controversy in *Paradiso* 12 (especially ll. 121–6), Clement's interpretation of the issues in *Exivi*, far from being a *laida opra*, would probably have seemed a reasonable and conscientious solution.[151] As in the case of Nicholas III and *Exiit qui seminat*, it is not Clement's declared view on Franciscanism that is the reason for his Dantean damnation. It is, once again, the discrepancy between pious intentions and simoniac deeds that calls this pope's authority in question and leads him to be identified in apocalyptic terms as one of the 'pastors' whose 'avarice brings the world to grief'.[152] Dante's appropriation of Spiritual discourse as a way of speaking about such pastors can be seen, therefore, not as a response to particular papal pronouncements, but rather as reflecting a wider awareness of the long debate about Franciscan poverty that was intensifying at and around the Avignon inquiry of 1309–12 and would reach a brutal conclusion a few years later under another (and very different) pope: John XXII.[153]

Further evidence of such appropriation can be found in Dante's own writing very shortly after the death of Clement V and possibly at the very time when he was revising *Inferno* 19. Some time between May and June of 1314 he wrote a letter (*Epistola* 11) to the Italian cardinals who were in conclave at Carpentras and attempting to elect Clement's successor. His subsequent description of the cardinals as 'wedded to avarice' deploys language and ideas markedly similar to those of the pilgrim's denunciation of the corrupt papal 'pastors' in *Inferno* 19.[154] The concern in the letter about the cardinals' betrayal of the Church as bride (*sponsa*, 4 and 11) in favour of a marriage to avarice ('Cupiditas

150 See Lambert 1998: 215–16. Clement was eventually (in July 1312) forced to take repressive measures in the face of outright rebellion by the Tuscan Spirituals; see Ini 1973: 318.

151 On Dante's likely view of *Exivi*, see Mellone 1987: 52.

152 *Inf.* 19. 104–6. See above, p. 44.

153 John XXII and his treatment of the Spirituals are discussed in Chapter 4, pp. 164–8, below.

154 Compare *Inf.* 19. 53–57, 71–72, 104, 112, and 115–17 (on the avarice of Boniface and Nicholas). The speakers in both texts are also conscious of adopting a prophetic and admonitory role from a position of (relatively) low status; see *Inf.* 19.88–9 and 100–3, and *Epistola* 11.9: 'Pudeat ergo tam ab infra, non de coelo ut [vos] absolvat, argui vel moneri.'

unusquisque sibi duxit in uxorem', 7) recalls the way in which wedlock and greed are drawn together on several occasions in the canto.[155] Both texts also contrast sharply in this respect with the Franciscan tradition of devotion or marriage to Poverty, a tradition which Dante will draw upon later in the *Commedia*.[156] The cardinals in the letter are thus seen as the legatees of Clement V, who is portrayed as a venal and simoniac 'high priest' in *Inferno* 19 (84–6) – an accusation that falls harshly upon those of them who (like Giacomo Colonna and Napoleone Orsini) sympathized with the Spiritual Franciscan views on poverty.[157]

In this letter Dante also ironically equates poverty with the power to prophesy, particularly when he claims the right to address those in authority, 'nulla pastorali auctoritate abutens quoniam divitiae mecum non sunt' ('not abusing any pastoral authority since I have no wealth').[158] He then envisages himself as the newly sighted blind man whose voice the Pharisees sought to suppress, and who had appeared in St John's account as a common man confronting and even mocking the 'blind' complacency of those who claimed authority over him (John 9: 25, 27 and 30). Concern about and justification of the possible presumption of such a speaker and truth-teller comes to dominate the middle of the letter, to such an extent that at points Dante seems to be talking to himself rather than the cardinals. His self-consciousness here has much in common with the pilgrim's anxiety about being a 'fool' before the pope in *Inferno* 19 (88).[159] His recognition of his 'garrulous' tone in the letter, however, spells out what has been left implicit in the canto: 'Iam garrulus factus sum: vos me coegistis' (9). Vociferousness, he claims, has been forced upon him, as part of a situation in which those in authority now have to be warned and corrected not from above but from 'so far below' ('tam ab infra').

155 Notably in Nicholas's description of Boniface VIII's deception and violation of the Church (*Inf.* 19. 55–7) and the pilgrim's apocalyptic view of the history of the Papacy's 'marriage' (109–11).

156 On St Francis's 'marriage' to Lady Poverty as represented in *Par.* 11, see Chapter 4 below, p. 000 with nn. 20–23.

157 On the role of Orsini and the Colonna cardinals as protectors of the Spirituals at Avignon, see this chapter above, pp. 75 and 78 with nn. 108–9 and 127.

158 On Dante's prophetic stance in this letter and its kinship with 'Spiritual' discourse in the *Commedia*, see Frugoni 1969: 81–87 and 90–91.

159 On Dante's 'folly' in *Inf.* 19, see this chapter above, pp. 60–1, with nn. 61 and 64.

Near the end of the letter, Dante singles out Cardinal Napoleone Orsini 'above all' ('tu prae omnibus, Urse', 10), as responsible for the 'widowing' and 'eclipse' of Rome. This specific appeal is significant in several ways. Napoleone Orsini is known to have helped to bring about the election of Clement V in 1305 and was said to have subsequently regretted doing so.[160] As the use of the vocative *Urse* ('Bear') reminds us, he was a nephew of Nicholas III and hence one of the *orsatti* ('bear-cubs') to whom Nicholas refers in *Inferno* 19 (71). The implied scenario at this point in the letter – with the dispossessed exile raising his voice prophetically against the powerful prince of the Church – thus parallels that in which the Dante persona rebukes a close relative of that prince in *Inferno* 19.[161] The writer of the letter to the Avignon cardinals may thus disclaim a 'pastoral authority', but he nonetheless wishes, like the Apostles and apostolic Franciscans, to speak with the authority of poverty.

If Dante thus appropriates Spiritual Franciscan discourse in his representation of decadent papal or prelatical authority, he is also highly distinctive in what he does with it. For a final example of this kind of reinvention, we should return to the description of Clement V in *Inferno* 19 as 'di ver' ponente, un pastor sanza legge' ('from out of the west, a pastor without principle', ll. 82–4). Here the acceleration of papal decline through the Clement's *laida opra* is reinforced by the connotations of the phrase that describes the pope's origins: 'di ver' ponente'. The noun *ponente* ('west') literally identifies Clement's origins (he was a Gascon and had been Archbishop of Bordeaux). But it also derives from a verb (*ponere*) which in late Latin referred to the setting of the sun. As an image of decline, it forms part of a larger pattern of descent and ascent in the canto and subsequently in the *Commedia*. Nicholas III is, as he says in lines 76–84, due to 'fall' further into the rock ('Là giù cascherò') when first Boniface and then Clement descend into Malebolge. We are later to be forcefully reminded, by Beatrice's last words in *Paradiso* 30 (145–8), of the repeated process of descent in which Clement is to participate – forcing his predecessor, Boniface, down 'più giuso'. By contrast, the *ascent* of the Dante persona is stressed at the end of *Inferno* 19: he is

[160] On Napoleone's role in the election of Clement V and his subsequent regrets, see Willemsen 1927: pp. 13–24 and 68–71.

[161] The difference in the letter, of course, is that Nicholas's nephew, Napoleone, now has the chance to atone.

shown being gathered up into the arms of Virgil, who 'rimontò per la via onde discese' (l. 126). In this context, the term *ponente* seems also capable of suggesting the decline of the spiritual authority of the 'sun' as the traditional image of papal authority, deriving from Genesis 1:16.[162] Dante had previously, in his letter to the princes of Italy (September 1310), associated the light of this sun very positively with Clement's 'apostolic blessing' of Henry VII, and he continued to represent papal authority more problematically through such imagery in *Purgatorio* and *Monarchia*.[163]

This pattern of decline will be strikingly reversed when Dante reaches the sphere of the Sun in *Paradiso* 11. Here the imagery of resurgent light is explicitly associated with the energies of the mendicant Orders, and particularly with the initial apostolic mission of St Francis.[164] St Dominic's origins are of course located in the *west* (*Par.* 12. 46–57), which is defined as the source of the wind of Spring ('Zeffiro') and the place where the sun hides itself ('si nasconde') from earthly gaze at times ('talvolta'). But St Francis (like Henry VII at the beginning of Dante's confident letter of 1310) is unequivocally identified with the rising sun:

> . . . chi d'esso loco fa parole,
> non dica Ascesi, ché direbbe corto,
> ma Orïente, se proprio dir vuole.
>
> [Whoever makes mention of this place should not call it *Ascesi* ('Assisi'/'I ascended'), which would fall short of the truth; but if they wished to speak true, they would call it 'the Orient'.] (*Par.* 11. 52–4)

St Francis's mission is thus associated through wordplay with the dawn, in a way that is diametrically opposite to Clement's association with the sunset of papal authority; and the opposition between *ponente* and *orïente* highlights the contrast between the ominous origins of the first

162 The noun *ponente* occurs only twice in the *Commedia* (the other occasion is *Purg.* 2. 15), and Giovanni Buti and Renzo Bertagni suggest that there may well be a *significato allegorico* here, since the west is 'la parte contraria a quella considerata auguralmente benefica, l'oriente'; see *ED* 4. 593–4. The other word for 'west' (*occidente*) occurs four times in the *Commedia* (*Inf.* 26. 113; *Purg.* 26. 5; 27. 63; *Par.* 6. 71) and is on the first occasion (in the *Inferno*) associated with a fatal journey. On the Papacy as the 'greater light' of Genesis 1:16, see Tierney 1980: 156 (citing Henry of Susa), and Ullmann 1974: 224.

163 See *Purg.* 16. 106–9 and *Mon.* 3.4.2–3 and 13–22.

164 See *Par.* 11. 19–21, 37–39 and 43–57.

Avignon Pope and the auspicious quarter from which the first Franciscan is said to have 'arisen'.[165] Between these two poles, of papal decline and the celebration of early Franciscan ideals, however, lies the process of ascent through Purgatory. The Franciscan features of that ascent now need to be traced.

[165] See Bosco 1966: 321–2. There is clearly also in this passage an allusion to the tradition of identifying St Francis with the angel of the sixth seal, 'ascenden[s] ab ortu solis' (Revelation 7: 2); see Da Campagnola 1971: 297–9.

3

Purgatorio: poverty in spirit

> Noi volgendo ivi le nostre persone,
> '*Beati pauperes spiritu!*' voci
> cantaron sì, che nol diria sermone.
> Ahi quanto son diversi quelle foci
> da l'infernali! ché quivi per canti
> s'entra, e là giù per lamenti feroci.
>
> [As we turned ourselves in that direction, voices sang in such a way that words could not describe it: '*Blessed are the poor in spirit!*' How different those crossing-points are from the ones in Hell! For here they go through in song, and down there with bitter lamentations.
> (*Purg.* 12. 109–14)]

Starting their first ascent within Purgatory itself, Dante and Virgil here turn away from the terrace of the Proud, and as they move towards a narrow flight of steps the first Beatitude (Matthew 5: 3) is sung. 'Blessed are the poor in spirit' is the first of seven Beatitudes that the pilgrim is to hear as he leaves each of the seven terraces of Purgatory.[1] Its immediate function here is to contrast the virtue of humility with the sin of pride, which is expiated in the terrace that Dante and Virgil are leaving. The significance of being 'poor in spirit' was, however, variously interpreted by the commentators, beginning with the Church Fathers. For Augustine and Chrysostom it meant being 'lowly' or deliberately humble; on the other hand, Jerome and Ambrose saw it as applying more literally to the value of poverty.[2] Nearer to Dante's own time, Aquinas thought that it could refer 'either to the contempt of riches, or to the

[1] The others are at *Purg.* 15. 38, 17. 68–9, 19. 50, 22. 6, 24. 151–4 and 27. 8. The scheme of contrasting Beatitudes to sins may derive from Hugh of St Victor (see Lansing in *DE* 89).

[2] See Aquinas, *Catena aurea*, tr. Newman 1997: I. 147–8.

contempt of honours out of humility'; whilst Marsilius of Padua argued that 'in spirit' meant through 'will or consent' and that the text thus applied to voluntary poverty as an ideal for the 'wayfaring Christian'.[3]

A wider view of 'poverty in spirit' as guide for the wayfaring Christians of *Purgatorio* thus seems appropriate, since (as the passage quoted makes clear) it is directly associated with the process of ascent: lines 112–14 of canto 12 explicitly contrast the soul's progression through this second kingdom with descents to damnation in the *Inferno*. Humility has certainly been essential to Dante's progress since he was girded with the 'lowly' reed on the very shore of the mountain (*Purg.* 1. 94–5 and 133–6); but the idea of voluntary poverty and austerity also – as we shall see – underlies the encounter with the angelic gatekeeper (*Purg.* 9), and will inform the imagining of both avarice and brotherhood later in the *cantica* (notably cantos 19–26 and 32).

Humility and brotherhood serve to constitute Dante's Purgatory as a restored Church – a community which stands as a reproach to the earthly institution and its leadership. This exemplary and monitory purpose is reflected in the *Purgatorio*'s allusions to Franciscanism, poverty and the Papacy. Its most exalted penitent is a pope expiating avarice and asserting the value of apostolic brotherhood; and it concludes with a vision of the Church in history that necessitates and evokes a prophecy of renewal. From early on it also alludes to Franciscan ideals and traditions; and in the process its discourse converges with that of several Franciscan texts. The first of these is one that also bases itself upon the first Beatitude and represents the ascent of a mountain in 'poverty of spirit'.

POVERTY ON THE MOUNTAIN: THE *SACRUM COMMERCIUM*

The paradoxical association of both humility and poverty with ascent – with 'attaining the kingdom of Heaven' – is recurrent from an early stage in Franciscan tradition. It is evident, for instance in St Francis's rewritings of the Beatitudes in his *Admonitions* (especially 14, 17 and 20).[4] It also comes to have structural significance in a later and highly influential thirteenth-century text: the *Sacrum commercium sancti Francisci*

[3] *S Th* 1a 2ae. 69, 3 and Marsilius, *Defensor pacis* 2. 13, 14.

[4] See Habig 83–4.

cum domina Paupertate.[5] The *Prologus* to the *Sacrum commercium* cites the first Beatitude in full and links it with Francis's determination to reach Lady Poverty 'to whom the Lord gave the keys to the kingdom of Heaven'.[6] Later on in the Franciscan work the Saint's homage to the personified figure of Lady Poverty repeats the same Biblical text.[7]

Like the *Purgatorio*, the *Sacrum commercium* is the narrative of an ascent. It describes a quest undertaken by St Francis, leading from the city to the plains up to a mountain and back down again to pursue a mission in the world. The saint and his chosen companions climb a steep, rugged and narrow path 'from the valley of wretchedness to the mountain of brightness', at the summit of which Lady Poverty stands.[8] The bulk of the text consists of Poverty's own allegorized account of her history, from the Fall through the ministry of the Apostles to the present threats of her rival, Avarice; and the work concludes with a *convivium* which seals the union between Lady Poverty and the friars who represent for her the 'the image of him to whom I am wedded in heaven' ('imaginem . . . eius cui sum desponsata in caelis') and who are urged by her to persevere in their 'conversion' to the renewed apostolic life.[9]

Some of the affinities between the *Sacrum commercium* and the *Purgatorio* are already quite well known; and a number of basic structural correspondences have already been noted. In the former, St Francis, casting off all possessions, climbs the mountain where Lady Poverty reviews the whole of human history, from the fall of Adam up to the present moment of reunion and renewal; and in the latter, Dante casts off all the sins as he ascends Mount Purgatory, encounters Beatrice and reviews with her the course of his own history and that of humanity.[10] There are also several verbal and metaphorical parallels from the moment of

[5] The *Sacrum commercium* will be cited here in the edition by S. Brufani (1990), with translations from Habig. For discussion of manuscripts and the controversy over its dating and ideology, see Appendix 1 below.

[6] Brufani 1990: 130–1, tr. in Habig 1550–1.

[7] Brufani 1990: 141, tr. in Habig 1562.

[8] Brufani 1990: 138 and 137, tr. in Habig 1560 and 1559.

[9] Brufani 1990: 174, tr. in Habig 1954.

[10] These basic parallels were pointed out by Carlo Paolazzi in his note on *Sacrum commercium* in *FF* 1635–6, n. 6 (my paraphrase).

arrival at the foot of the mountain.[11] Both Dante and St Francis are regarded as especially privileged by virtue of their access to the mountain; both groups of climbers, on arrival at the foot of the mountain, are immediately forced to pause and review the steepness of the ascent; and both are represented through similar imagery as they approach the summit.[12]

Mountains of course loom large in early Franciscan literature and culture. St Francis himself appears to have been recurrently drawn to the solitude of mountainous places in Umbria and Tuscany, and a large number (perhaps half) of the early thirteenth-century Franciscan houses were hermitages.[13] Remote, mountainous places feature as settings for the Saint's quests and miracles not only in the texts of the early Lives but also in the rich tradition of thirteenth- and early fourteenth-century Franciscan painting – from the Pescia panel of 1235 to the Bardi Dossal and the frescoes of Giotto in Santa Croce.[14] The mountainous wilderness continued to be a prominent feature in depictions of the

[11] In *Purgatorio* 3. 46 ('divenimmo . . . a piè del monte') may echo a phrase at the start of Francis's ascent in the *Sacrum commercium* ('devenit ad montem', Brufani 1990: 136). For the suggested parallel, see Paolazzi in *FF* 1636 (n. 6).

[12] Dante says that he and Virgil 'trovammo la roccia sì *erta*' (*Purg.* 3. 47), while Francis and his companions 'considerarent montis ascensum propter nimiam *altitudinem et asperitatem* eius' ('They thought again about ascending the mountain, because of its extreme steepness and ruggedness', Brufani 1990: 136). On the process and significance of achieving the summit, see also *Purg.* 27. 127–42, with *Sacrum commercium*, Brufani 1990: 166. The free, unburdened movement of the climbers as they approach their goal is in both texts compared to flight (see *Purg.* 27, 123 and *Sacrum commercium*, 137); for Paolazzi's comments on this parallel, see *FF* 1637, n. 8.

[13] See Brady in Cirino and Raischl 1995: 199. The early biographies, such as the *Vitae* of Thomas of Celano and Bonaventura's *Legenda maior*, stress this eremitical impulse by alluding to texts like '[my dove] that art in the clefts of the rock', and 'Thou hast exalted me upon a rock'; see *1 Celano* 71 and *2 Celano* 165, in *Analecta Franciscana* 1926–41: 53 and 226, and Habig 288, 495. Further discussion of this aspect of St Francis's life, as constructed by the early biographies, is in Wolf 2003: 65.

[14] Among such miracles are: the finding of the spring (*2 Celano* 46, *Legenda maior* VII, 12, and *Legenda minor* V, 3); the drinking-vessel that turned into a bee-hive (*2 Celano* 169); the discovery of relics at Monte Casale (*Legenda maior* VI, 7); and, above all, the scene of the Stigmatization at the hermitage of La Verna, below the summit of Monte Penna (*1 Celano* 94–5, *Legenda maior* XIII, 1–7, and *Legenda* VI, 1–5). The 'Miracle of the Spring' fresco in the Upper Church at Assisi is a further example; see Stubblebine 1985: 88–9 and plate 14; also *2 Celano* 46 (Habig 403–4). On mountainous landscapes in the Bardi Dossal at Santa Croce in Florence, see Appendix II, below.

Stigmatization and other legends and miracles in Franciscan art during Dante's lifetime; and the relevance of these to Dante's portrayal of St Francis in the *Paradiso* will be apparent in the next chapter.[15] Meanwhile, it is likely that the location of an apostolic quest upon a mountain in both the *Purgatorio* and the *Sacrum commercium* would, for contemporary readers, evoke powerful images of the eremitical life. A number of the radically inclined Franciscan texts of the early fourteenth century similarly stress St Francis's eremitical impulse and his avoidance of buildings in favour of mountain crags – a preference that was also transmitted to the culture of the Italian Spiritual Franciscans.[16] The Franciscan tradition of seeking and imagining wildernesses – evident as it is in both the texts and the painting of the period – thus provides a wider context for the parallels between the *Sacrum commercium* and the *Purgatorio*.

The archetype of the mountain as place of trial and purgation is of course, as Jacques Le Goff has shown, widely manifest in Hebrew, Germanic, Irish and Italian mythology, as well as in the visionary and homiletic literature of the Middle Ages.[17] The symbolism of the mountain in *Purgatorio*, as in the Franciscan texts, draws upon a variety of Old and New Testament sources (such as those which are quoted before the ascent of St Francis and his companions in the *Sacrum commercium*).[18] Both the *Sacrum commercium* and the *Purgatorio*, however, envisage the ascent of the mountain not only as a process of increasingly unburdened flight, but also as a religious enterprise for which the climber has to be formally (even ritually) prepared. At the start of their ascent in the *Sacrum*

[15] See Chapter 4 below, pp. 139–44 with nn. 39–50.

[16] Texts which stress Francis' eremitical preference in this way include the *Legend of Perugia* (MS of 1311) 13, in Habig 990; and the *Speculum perfectionis* 9, in Habig 1135. See also Stubblebine 1985: 84–5, on the *Actus beati Francisci et sociorum eius* (circulating in the 1330s). During the thirteenth and early fourteenth centuries the Spirituals had their strongholds in the high hermitages of Umbria and the March of Ancona. Their successors during the fourteenth century (the early Observants) were likewise drawn to remote places in the same mountainous region, although the Observant movement seems subsequently to have evolved a more workable relationship between the city and the hermitage (see: Merlo in Cirino and Raischl (eds.) 1995: 273–6; Moorman 1968: 188–9 and 369–73; and Peck 1980: 94).

[17] Le Goff 1984: 27, 109–10, 116–17, 126–7, 190, 195, 203–6, 250–6, and 337–8.

[18] The texts include Psalm 24 (Vulgate 23): 3 ('Quis ascendet in montem Domini'), Isaiah 2: 3 ('Ascendamus ad montem Domini . . . et docebit nos vias suas') and Revelation 21: 10 ('et sustulit me in spiritu in montem magnum et altum') – all cited in the *Sacrum commercium* (paras. 10 and 12, Brufani 1990: 134 and 136).

commercium St Francis exhorts his companions to 'gird yourselves and be valiant men' ('accingimini tanquam viri potentes').[19] In *Purgatorio* I Dante's girding with the *umile pianta* (the reed) is a ritual preparation for the ascent of the mountain. Cato, the guardian of the mountain, requires the adoption of this symbol (*Purg.* I. 94–9); and, as Benvenuto da Imola emphasized, it is a necessary part of the purgatorial process:

> primo praecepit quod muniat ipsum cingulo humilitatis, quia prima via accedendi ad poenitentiam, causa ascendendi ad montem altissimum virtutis, est humiliatio . . .
>
> [first he tells him to equip himself with the girdle of humility, because the first way of approaching penitence, the means of ascending the lofty mountain of virtue, is humiliation . . .][20]

There are thus some broad parallels between the initial stages of the journey in the *Purgatorio* and the *Sacrum commercium*; and there is thus a Franciscan precedent for Dante's association in canto 12 between the ascent of the mountain and the necessity for 'poverty in spirit'. Earlier than this, however, another highly ritualized episode has made a similar kind of connection.

THE ANGEL AT THE GATE: CANTO 9

At the very entrance of Purgatory itself the angel-gatekeeper draws forth the keys that are to admit Dante from beneath a robe that is notably more sombre in colour than the other angels' clothing:

> Cenere o terra che secca si cavi,
>   d'un color fora col suo vestimento;
>   e di sotto da quel trasse due chiavi.
> L'una era d'oro e l'altra era d'argento . . .
>
> [Ash or dry earth when it is dug up would be the same colour as his clothing, from beneath which he drew two keys. One of these was of gold and the other was of silver . . .] (*Purg.* 9. 115–17)

[19] Brufani 1990: 136, tr. in Habig 1557 (possibly drawing upon 1 Maccabees 3: 58).

[20] Benvenuto da Imola, *Comentum*, ed. Lacaita 1887: 3.41. Earlier than Benvenuto, Pietro Alighieri, commenting on Dante's ascent in a different context (the dream of the eagle in *Purg.* 9), had noted the relevance of Psalm 17 (AV 18), which (in his version) includes the phrases 'in te enim curram *accinctus*' and 'Deus qui *accinxit* me fortitudine'; see his *Commentarium*, ed. Nannucci 1845: 358–9.

As several commentators have pointed out, the symbolism of the gold and silver keys being drawn from beneath the angel's coarse, dull robe vividly reinforces the link between spiritual wealth and material poverty; and in this context some have noted the similarity between the greyish-brown colour of the robe and that of the early Franciscan habit.[21]

The colour that Dante so carefully describes here is the same as the brownish-grey 'russet' portrayed in the late thirteenth- and early fourteenth-century paintings of St Francis and his followers (e.g. by Cimabue or Giotto), or indeed as the habit (now in the Basilica at Assisi) that is said to have been worn by St Francis himself.[22]

There is also documentary evidence (not so far noted by modern commentators) that the specific comparisons with ash (*cenere*) and earth (*terra*) were precisely those used in Franciscan texts of the Trecento to describe the Order's habit. Early specifications for the Franciscan habit (such as the Rules of 1221 and 1223, Bonaventura's *Expositio Regulae*, and the Statutes of 1260 and 1316) mention 'poor clothing', 'sackcloth', 'undyed' and 'uncarded' wool and 'poorness of quality as well as colour' ('vilitas . . . in pretio pariter et colore').[23] But there are two Franciscan texts of Dante's time that are much more precise in the terms they use to describe the habit's colour. These are the *Scripta Leonis, Rufini et Angeli sociorum S. Francisci* (also known as the *Legend of Perugia*), of which the earliest manuscript is dated c. 1311; and the *Speculum perfectionis* of 1318.[24]

Both of these early fourteenth-century Franciscan texts present similar references to the colour of the Franciscan habit in the form of anecdotes that may well be much earlier in origin. Chapter 101 of the *Scripta Leonis* describes how, during his last days, St Francis asked his companions to obtain (from Lady Jacoba of Settesoli) 'cloth for a tunic, of religious stuff which is like the colour of ashes and which is like the cloth the

[21] See, for example, Porena (ed.) 1947: 2. 86. More recently, Armour allows that this may be 'a secondary reference', whilst Bosco and Reggio acknowledge that a Franciscan allusion at this point is 'highly suggestive'; see Armour 1983: 49 and BR 2: 160.

[22] For a description of this garment (as recorded in 1912), see Da Alençon 1925: 5a.

[23] For the account of the Franciscan habit in the Rules, see Habig 33 and 59; for Bonaventura's *Expositio*, see *Opera omnia* (Quaracchi edn), vol. 8, 405. For the references in the Statutes of 1260 (Narbonne), see Bihl 1941: 42; and for those in the Statutes of 1316 (Assisi), see Carlini 1911: 278–9.

[24] On the dating of the earliest, *Scripta Leonis* MS (P), see the edition by Brooke 1970: 27–32 and Habig 962; and on the dating of the *Speculum perfectionis*, see Habig 1108–9.

Cistercian monks produce in places overseas' ('pannum pro una tunica de panno religioso qui colori cineris assimiletur et est tanquam pannus quem faciunt monachi Cistercienses in ultramarinis'); it then states that Jacoba appeared bringing with her (unasked) 'the cloth for the dead, that is, of the colour of ashes' ('pannum morticinum, uidelicet cinerei coloris').[25] In the *Speculum perfectionis* the same story is told, giving slightly less detail about the cloth but still describing it twice as 'ashen-coloured' ('qui in colore assimilatur cineri . . . cinerei coloris').[26]

Amongst the sayings and legends that appear in the later part of the *Scripta Leonis*, Chapter 110 records St Francis's comparison between the plumage of the lark and the habit of the true religious:

> 'As she flies she praises God, like a good religious despising earthly things, for her life is always in the heavens. Moreover her clothing is like the earth, her feathers that is, giving an example to religious that they ought not to have coloured and fancy clothing but as if dead, looking like soil.'
>
> ['uolando laudat Dominus [*sic*] sicut boni religiosi despicientes terrena, quorum semper in celis est conuersatio. Praeterea, eius uestimentum terre assimilatur, uidelicet penne eius, exemplum prebens religiosis ut non colorata et delicata uestimenta habere debeant, sed quasi mortua ad modum terre.'][27]

A very similar version of this speech again appears a few years later in the *Speculum perfectionis* (Chapter 113):

> 'Her plumage resembles the earth, and she sets an example to Religious not to wear fine and gaudy clothing, but cloth of a humble price and colour, just as earth is inferior to the other elements.'
>
> ['Cuius vestimenta assimilantur terrae, id est pennae ejus, et dat exemplum religiosis ut non delicata et colorata vestimenta habeant sed vilia pretio et colore sicut terra est vilior aliis elementis.'][28]

The wording in this second example relates even more closely to the official specifications (in the Constitutions of Narbonne in 1260) concerning the 'vilitas in pretio . . . et colore' of the Franciscan habit.

[25] Ed. and tr. Brooke 1970: 266–7.

[26] *Speculum perfectionis* Chapter 112, in Sabatier 1898: 221–2, tr. in Habig 1249–50.

[27] Ed. and tr. Brooke 1970: 282–3.

[28] Ed. Sabatier 1898: 224, tr. in Habig 1252.

A later Trecento Franciscan text, Bartholomew of Pisa's *Liber de conformitate vitae Beati Francisci ad vitam Domini Iesu*, is an important source of information about the early Franciscans and perceptions of them during this period.[29] The twelve sections of the *Liber* develop in exhaustive detail the parallels between the life of St Francis and that of Christ, and in one of these Bartholomew describes St Francis's instructions about the material of the habit and the nature and significance of its colour:

> As for the material, he instructed that it should be of coarse cloth and of an ashy, pale or earthy colour, to act as a reminder of the mortification of the body of Christ . . .
>
> [Quoad materiam docuit, quod esset de panno vili et coloris cinerei, vel palidi, vel terrei, corporis Christi mortificationem repraesentantis . . .][30]

Like the passage describing the angel-gatekeeper's robe in *Purgatorio* 9, all these contemporary and later Trecento Franciscan texts emphasize the comparisons between the colour of true religious clothing and that of ash (*cinis/cenere*) and earth (*terra*). St Francis's speech about the lark in the two earlier versions also stresses the paradoxical association between the earthy colour of the religious and their concern with the things of Heaven ('semper in celis est conuersatio . . . uestimentum terre assimilatur'); and a similar paradox is implicit in the encounter at the gate of Dante's Purgatory.

The notion that Dante's angel primarily represents a kind of confessor-figure has been persuasively refuted.[31] We can, however, recognize in the angel-gatekeeper an allusion to Franciscan poverty, together with some significant implications for the future of the Church and the Papacy as imagined in the *Purgatorio*. The angel's sword and keys are versions of those symbols of authority wielded by the papal apologists; the latter are explicitly said to have been 'entrusted by [St] Peter'

[29] Bartholomew's *Liber* is edited in *Analecta Franciscana*, vols. 4–5 (1906–12). It was begun in 1385 and presented to the Chapter General of the Order at Assisi in 1399. According to one source, Bartholomew was subsequently rewarded with a habit that had been worn by St Francis himself; see Moorman 1968: 396, quoting Wadding, *Annales Minorum* 9. 158.

[30] Bartholomew, *Liber de conformitate*, ed. in *Analecta Franciscana*, vol. 5 (1912): 104, lines 8–10 (my translation).

[31] Armour 1983: 35–52.

(*Purg.* 9. 127); and the robe – as described immediately before the keys – invests this figure, as 'St Peter's vicar' with 'those elements of humility, poverty, and simplicity which Dante, with the Franciscan Spirituals, saw as the basis of the ideal of the reformed Church'.[32]

Dante's authoritative, quasi-papal angel here may also allude to contemporary prophetic beliefs about the 'Angelic Pope', the figure who would guide and protect the beleaguered Christian community during the Last Days. This idea had been foreshadowed by Joachim of Fiore and was being fully articulated in Joachimist thinking of various kinds from the late thirteenth century onwards – and gaining stimulus from the election and resignation of Celestine V (1294). Sources for the idea around Dante's time include Roger Bacon, the *Liber de Flore*, Gentile of Foligno and (in a more extreme form) Fra Dolcino, to whom Dante's Mahomet had ironically addressed a prophecy in *Inferno* 28 (55–60).[33]

In this scene Dante can also be seen developing the powerfully instrumental role of Poverty as it is envisaged in the *Sacrum commercium*. The prologue to the *Sacrum commercium* ends by describing St Francis's overriding 'desire to come to her [Poverty] to whom the Lord gave the keys of the kingdom of Heaven' ('optio . . . ut posset pervenire ad eam, cui Dominus tradidit claves regni celorum').[34] In *Purgatorio* 9, the very moment at which we are reminded of the outward and visible signs of Franciscan poverty and humility is crucial: it is precisely the moment when the angel performs the authoritative act of drawing forth the keys to unlock the gate and enable the pilgrim to join the community of Purgatory itself.

The consequences for the ensuing ascent are considerable. If Dante's representation of the angel at the gate does indeed deliberately and specifically invite comparison with Franciscan imagery and narrative, then a number of the encounters that follow on the terraces of *Purgatorio* take on a further dimension, especially when forms of asceticism,

[32] On the swords (Luke 22: 38) and keys (Matthew 16: 19) as images of papal propaganda, see Tierney 1988: 142 and 148–9, and (more extensively on the 'two swords') Watt in *CHMPT*, ch. 14 (for further details and references, see Chapter 4 n. 86, below). On the associations of Dante's angel with humility, poverty and simplicity and a reformed Church, see Armour 1983: 39–41, 44–8, and 51.

[33] On ideas about the 'Angelic Pope' see Reeves 1969: 47, 194, 245–6, 252–3 (with n. 5) and 401–10; McGinn 1978; and Mineo 1998: 31 with n. 26.

[34] Brufani 1990: 131, tr. in Habig, 1551.

humility and brotherhood are involved. This is not to argue that Dante is seeking to convert his second kingdom into a Franciscan convent, but rather that – as with his 'cultivation of liturgical language' in this *cantica* – he is appropriating a discourse of Franciscan poverty in order to imagine Purgatory as a restored Church.[35] Allusions to early Franciscan tradition and imagery at this moment of initiation and rededication have implications for the subsequent development of *Purgatorio*'s vision. Contemporary readers who perceived such appropriations and parallels in the portrayal of the angel at the gate might subsequently have been readier to interpret the beatitude that accompanies the pilgrim's ascent from the terrace of Pride (*Beati pauperes spiritu*) in terms of that broader ecclesiological vision. The challenge posed by the Franciscan connotations of the angelic and apostolic gatekeeper creates resonances that extend to the idea of brotherhood and humility in the community of Dante's Purgatory, as well as to the specific representations of avarice and poverty, and eventually to the apocalyptic sequence at the end of the *cantica*.

FROM PRIDE TO BROTHERHOOD: CANTOS 11–19

> Nella Chiesa primitiva s'incominciarono tutti li cristiani a chiamare *frati*, e aveano ogni cosa in comune.
>
> [in the early Church Christians all began to call each other 'brother', and they held everything in common.][36]

The Dominican friar Domenico Cavalca (c. 1270–1342) was a near contemporary of Dante, and he here associates the word *frate* ('brother') with the origins of the Christian community. The use of *frate* to mean 'sibling' was, however, rather uncommon in Dante's time: in ordinary Florentine usage the term normally referred to the religious and mendicant orders.[37] In the *Inferno*, *frate* usually (in nine cases out of eleven, and notably in canto 19) means 'friar' – whilst that meaning does not

[35] On this view of the function of the liturgy in *Purgatorio*, see Barnes in *DE* 570.

[36] Cavalca 1763: I. 313.

[37] See Onder's article (*s.v. frate*) in *ED* 3. 50. The alternative form, *fratello*/*fratei*, is relatively infrequent in the *Commedia*.

obtain in any of the thirteen instances of the word in the *Purgatorio*.[38] This difference of usage suggests that there is a deliberate attempt in this *cantica* to recover and extend the broadly 'apostolic' sense of the word. *Frate* is used to express community and solidarity, from its first employment in Purgatory proper, by the artist Oderisi, through its use by souls in the circle of the Envious, by Marco Lombardo, Pope Hadrian V, Statius, Virgil, Forese, Bonagiunta, Guinizzelli, and Matelda, to its final appearance at the beginning of Beatrice's prophecy in the last canto.

During the journey through the terraces of Purgatory the word also accompanies gestures of humility. Amongst the spirits of the Proud in cantos 11–12, Dante is addressed for the first time in Purgatory proper as *frate*. This is when Oderisi da Gubbio is disclaiming supremacy in his art and yielding it to another (*Purg.* 11. 82). Oderisi is, of course, among the souls who are acquiring humility after the examples of the Virgin, King David and Trajan, depicted by divine art in the previous canto (*Purg.* 10. 34–93), and are thus aiming to become *pauperes spiritu* in the Augustinian sense. Humility as a model is also apparent in the next terrace and canto, where reference is made to a member of the Franciscan Order: Pier Pettinaio. This reference is also preceded by an address to Dante as *frate*. The voice which answers his request to hear from any Italian soul is both anonymous and dismissive of merely local allegiances:

> 'O frate mio, ciascuna è cittadina
> d'una vera città; ma tu vuo' dire
> che vivesse in Italia peregrina.'
>
> ['My brother, we are all citizens of the one true city; but you mean to speak of those who lived as pilgrims in Italy.'] (*Purg.* 13. 94–6)

The form of address (*frate*) here asserts the values of the wider spiritual community above those of individuality and implicitly invites Dante's participation in the former. It is in this immediate context that the model of Franciscan humility is invoked by the penitent Sapia, and the figure of Pier Pettinaio as bringer of 'peace' is named by her:

38 *Frate* in *Purgatorio* occurs at 4. 127, 11. 82, 13. 94, 16. 65, 19. 133, 21. 13 and 131, 23. 97 and 112, 24. 55, 26. 115, 29. 15, and 33. 23. On its uses and their significance in *Paradiso*, see Chapter 4 below, pp. 128–9 with nn. 10–14.

'Pace volli con Dio in su lo stremo
  de la mia vita; e ancor non sarebbe
  lo mio dover per penitenza scemo
se ciò non fosse, ch'a memoria m'ebbe
  Pier Pettinaio in sue sante orazioni,
  a cui di me per caritate increbbe.'

['I sought peace with God at the very end of my life; and my dues would still not be discharged by penitence, were it not that Pier Pettinaio in his charity took pity upon me and remembered me in his devout prayers'.] (*Purg.* 13. 124–9)

A member of the Franciscan third order, Pier lived mostly in Siena, where he died in 1289 and where his saintliness was officially venerated by the city; but towards the end of his life he also seems to have been associated with the group of Spiritual Franciscans at Santa Croce in Florence, where, in the later 1280s, Ubertino da Casale as well as Dante came to know of him.[39] Mention of him at this point thus reflects something of the strength of Dante's continuing interest in the Florentine Franciscan community.[40] More specifically, it contrasts Franciscan ideals of apostolic brotherhood with the divisive rivalries within and between cities. As a citizen (in a sense) of both the earthly cities mentioned in this context (Siena and Florence), Pier is well qualified to act as a potential symbol of reconciliation for them as well as for the fractious Sapia. Hence he also illustrates most fully the ideal articulated by souls in this circle: that of being a 'brother' (*frate*), seeking citizenship of 'the one true city' and guiding others towards it (94–5).

The idealistic political implications of the term *frate* are not of course restricted to specifically Franciscan figures or contexts in *Purgatorio*. Political vision and prophecy in this *cantica* are often directed to the

[39] Pier was subsequently honoured as a local saint ('Sampiero pettinagnolo' or 'Santo Pietro Novello') by Florentine *laudesi* (companies of devotees). Immediately after his death the Comune voted to place a 'noble sepulchre' with altar and ciborium above his grave in the Franciscan church; see the article by Manselli in *ED* 5. 493a. Ubertino refers to the influence of Pier's sanctity upon him in his prologue to the *Arbor vitae crucifixae*, 1485 print, f. 2v b. In this passage Sapia's tribute to his piety and its influence indicates that she is now adopting towards this Franciscan tertiary the kind of role that was actually played by the *pinzochere*, the groups of female penitents ('femine penitentie de vestitis S. Crucis') who were congregating around the Florentine Franciscan convent of Santa Croce in Dante's time (see Davidsohn 1900–8: 4. 487 and Manselli 1973: 327–8).

[40] *ED* 4. 493a.

Dante persona through this form of address. Marco Lombardo uses it to introduce his account of the wayward world (*Purg.* 16. 65), and so does Forese when about to prophesy disaster for his and Dante's fellow-Florentines (*Purg.* 23. 97). Above all, Beatrice herself will use it near the end of the *cantica* to preface her interpretation of the apocalyptic vision of the Church that Dante himself witnesses (*Purg.* 33. 23); but before turning to that final vision and its implications we should take into account occasions in the later cantos of *Purgatorio* when the word not only raises questions about the Church and Papacy but also helps to dramatize the relationships between authority, poverty and community.

On the terrace where avarice is expiated and poverty exalted (*Purg.* 19–21), *frate* occurs several times in a context where (as we shall see) there are recognizable Franciscan allusions.[41] At the beginning of this phase in the *Purgatorio* there are also some further parallels with the *Sacrum commercium.* Immediately before the ascent to the terrace of Avarice, Dante's enigmatic dream (*Purgatorio* 19. 1–33) stages a confrontation between two allegorical figures: the *femmina balba* (or *dolce serena*) and the *donna santa e presta*. Representations of vices and virtues as contrasting female figures are of course widespread in the art and literature of Dante's time and before; nonetheless, there are some quite specific parallels between this problematic scene in *Purg.* 19 and the *Sacrum commercium*'s account of the rivalry between Lady Poverty and her devious adversary, Lady Avarice.[42] Avarice in the *Sacrum commercium*, like the *femmina balba* of Dante's dream, takes on a more acceptable appearance in order to attract followers. She even adopts the name of 'Discretion' ('nomen Discretionis assumens'), and she is recurrently associated with plausible and pleasing disguises – with the 'sheep's clothing' of Matthew 7: 15 and 'the semblance of piety'.[43] Yet the 'appearance of holiness' ('specie sanctitatis') in Avarice's followers is subsequently shown to change, as outward signs of inner corruption ('dissolutio interior') begin to break out ('erumpebant foris').[44] This vivid disclosure shows some affinity to the stench that rouses Dante from his dream of the Siren

41 On Franciscan allusions at this stage in the *Purgatorio*, see Gardner 1926: 77.

42 Brufani 1990: 154–66.

43 *Sacrum commercium,* paras. 43 (Brufani [ed.]: 157, Habig 1578), 38 (Brufani 1990: 154, Habig 1576), and 40 (Brufani 1990: 155, Habig 1577).

44 *Sacrum commercium,* para. 48 (Brufani 1990: 162, Habig 1582).

(*Purg.* 19. 33), and both episodes reflect a violent revulsion from earthly goods, of the kind that led the early Franciscans to 'look on them all as dung' ('velut stercora omnia reputabant').[45] Commentators on the *Purgatorio* passage stress the Siren's identification with *cupiditas* in general, rather than *avaritia* alone – a view supported by the description of 'alludens cupiditas, more Sirenum' ('Greed, beguiling like the Sirens'), in *Epistola* 5.4, and by the development of ideas about *ricchezze*, *avarizia* and *cupiditate* in *Convivio* 4.12.[46] And although, in the *Sacrum commercium*, Lady Poverty explicitly identifies her adversary as *Avaritia*, that figure's forms and effects come, like Dante's Siren, to constitute a total view of the world rather than the limited representation of a single vice.

In *Purgatorio* 19 the main speaker for the avaricious souls is a pope: Hadrian V (d. 1276). Dante's encounter with this figure carries important implications for the association of poverty with the Papacy. Like the encounter with Nicholas III in the corresponding canto of the *Inferno*, it strikes several kinds of Franciscan resonance. Like Nicholas, Hadrian also had some significant links with the Franciscan Order. Both of them were said to have befriended and protected the radical Minister General of the Order, John of Parma, at a time of crisis in the middle of the thirteenth century.[47] Salimbene, moreover, acknowledges Hadrian's 'great love' for the Franciscans, which also seems to be attested by his choice of burial site, in the Franciscan church at Viterbo.[48] Such Franciscan associations – as well as the brevity of his own tenure of papal authority (little more than a month, from 11 July to 18 August 1276) – lend further force to this pope's renunciation of material wealth, to his abrogation of worldly status, and to his insistence on being regarded as a fraternal equal with Dante and the other souls in Purgatory. Conversely, as we have seen, in *Inferno* 19 the Franciscan associations of Nicholas III have

[45] *Sacrum commercium*, para. 44 (Brufani 1990: 158; Habig 1579).

[46] *Epistolae*, ed. Toynbee, 1966: 52; the passage is cited, for instance, in Vallone and Scorrano 1986: 281. For discussion of the Siren as *cupidigia*, in relation to *Convivio* 4.2, see Paparelli 1967: 14–16.

[47] See Moorman 1968: 146; Salimbene, *Cronica*, ed. Holder-Egger 1905–13: 302, 663–4; and Clareno, *Historia* in *ALKG* 2: 276–7 and 285–6.

[48] Holder-Egger 1905–13: 666; see also Gardner 1926: 78. Soave-Bowe 1987 also discusses the evidence for Hadrian's broader commitment to 'a mission of peace, conciliation and reform' during his earlier career (as Cardinal Ottobuono Fieschi).

served to intensify the extent of his betrayal and of his distance from the pilgrim who stands over him 'like a friar' ('come frate, *Inf.* 19. 49).

There are some further crucial differences in the scenario of *Purgatorio* 19. When Dante here kneels (127) as pilgrims would normally do before a pope, the gesture of respect for authority is rebuffed, and Hadrian explains his new position thus:

> 'Non errar: conservo sono
> teco e con li altri ad una podestate.'
>
> ['Do not mistake: I am a fellow-servant, along with you and the others, of a single authority.'] (*Purg.* 19. 134–5)[49]

As Benvenuto da Imola and later commentators point out, there is a clear allusion in these lines to the scenario in Revelation 19: 10, where the angel rejects St John's homage in closely similar terms ('conservus tuus sum, et fratrum tuorum'). By implication, then, Dante is here endowing himself with the authority of the visionary, or, as Benvenuto puts it, 'Dantes vir summe speculativus potest assimilari Joanni summe contemplativo' ['Dante, the supremely speculative man, may be compared to John, the supreme contemplative'].[50] For his fictional speaker too – Hadrian V – the allusion has further implications: the penitent's vernacular use of the angel's *conservus* in Revelation 19 signals a stage in his transformation from earthly to angelic pope. Significantly also in Revelation 19: 10 the angel's words herald the final Judgement and the restoration of the 'new Heaven and new earth' about which the visionary is called upon to testify.

Another term that the angel of Revelation 19 uses to describe John and his fellow apostles is *fratres* ('brothers'); and the equivalent has occurred in the previous line of *Purgatorio* 19 to describe and encourage Dante himself. The pope's use here of this mode of address (*frate*) thus becomes one of the most striking instances of Dante's recovery, during the course of his journey through Purgatory, of the word's communal and apostolic meaning:

> 'Drizza le gambe, lèvati sù, frate!'
>
> ['Straighten your legs, rise up, brother!'] (*Purg.* 19. 133)

[49] Compare the posture of humility Dante adopts before the 'papal' angel in *Purg.* 9.109, and see the comment on this passage in Armour 1983: 60.

[50] Benvenuto da Imola, *Comentum*, ed. Lacaita 1887: 3. 515.

Hence, concentrated within this single line of speech from the prone pontiff, the scene conveys both the rejection of avarice (including what Pope Gregory had called 'the avarice of high position') and the urge to a more positive form of ascent: that which is associated with 'poverty in spirit'.

POVERTY AND THE POETS: CANTOS 20–26

On the terrace of the Avaricious, the leading example of poverty invoked by the penitent souls is the Virgin Mary (*Purg.* 20. 16–24). The Virgin provides the first instance, of course, for all the exempla of virtue in the *Purgatorio*, and for this wider scheme it is thought that Dante may actually have followed the precedent of a Franciscan text, Conrad of Saxony's *Speculum Beatae Mariae Virginis*; but in *Purgatorio* 20 the prominent reference to the poverty of the Virgin Mary recalls a motif that was recurrent in Franciscan writing.[51] Here Dante presents the poverty of the Virgin Mary at the Nativity in the style of a Franciscan *lauda*, as the first of the short exemplary scenes performed by the souls of the penitent avaricious on this mountainside stage:

> Noi andavam con passi lenti e scarsi,
>   e io attento a l'ombre, ch'i' sentia
>   pietosamente piangere e lagnarsi;
> e per ventura udi' 'Dolce Maria!'
>   dinanzi a noi chiamar così nel pianto
>   come fa donna che in parturir sia;
> e seguitar: 'Povera fosti tanto,
>   quanto veder si può per quello ospizio
>   dove sponesti il tuo portato santo.'

> [We were moving onward with slow, short steps, as I gave heed to the souls whom I could hear piteously weeping and wailing; and I chanced to hear ahead of us a cry of 'Sweet (Virgin) Mary!', just like

[51] On the *Speculum Beatae Mariae Virginis*, see Mezzadroli in *DE* 870b and Girotto 1952. One of the earliest texts (after Luke's Gospel) to associate poverty with the birth of Christ is Paul, Philippians 2: 5–9. As Wolf (2003: 42) points out, St Francis emphasized the Pauline connection between the Incarnation and voluntary poverty in the second version of his *Letter to the Faithful*; see n. 53 to this chapter, below.

> the appeal of a woman in labour, followed by: 'You were so poor, as we can see from that lodging where you laid down your sacred burden.'] (*Purg.* 20. 16–24)

The vivid plainness of the penitent's language here contrasts with the more metaphorical and invocatory style of the narrator's preceding denunciation of avarice as 'antica lupa' (15). There is a degree of stylistic and thematic similarity between this Dantean scene and an actual early fourteenth-century Umbrian *lauda* of the Nativity. In its later stages the *lauda* (which was performed by the *disciplinati* in Perugia) lays recurrent stress on the theme of poverty, on the infant Christ's appearance (in Franciscan guise) as 'el poverello', and on the Virgin's role as 'la madre poverella'.[52] Near the end of the play, the exemplary nature of the scene is stressed through a sharp admonition directed by the shepherds to the avaricious man:

> Or te confonda, avaro,
> che non te sazie d'adunar moneta:
> lo suo Figluol sí caro
> Dio l'ha mandato a casa sí fornita.
> Correge la tua vita
> e faccia frutto en te 'l Figliuol de Dio,
> che tanto s'avilio;
> en sí gran povertà l'avem trovato.

> [Now, miser, never tired of heaping up money, be stricken with wonder: to a house furnished like this God has sent his most precious son. Set your life in order and let the son of God who made himself so humble bear fruit in you; for we have found him in such great poverty.] (*La Natività del Signore*, 345–52)

The poverty of the Virgin and of the Nativity scene is also a theme that recurs in the *Sacrum commercium*, as well as other Franciscan texts from St Francis onwards.[53] In the *Sacrum commercium* also (a text which itself has affinities with Franciscan drama) St Francis and his followers during

[52] The *lauda* is the anonymous *La Natività del Signore*, ed. Faccioli 1975: I. 47–60, esp. lines 138 onwards.

[53] The emphasis on the deliberate choice of poverty by Christ and the Virgin (despite the former being 'rich beyond measure') can be found in St Francis's 'Letter to All the Faithful' of 1224–6; see Habig 93 and *FF* 151 (section 182). On the biblical sources, see also n. 51 to this chapter, above.

their initial address to Lady Poverty stress the appropriateness of the Virgin's extreme poverty as a 'throne' and 'couch' for Christ:

> 'Prius enim quam de luminosa patria veniret ad terras, preparasti sibi locum congruentem, thronum in quo sederet et thalamum in quo quiesceret, pauperrimam scilicet Virginem . . .'
>
> ['For before he came upon earth from his home full of light, you prepared a place that would be suited to him, a throne upon which he would sit and a dwelling in which he would rest, namely, the most poor virgin . . .'][54]

The ways in which the traditional motif of the Virgin's poverty is realized in the *Sacrum commercium*, the *lauda* and *Purgatorio* 20 thus suggest that both Franciscanism and the dramatic culture that it fostered form contexts for Dante's representation of poverty on the terrace of Avarice.[55]

Brotherhood continues also to be a way of representing poverty in spirit here; and the term *frate* is used twice between poets in the next canto (*Purg.* 21. 13 and 131). For the first instance, near the beginning of the canto (line 13) the context is that of Christian, or more specifically apostolic, wayfaring. Dante and Virgil, as they move along the terrace of Avarice – with Dante silently considering the significance of the cry and the earth tremor at the end of the previous canto – are explicitly compared to the 'due ch'erano in via' (8): the two disciples on the road to Emmaus.[56] It is at this point that the shade of another poet, Statius, confronts them with the words:

> 'O frati miei, Dio vi dea pace.'
>
> ['My brothers, may God give you peace.'] (*Purg.* 21. 13)

This greeting is based in part on the words of Christ appearing to the Apostles in the scene that follows the episode on the road to Emmaus (Luke 24: 36). The biblical phrase there and in the parallel scene in John (20: 19 and 26) is 'Pax vobis'. Dante's phrase here is, however, verbally closer to the greeting that was appropriated by St Francis in his Testament of 1226, as a sign of apostolic renewal: 'Dominus det

54 Brufani 1990: 140; Habig 1561–2.
55 See Bosco, 1977: 1, esp. 135–41, and Armour 1991, esp. 11–12.
56 Luke 24: 13–16.

vobis pacem.'[57] The phrase in this form is described as a 'revelation' in both the Testament and Bonaventura's *Legenda maior* 3.2.[58] The strong impression made by its use by St Francis and his early companions *per viam* is mentioned in a text contemporary with the *Purgatorio*: the *Scripta Leonis, Rufini et Angeli* of c. 1311. Apparently it caused much astonishment (as well as some indignation) because 'people had never before heard such a greeting given by religious'; and St Francis himself saw this as validating the Order's apostolic mission.[59]

The apostolic role of the pagan poet Statius – resurrected in the guise of a contemporary Christian wayfarer – is reinforced by his use of the word *frati* in the same line as the Franciscan greeting. Parallels between his individual progress, that of *Purgatorio*'s community of souls and the life of the religious are also indicated by a metaphor he uses when explaining the cause of the previous canto's earth tremor and cry. These happen, he explains, when the individual's will feels itself to be 'wholly free to seek another community' (*Purg.* 21. 62). The word I have translated as 'community' here is *convento*; and this is its first use in the *Commedia.* It is not a frequent term, even in the figurative sense (as here); and Dante's next use of it (in *Paradiso* 22. 90) will apply to the early Franciscan Order.[60]

Meanwhile, as Statius' greeting to them has suggested, all three of the poets here seem to represent a new wayfaring community. Both the classical poets in this canto invoke the presiding authority of the austere gatekeeper of *Purgatorio* 9; and Statius refers to the angel as an apostolic or even papal figure ('vicario di Pietro').[61] The phrase *in via* has (as we have seen) suggested apostolic parallels for Dante's and Virgil's progress as pilgrims at the start of the canto (l. 8). Later on in his account of his work, Statius will describe the process of poetic composition in the same two words (l. 93). Familial terms such as those for sister, mother and (repeatedly) brother also link the poets at points throughout the canto – from Statius' greeting near the beginning to Virgil's refusal of Statius' attempt to pay homage to him at the end:

[57] The parallel was noted by Gardner 1926: 77–8.

[58] In Habig 68 and 647. [59] *Scripta Leonis*, ed. Brooke 1970: 204–5.

[60] On the idea of community in *Par.* 22, see Chapter 4 below, p. 176 with n. 148. The word *convento* is also used subsequently in the *Commedia* to describe Christ's Apostles (*Par.* 29. 109) and the community of souls within the celestial rose (*Par.* 30. 129).

[61] *Purg.* 21. 23–4 and 54.

Già s'inchinava ad abbracciar li piedi
al mio dottor, me el li disse: 'Frate,
non far, ché tu se' ombra e ombra vedi.'

[Already he was stooping to embrace my teacher's feet; but he said to him: 'Don't do that, brother: you are a shadow and what you see is a shadow.' (*Purg.* 9. 130–2)][62]

This second occasion in the canto when one of the poets addresses the other as *frate* has parallels with that earlier occasion on this terrace when the Pope (Hadrian V) had disclaimed Dante's attempt at homage and urged him as a brother (*frate*) to rise. Here again status (and the terms associated with it) gives place to humility and the word that in *Purgatorio* repeatedly expresses it. And this 'poverty in spirit' (in the Augustinian sense of humility) is once again associated with the process of ascent. The words that immediately follow this passage and introduce Statius' verbal tribute in the canto's final *terzina* are 'And he, arising' ('Ed ei surgendo'); and they remind us of his own status as resurrected soul and redeemed poet.

The three poets of *Purgatorio* 21 (two Christian, one pagan) can thus be seen as a community of wayfarers whose shared identity and purpose are strengthened by the terms that apply to the apostolic, the religious and even on occasion the Franciscan life. A similar function seems to be served in subsequent cantos by the recurrence of *frate* as a mode of address by other poets. Dante's friend and fellow-Florentine poet Forese Donati uses the term twice in quite quick succession, at the beginning and end of his prophecy about Florentine excess and the judgement that awaits it (*Purg.* 23. 97 and 112). The word of course expresses friendship and equality here, but it may also form part of Forese's renunciation of the contest for material status that (as we have seen) seemed to underlie the invective of the *tenzone* that had been exchanged between him and Dante in the 1290s.[63]

Concern about material status and 'the excessive love of secondary goods' is at issue in various ways throughout the last three terraces of Dante's Purgatory; and renunciation and humility correspondingly

[62] Other notably familial terms in *Purg.* 21 are *serocchia* (Virgil describing Dante's soul in 28) and *mamma* (Statius referring to the *Aeneid* in 97).

[63] See Chapter 1 above, pp. 11–12 and nn. 14–19.

take a variety of forms in the later cantos of the *Purgatorio*, as the two subsequent encounters with poets (Bonagiunta da Lucca and Guido Guinizelli) suggest.[64] In the first of these (*Purg.* 24. 34–63) Dante the pilgrim, in his speech to Bonagiunta, himself seems to adopt a rather haughty or dismissive attitude towards his poetic predecessor. Dante the poet may be redressing the balance by allowing Bonagiunta to call him *frate* in reply and thus to claim a more secure place within the literary tradition that is being constructed here. Conversely, when Guinizelli responds to Dante's tribute to his *dolci detti* by addressing him in this same way (*Purg.* 26. 115) the scenario has much more in common with the occasions on which (as we have seen) both Hadrian V and Virgil disclaim homage. Dante has shortly before this spoken of Guinizelli as the poetic 'father (*padre*) to me and to my betters' (97–8); and the latter's use of *O frate* to begin his response can be construed as a gesture of renunciation and humility – a gesture that is completed by his yielding place to another poet as 'the better craftsman in the vernacular' (117) and by his request for Dante's prayers when he reaches 'the abbey (*chiostro*) where Christ is head of the community' (128–9). Paradoxically, then, this language of renunciation and humility has the effect of exalting the status of Dante's poets in the later stages of the *Purgatorio* – strengthening their affinities with the apostolic religious and giving them prominence among those who are *pauperes spiritu.* This development is paralleled and eventually transcended by that of Dante's own role as visionary vernacular poet here and especially in the closing stages of the *cantica.*

BETWIXT THE CHURCH DESTROYD AND CHURCH RESTOR'D: CANTOS 32–33

By the end of his ascent through Purgatory, the Dante persona has in several ways followed the prompting of the pope in *Purgatorio* 19 and 'risen up' as a 'brother'. In the Earthly Paradise, as he turns to the east and towards the procession bearing Beatrice, his guide Matelda addresses him once again as 'brother':

[64] On this wider concern with 'secondary goods' in the later cantos of *Purg.* (from 17 on), see Armour 1994: 19.

'Frate mio, guarda e ascolta.'

['My brother, look and listen.'] (*Purg.* 29. 15)

There are further harsh lessons in humility that he has to learn from Beatrice in the subsequent cantos (30–1), but in the final scenes of the whole *cantica* (32–3) this 'brother' appears both as a member of a community and as a privileged prophetic and even apostolic voice – in a role which is comparable to that of John in Revelation, as a writer of a vision and a writer to churches. Such a role has also been suggested by Pope Hadrian V when in speaking of the pilgrim as *frate* and *conservo* (*Purg.* 19. 133–4) he alludes to the angel's identification of himself as the 'fellow-servant' of John 'and [his] brothers' in Revelation 19.[65] The relationship between angelic *conservus* and visionary *frater* is re-enacted at several points by Dante and Beatrice in *Purgatorio* 32–3. Immediately before the descent of the eagle upon the tree and the chariot in *Purgatorio* 32 Beatrice urges Dante to write down what he sees ('quel che vedi . . . fa che tu scrive', 104–5) in terms that closely parallel the injunctions to the visionary in Revelation 1: 11 and 19 ('Quod vides, scribe' and 'Scribe ergo quae vidisti').[66] Like Dante's St Peter later in *Paradiso* (whom she resembles in other respects too), she thus emphasizes the individual responsibility of the prophet's task.[67]

The Dante persona is thus assigned a distinctive prophetic role; yet at the moment of this vision he is far from being alone. From canto 29 onwards he continues to be in the presence of the groups of figures around the chariot; and not only is he included as *frate* by Matelda, but he also remains in the company of Statius, who had joined him and Virgil as *frati* ten cantos earlier.[68] Moreover, at the start of canto 32, as the procession begins to move towards the tree that is to be the location of the vision, it is described in military terms as *essercito* (17)

[65] 'Conservus tuus sum et fratrum tuorum', Rev. 19:10. See this chapter above, p. 103 with nn. 49–50.

[66] On the parallels between Dante and John as impoverished exiles and visionaries, see also Herzman in Emmerson and McGinn 1992: 403 and 405.

[67] *Par.* 27. 64–6. There is also a parallel between Beatrice's appearance 'colorata come foco' in *Purg.* 33. 9 and the transformation of St Peter in *Par.* 27.10–15, 19–21 and 28–36, as noted in BR 2: 557.

[68] The group of figures (*gente*) is referred to in *Purg.* 29. 64 and 152, and 30. 7 and 59; and reminders of Statius' presence are at *Purg.* 32. 29 and 33. 135.

and *milizia* (22) – both words which, later in *Paradiso*, will be applied to the community of which St Francis and St Dominic became leaders.[69] Furthermore, as Dante 'awakens' at the beginning of the vision itself, he compares himself at length (ll. 73–81) not with a lone prophet nor even with St John in Revelation, but with a group of apostles (Peter, James and John) witnessing the Transfiguration of Christ on the summit of Mount Tabor, and becoming temporarily the companions (*scuola*) of Moses and Elijah.[70]

After this explicit reference to the Apostles as a group there follow allusions to the ideals of the apostolic life, which likewise serve as preliminaries to the main events of the vision. Beatrice, whom the awakened Dante anxiously seeks as a guide, is said by Matelda to be seated by the tree surrounded by the *compagnia* of the seven Virtues (32. 86–8); but the text shortly afterwards describes her again as 'seated alone upon the bare [or 'very'] ground', with the circle of the Virtues drawn as an enclosure (*claustro*) around her:

> Sola sedeasi in su la terra vera,
> come guardia lasciata lì del plaustro
> che legar vidi a la biforme fera.
> In cerchio le facevan di sé claustro
> le sette ninfe . . .
>
> [She was sitting alone upon the bare ground, as if left there as guardian of the chariot which I had seen tied [to the tree] by the two-natured beast. Around her the seven nymphs formed themselves into an enclosure . . .] (*Purg.* 32. 94–8)

The shift of scene here is suggestive. The 'bare ground' ('terra vera') upon which Beatrice sits 'alone' suggests asceticism of the kind associated with the eremitical and Franciscan traditions. Indeed, there is a possible parallel here with descriptions of St Francis having himself placed 'upon the bare earth' ('in nuda terra') at the point of death – an episode that Dante will later adapt in his own description of Francis' death (*Par.* 11.

[69] *Par.* 12. 37 and 41. *Essercito* is used more broadly twice earlier in the *Commedia* to mean 'crowd' or 'group' (*Inf.* 18. 28 and *Purg.* 8. 22), both times, however, within a context of communal devotion. *Milizia* occurs here for the first time in the poem, but will be frequently used of the souls in *Paradiso* (e.g. 5. 117, 8. 83, 9. 141, 12. 41, etc.).

[70] Matthew 17: 1–9, Mark 9: 1–9 and Luke 9: 28–36.

115–17).[71] The very word *claustro* ('enclosure') that describes the circle formed by the lamp-bearing nymphs derives from the same Latin root as Dante's word for 'cloister' (*chiostro*) and hence – like Statius' use of *convento* in *Purgatorio* 21. 62 – conveys the sense of a religious community, in this case with Beatrice as its centre and leader.[72] There is also a parallel between the imagery and wording of this episode and those of a scene towards the end of the *Sacrum commercium sancti Francisci cum domina Paupertate*. In the latter, Lady Poverty, after her rather austere 'banquet' with St Francis and his companions takes a rest 'upon the bare ground' ('supra nudam humum') and then on awaking asks to be shown the Franciscans' cloister ('petens sibi claustrum ostendi'), upon which they lead her to a hilltop from which the whole world can be seen and tell her that 'this is our cloister' ('hoc est claustrum nostrum').[73] Both texts thus represent the idealized contemplative female resting on the ground, and both give new significances to the idea of the 'cloister' (*claustrum/claustro*). They thus also link the idea of 'poverty in spirit' with those of vision (the Franciscan vision of the world and *Purgatorio*'s subsequent vision of the Church) and community. Many of the correspondences between Dante's Beatrice and the *Sacrum commercium*'s Lady Poverty are not of course unique, but this particularly close convergence strengthens the link between the processes of ascent and vision in the *Purgatorio* and the culture and literature of Franciscan poverty.[74]

From the centre of this *claustro* in *Purgatorio* 32, Beatrice addresses Dante first as a member of several communities – the 'forest-dwellers' of the *Paradiso terrestre* and 'that Rome of which Christ is a citizen' – and then as an individual charged with the task of writing home to the

[71] Such descriptions are, for example, in *2 Celano* 214 (Habig 534); Bonaventura, *Legenda maior* 1.14.3 (Habig 738); and in the third of the 'additional stories' in a manuscript (Bodley MS Lat. th. d. 23) containing the *Scripta Leonis* (ed. Brooke 1970: 296–7). In the case of the lines in *Purg.* 94–8, BR (2: 547) note the strangeness of the epithet (*vera*), but reject the possibility of an allusion to poverty on the (somewhat narrowly defined) grounds that 'Beatrice does not symbolize the Church so much as Theology.'

[72] *GDLI s.v. claustro. Claustrum* was, moreover, the term that St Francis himself used to describe an eremitical enclosure in the woods or up in the mountains; see Brady in Cirino and Raischl 1995: 201. For examples of *claustrum* to describe remote Franciscan hermitages, see Esser in Cirino and Raischl 1995: 164–5 and 184.

[73] Brufani 1990: 173; Habig 1593.

[74] On Lady Poverty and Dante's Beatrice, see Paolazzi in *FF*, pp. 1635–6 (n. 6), 1638 (n. 9), and 1643–4 (n. 16); and Havely 1996: 238–9.

'erring world' his vision of the apocalyptic events and transformations that occupy the rest of the canto (109–60).[75] It seems generally agreed that the vision itself represents in some form the process of the corruption of the Church; and its specific stages and the symbolism of the eagle, fox, dragon, prostitute and giant have been subject to extensive commentary from the Trecento onwards.[76] In relation to the ascetic and apostolic context that has been established for the vision, several features of this sequence are particularly significant. Once again, cupidity is at issue; and recurrent here, especially in the later stages, are acts of greed, rapacity and theft. The eagle strips (or as it is later said, 'robs') the tree of blossoms and leaves for a second time (113–14; compare *Purg.* 33. 57). The gift of plumage with which it invests the chariot (whether or not it signifies specifically the Donation of Constantine) is clearly an 'evil burden' for this vessel to carry (32. 129); it obscures its original identity and forms a stage in its monstrous metamorphosis (142–7).[77] The fox which emerges from the 'cradle' of the chariot in between the two descents of the eagle (118–23) bears some resemblance to the ravenous wolf of *Inferno* 1. 50–1 and 97–9, and it may, as Armour suggests, represent falsehood or greed rather than heresy (with which it is usually identified).[78] The dragon that emerges from the earth beneath the chariot not only 'breaks the vessel' (as Beatrice later says in 33. 34) but also literally steals a fragment of its base ('trasse del fondo', 135). The prostitute who then appears seated, like the *meretrix magna* of Revelation 17: 1–6, upon the monstrous chariot is said to have a 'greedy glance' ('l'occhio cupido', 154) and is later referred to as a 'thief' ('fuia') by Beatrice (33. 44); whilst the giant who consorts with her not only fears jealously that she will be stolen from him (151), but also ends up by abducting both her and the whole 'nova belva' (158–60). This entire process – and especially its culmination in the appearance and disappearance of the 'puttana sciolta' and the giant – thus recalls

[75] The contrasting locations of 'forest' and 'city' in the first three lines of Beatrice's speech (100–2) evoke the dialectic of eremitical life up to and including the Franciscans. On this tradition, see Chapter 1 above, pp. 24–6 ; this chapter above, pp. 91–2 with n. 13–16; and Cirino and Raischl 1995: 265–6.

[76] For some more recent accounts, see, for instance: Kaske 1961, 1971, 1973–4 and 1983; Armour 1989: 215–38; Scott 1996: 198–202.

[77] On the question of the eagle's gift and the possibility that the scene 'does not refer specifically or only to Constantine', see Armour 1989: 219–21.

[78] Armour 1989: 219 and 1994: 19–20.

the kinds of cupidity and theft that have been associated with avaricious 'pastors' and the corrupt Papacy in *Inferno* 19.[79] During the pilgrim's denunciatory 'song' to Nicholas III in *Inferno* 19 104–11, the avaricious 'pastors' like him had been directly identified with the *meretrix magna* of Revelation 17, and it seems likely that a similar association of avarice with apocalyptic imagery is taking place here.[80]

The linking of avarice with apocalypse is not of course unique to Dante, or even to this particular period; and it can be seen as part of the long association of prophecy with criticism of society and the Church. The linkage, however, seems to have been strengthening in exegesis and polemic, from the Joachimist commentary *Super Jeremiam*, written in Southern Italy in the 1240s, through to the work of Franciscans of the later thirteenth and early fourteenth centuries such as Bonaventura, Olivi and Jacopone da Todi. The Jeremiah commentary had applied apocalyptic imagery to (amongst other things) the corruption and greed of both the Church hierarchy and the Empire; and the corruption of the ideal of Franciscan poverty was also placed within a similar framework by Bonaventura in his *Collationes in Hexaemeron* (1268).[81] Olivi, however, went much further than Bonaventura in this direction, presenting the threat to evangelical poverty as an intrinsic part of the apocalyptic scenario itself and as coming from within the very hierarchy of the Church.[82]

As we have seen, Olivi was an important presence in the Franciscan community at Santa Croce during (or shortly before) the time when Dante frequented the *studium* there; and his influence on Dante's apocalyptic language has already been apparent in the pilgrim's denunciation of popes in *Inferno* 19.[83] His eighth *Quaestio* on Evangelical Perfection was written in 1278/9 – well before his lectorship in Florence – and it concludes by presenting the argument for Franciscan poverty in apocalyptic (even Joachimist) terms: if the end were at hand and the Franciscans were its prophets, then it would be even more necessary for them to

[79] On avarice and apocalyptic language in *Inf.* 19, see Chapter 2 above, pp. 57–8 with nn. 50–2.

[80] For comparison of the two passages (in *Inf.* 19 and *Purg.* 32) as conveying a 'crescendo of evil', see Davis 1984: 62.

[81] See Burr 1993: 6–7, 22 (n. 28) and 105.

[82] Burr 1993: 105.

[83] See Chapter 2 above, p. 53 with nn. 34–5.

maintain the rigour of their Rule.[84] Olivi's vision of the corruption of the Church and its leadership thus takes him along a path that differs not only from Bonaventura but also from earlier apocalyptic exegesis.[85] In his subsequent commentary, the *Lectura super Apocalypsim* (late 1290s), he sees the fifth of the seven periods of Church history as one of peace but also of the relaxation of rules and the transformation of the Church from 'top to toe' into a 'new Babylon'.[86] In defining this latter process he lays particular stress upon forms of clerical cupidity, especially simony; and since the problem might go all the way *ad verticem*, he acknowledges that those 'spiritual men' who seek to defend the ideal of evangelical poverty might have to not only question but also eventually disobey ecclesiastical authority.[87]

The culmination of this process for Olivi – as for Dante in *Inferno* 19 and *Purgatorio* 32 – is represented by the figure at the start of Revelation 17: the *meretrix magna*. His comments on the *meretrix* could be read by both allies and adversaries as implying an identification of her with the Papacy and of Babylon with the institutional Church. As we have seen, his follower, Ubertino of Casale, at the Avignon inquiry of 1309–12, some ten years after Olivi's death, was publicly concerned to rebut this reading, but, as the 1319 commission on the *Lectura* showed, it was a charge that remained on the books.[88] Indeed, Olivi himself is careful early on in his commentary on Revelation 17 to emphasize that the *meretrix* is not to be identified with 'the Church of the just on pilgrimage', but rather with 'the multitude of the reprobate who assault and blaspheme against

[84] On Olivi's eighth *quaestio* see Burr 1993: 66 and n. 20; see also Burr 1989: 177–83, esp. (for the sentence quoted) 180. On the link between Joachimism and the justification of Franciscan poverty, see also Leff 1966: 52 and Reeves 1969: 175.

[85] Important earlier commentaries on the Apocalypse include Richard of St Victor and the Pseudo-Thomas; see Mineo 1998: 37–8 and nn. 74–7. For a survey of Franciscan commentaries on the Apocalypse – including non-Joachimist examples (such as Vital du Four, John Russel and William of Meliton) – see Roest 1994.

[86] See Burr 1993: 85 (nn. 37–9) and 94 (n. 62).

[87] See ibid., 85 (n.39) and 93. On the problem of obedience to authority, as experienced by the Sprituals, see also Burr 2001: 165–7.

[88] On the *meretrix* in Olivi's *Lectura super Apocalypsim* and Ubertino's interpretation of her at the Avignon inquiry, see Chapter 2 above, pp. 79–80 and nn. 132–8. It has been pointed out that of the sixty articles in the *Lectura* censured by the commission of 1319, thirty-eight concern the *meretrix magna* (Burr 2001:208).

the pilgrim Church through unjust acts'.[89] As Olivi's interpretation of the passage in Revelation 17 progresses, however, it becomes easier to see how it could allow those so inclined to read the *meretrix* in terms of official persecutors, such as the Spirituals deemed Boniface VIII and (later) John XXII to be. Such a dissident reading seems feasible when Olivi goes on to identify her with 'the Roman people and Empire, both as it once was in its most pagan state and as it subsequently was through the Christian faith, still striking fear into many and fornicating with this world'; and, when commenting on Revelation 17: 3, he argues that 'just as this beast in the time of paganism and heresy was surely stained with the blood of martyrs, now on the other hand she is stained with the blood or the slaughter of souls and the impious persecution of the spirit and spiritual persons'.[90]

Revelation 17: 2 gives the 'kings of the earth' a relatively subordinate role with regard to the *meretrix magna*. On the other hand, both Olivi in the *Lectura* and Dante at the end of *Purgatorio* 32 give them (as the secular power, engaged in a process of mutual corruption) a more significant and complementary part to play. Dante's portrayal of the partnership of the whore and the giant on the monstrous chariot in several ways parallels Olivi's commentary on Revelation 17. The relationship between the two Dantean figures is – if we envisage them as (respectively) ecclesiastical and secular authorities analogous to Olivi's imagined alliance between the 'mystical Antichrist' – comparable to 'Caiaphas the priest' – and the 'great Antichrist', comparable to 'the pagan Nero governing the whole world' in the *Lectura super Apocalypsim*.[91] The unholy union on the *carro* can also be compared with the *Lectura*'s imagining of

[89] 'Non quoad ecclesiam iustorum que peregrinata est apud eam, sed quoad multitudinem reproborum que eandem apud se peregrinantem ecclesiam iniquis operibus impugnant et blasfemant', *Lectura* in Rome Bibl. Ang. MS 382, f.103rb (my translation); also (transcribed from Florence MS Laur. conv. soppr. 397, f. 192v) in Tocco 1903: 39–40.

[90] As will be seen in Chapter 4 below (pp. 173–5 with nn. 138 and 142–4), it would not take much ingenuity on the part of Olivi's later followers to identify this kind of persecution with that which led to the burnings at Marseilles in 1318 and the martyrdom of a number of Spirituals in the early years of John XXII's pontificate.

[91] For Olivi's views on the Antichrists, see Burr 1993: ch. 6, esp. 148–9; for the parallels with Dante, see Davis 1955: 209ff. and 1984: 62–5 and Scott 1996: 202 and n. 78. A related pattern in the *Lectura* is the alliance between a treacherous Christian leadership and a pagan ruler (Burr 1993: 148).

ecclesiastical corruption as adultery at a specific point in its commentary on Revelation 17:

> She is therefore called 'the great whore' because, abandoning the faithful devotion and the love and delight of Christ her spouse, she cleaves to this world and its pleasures and wealth, and hence to the devil, and *furthermore to the kings and magnates and prelates and all other lovers of this world* . . .
>
> It is then said that 'the *kings of the earth* have fornicated with her', namely *both secular* [rulers] *and ecclesiastical ones*. Those who share her carnal glory, wealth and pleasure are one with her carnally and in repeated crimes.[92]

Such parallels do not necessarily contradict the traditional view (going back to the early commentators), which identifies the giant with Philip IV of France and the abduction of the *carro* with the removal of the Papacy to Avignon.[93] They imply, rather, that we should read such figures and images (like those in the letter to the Avignon cardinals or the portrayal of Clement V in *Inferno* 19) rather more flexibly and within a wider context of reformist apocalypticism.

In more obviously polemical writing by Spiritual Franciscans a comparable convergence of ideas is also at times perceptible – for instance in the work of Jacopone da Todi.[94] Jacopone's most apocalyptic poem is the satirical *lauda De pugna* ('De la grande battaglia de Antecristo').[95] Here he represents the corruption of the Church in the Last Days through the liberation of 'the ancient dragon' ('l'antiquo serpente', 6) from his bonds, and through the emergence of Avarice, along with pride in learning and false sanctity, as the dragon's main champions:

> L'Avarizia ne lo campo è 'ntrata,
> fatt'à sconfitta e morta molta gente;
> e pochi so' che voglia contrastare.
>
> [Avarice has entered the field; she has conquered and killed many people, and there are few who wish to stand up against her.] (43–5)

92 *Lectura* in Bibl. Ang. 382, f. 103r (my translation and italics); also in Tocco 1903: 40 (Laur. conv. soppr. 397, f. 192v).

93 For a review of interpretations of *Purg.* 32's Whore and Giant, see Scott 1996: 201–2.

94 On Jacopone, see Chapter 1 above, pp. 29–31; also (for parallels with Dante) Chapter 2, p. 60 with nn. 59–61, and pp. 69–70 with nn. 88–94.

95 In Mancini 1974: no. 6.

Before this stage of the conflict the whole of the Church has been seen in cosmic terms as a darkened moon 'which used to give light to the world by night' (19), and then in a striking shift of metaphor the clergy are imagined as an unbridled horse:

> Papa e cardenal, con' l'ò guidata,
> la luce ène tornata en tenebria;
> la universitate clericata
> l'<ò> encursata e pres'à mala via.
> O scire Deo, e chi porrà scampare?
>
> [Popes and cardinals have governed it in such a way that its light has been turned into darkness; they have given the whole body of the clergy its head and it has gone astray. O Lord God, who then can escape?] (*De pugna*, 20–4)

Jacopone's highly unusual verb *encorsare* thus imagines the Church metamorphosing into an uncontrolled beast.[96] Through this single compressed image, the path to destruction taken by his unbridled clergy begins to resemble the errant career taken by the grotesquely transformed *carro* at the very end of the vision in *Purgatorio* 32.

Faced with these kinds of transformation and distortion, both Jacopone's *lauda* (ll. 24, 31, 59) and Dante's *Purgatorio* look for divine intervention. Beatrice, in the final canto of *Purgatorio*, foresees the 'vengeance of God' which will strike down both the whore and the giant by means of the enigmatic 'cinquecento diece e cinque' (*Purg.* 33. 34–45).[97] Dante's prophecy is cast in broad terms that resist specific identifications, and it is important in this context, as has been recently argued, 'not to establish *who* the "515" may be but *what* it represents from the apocalyptic and eschatological point of view'.[98] In addition to the many other traditions that have been adduced, there are also two ways in which the discourse of the prophecy can subsequently be seen as converging with that of Franciscan apocalyptic.

[96] Mancini 1974: 351 glosses Jacopone's phrase as meaning that the popes and cardinals have urged the clergy 'al galoppo sfrenato'; this interpretation is confirmed by Ageno (1953: 199) and by *GDLI, s.v. incorsare*[3].

[97] For recent approaches and reviews of interpretations see Armour 1989: 238–51 and Scott 1996: 202–11.

[98] Mineo 1998: 42 (my translation).

First, there is the notion of the returning hero who comes in the Last Days to combat evil and inspire the faithful, as Dante's 515 is destined to do.[99] The myth is of course recurrent in other cultures and contexts; but a similar return is known to have been anticipated by the radical followers of St Francis.[100] Olivi, for example, on several occasions attributes to a companion of Brother Leo a belief in the saint's coming resurrection, most notably in the *Lectura*, when developing the Franciscan tradition which envisaged St Francis as the angel of the sixth seal in Revelation 7: 2. This return of the saint, Olivi explains, is particularly appropriate, since

> just as he was singularly assimilated to Christ in his life and in the stigmata of the cross, so he will be as, assimilated to him in a resurrection necessary for confirming and informing his disciples, just as Christ's resurrection was necessary for confirming the apostles and informing them concerning the foundation and governance of the future church.[101]

Olivi had also referred to this same belief in very similar terms in his commentary on Matthew (ch. 27), some twenty years before the *Lectura*.[102] Its continuing appeal to subsequent Spiritual Franciscans is reflected by its repetition a few years after the *Lectura* in the apocalyptic fifth book of Ubertino da Casale's *Arbor vitae crucifixae*, where the prophecy is said to have come from Brother Leo and to have been transmitted through 'Brother Conrad [of Offida] and many others worthy of belief'.[103] This resurrection, Ubertino explains, will be in order to allay 'the confusion in the minds of spiritual men and his [Francis'] children because of the thoroughgoing assault upon his Rule'; and like Olivi Ubertino argues that

99 In the *Legenda maior* Bonaventura had seen apocalyptic significance in St Francis' role as Angel of the sixth seal and herald of Christ's second coming; see Emmerson and Herzman 1992: 36–9, 49 and 57.

100 On the development of the legend of St Francis' resurrection, see Manselli 1976.

101 'Sicut in vita et in crucis stigmatibus est Christo singulariter assimilatus, sic et in resurrectione Christo assimiletur necessaria tunc suis discipulis confirmandis et informandis sicut Christi resurrectio fuit necessaria apostolis confirmandis et super fundatione et gubernatione future ecclesie informandis.' In *Lectura*, Bibl. Ang. 382, f. 55va; as translated in Burr 1993: 121 and 130–1 (n. 64). See also Manselli 1976: 313–14.

102 *Lectura super Matthaeum* in Bodley MS New College 49, f. 155ra; see also Burr 1993: 131 and n. 67.

103 Ubertino da Casale 1485 print (repr. 1961): 442b–3a.

> just as Francis was uniquely similar to Jesus Christ in the likeness of his Passion, so is he also identical with him through anticipating the resurrection before others. And this will be greatly to the strengthening of belief and truth of the apostolic life, which he wished to renew in Francis and which is suffering in similar ways at the hands of the carnal Church.[104]

This should not, of course, lead us to assert that Dante's 515 'is' St Francis, but rather to recognize that contemporary Spiritual Franciscan exegesis was imagining a closely comparable kind of redemptive advent.

Secondly, there is a specific linguistic or semiotic similarity between Dante's imagining of apocalyptic intervention and Olivi's. The 515 of *Purgatorio* 33 has since the early commentators been translated into the Roman numerals and letters DXV.[105] Moreover, several of those who see these letters as an anagram of 'DVX' ('leader') have also referred to the title 'novus DVX' assigned to the Last Emperor in Joachimist prophecies.[106] The Joachimist prophecies are clearly an important context for both Olivi's apocalyptic ideas and Dante's, and the association can be reinforced by a linguistic (or rather, literal) parallel. If those many who have transliterated the 515 into DXV or DVX are right, then Dante's eschatology necessarily relates numbers to letters. Letter-prophecies of course were common enough in the period; and we know that Ubertino da Casale, for instance, took no little delight in noting that the number of the Beast could (according to a Greek commentary on the Apocalypse) be transliterated into Boniface VIII's former first name.[107] It may also be noted that Olivi's quest to establish an eschatological timescale leads him into an analogy between, on the one hand, the twenty-three centuries between the founding of Rome and the Last Judgement and, on the other, the twenty-three letters of the Latin alphabet.[108] In the course of this calculation he places particular stress upon three letters: the

[104] Ubertino da Casale 1485 (my translation).

[105] For concise reviews of interpretations of *Purg.* 33's DXV, see Davis in *ED* 2: 10–14 and Scott 1996: 204.

[106] On the connection between the DXV and the Joachimist *novus dux*, see Renucci 1965, Armour 1989: 247, 250, 266, 279, and Scott 1996: 205–7.

[107] The commentary in question was that of pseudo-Justin Martyr, which allowed 666 to be transcribed into *Benedictos* (Benedetto [Gaetani] being Boniface's former name); see Ubertino da Casale 1485 (repr. 1961): 465a.

[108] See Burr 1993: 172–3 and *Lectura* in Bibl. Ang. 382, f. 113r–v.

eighth, H (associated with the birth of Christ); the twentieth, V (associated with the time when 'the carnal church or Babylon will expire'); and the twenty-first, X (when 'the Cross of Christ will be restored and lifted up'). Olivi's use of an interchangeable triad of letters and numbers (HVX) thus has some affinity as a procedure with Dante's 515 triad, and it even shares two of the same characters if, like most commentators, we transliterate Dante's formula. Again, this is not to assume that Dante is alluding to Olivi's timescale or adopting his specific agenda, but rather to show that, along with the other discursive correspondences that have been noted throughout this chapter, he shares with the Franciscans (and on occasion the Spiritual Franciscans) a mode of expression and a way of articulating an optimistic and redemptive vision of history.

Interdiscursivity, however, is not the same thing as identity; and there are ultimately some significant differences between the *Commedia*'s vision of the Church and that of Olivi and his followers. For instance, the Spirituals' attitude towards Rome, the Empire and its earlier pagan culture seems to have been largely hostile; whereas Dante (despite the destructive actions of the Giant at the end of *Purgatorio* 32) continued to envisage a positive role for the temporal ruler and (for instance in *Monarchia* 3 and *Paradiso* 6) an ideal partnership between pope and Emperor – between (as Davis concisely puts it) 'a revitalized Empire and a repauperized Church'.[109] Moreover, Dante's view of evangelical poverty (for instance in *Monarchia* 3 and *Paradiso* 12, 21 and 22) is more inclusive than that of the Spirituals – extending to the whole of the Church and not just to the elite of the Franciscan Order.[110] For his vision of the Church in the *Purgatorio* – as elsewhere – Dante is thus appropriating the discourses of the Spirituals rather than adopting their full apocalyptic programme. He is also polysemously combining those discourses with a number of sources and traditions, Franciscan and other.[111] Bonaventura's eschatology in the *Legenda maior* probably informed his imagination to some degree; so also did Poverty's vision of Christian history in the *Sacrum commercium*; and so also did his

[109] Davis 1984: 48, 54–7 and 66–9. On the differences between Dante and the Spirituals on secular politics, see Mineo 1998: 28–31.

[110] With regard to the 'inclusivity' of Dante's thinking in this respect, I thus concur with Davis 1984: 53–4 and Mineo 1993: 562–9.

[111] For more discussion of the sources and traditions that Dante combines, see Mineo 1998: 44 and n. 115.

own personal reading of Revelation.[112] One important effect of these convergences is to confirm the authority of the pilgrim as visionary and eventually as vernacular poet – a figure who is addressed as *frate* by fellow-vernacular poets (*Purg.* 24 and 26), by a pope (*Purg.* 19) and by the prophetic Beatrice (*Purg.* 33), who is to guide him through the evolving visions of the apostolic ideal in the poem's final *cantica*.

[112] The relationship between Dante's apocalypticism and Bonaventura's is discussed by Herzman in Emmerson and McGinn 1992: 405–7. For the vision of Christian history in the *Sacrum commercium,* see Brufani (ed.) 1990: 143–66 (chs. 7–26) and this chapter above, p. 90 with n. 10. On Dante's personal reading of Revelation and how he 'transforms and turns it to his purpose as it best seems to him', see Francesco da Buti's comments on *Purg.* 32, cited in Mineo 1998: 44, n. 15; also Herzman in Emmerson and McGinn 1992: 412–13.

4

Paradiso: poverty and authority

'e tu, figliuol, che per lo mortal pondo
ancor giù tornerai, apri la bocca,
e non asconder quel ch'io non ascondo.'

['and you, my son, who because of the burden of mortality must return to earth, raise your voice; do not hide the things I have not hidden.'] (*Par.* 27. 64–6)

From the enclosing circles of Heaven, *Paradiso*'s vision glances back to the 'threshing-floor' of earthly history (22. 151) and the trajectories of human aspiration and folly, such as the 'errant course' steered by Ulysses (27. 82–3). Revisiting the *Inferno*, it also plumbs yet deeper, when St Peter describes Satan's delight in the 'blood and filth' now seeping down from papal Rome (27. 25–7), and when Beatrice imagines an inverted kind of papal succession receding into the fissures of the rock in Malebolge (30. 146–8). The vision of the Church, its leadership and its history, here adopts a prophetic stance, as it had in the pageant of *Purgatorio* 32; and in the speech of St Peter quoted above the lay writer is once again authorized – as he was by Beatrice after that vision in *Purgatorio* (33. 52–7) – to tell what he has seen and not to conceal what he has been shown.

Within this visionary framework the ideal of evangelical poverty is both celebrated and contested. The *poverello*, St Francis, is named three times in the course of the *cantica*: in the middle of the canto that presents his life-story and his relationship with Lady Poverty (11.74); during St Benedict's lament for the decline of monasticism (22. 90); and, finally, as a figure in the celestial Rose, beside John the Baptist, the saint of the desert (32. 35). There are two main issues involved in the authorizing of poverty in this *cantica*: the role of St Francis and the early Franciscans, and the relationship of evangelical poverty to papal power. The portrayal of St Francis, in *Paradiso* 11, should thus be placed in two kinds of context. Of immediate relevance, first, is the role of the saint's 'forerunners' and of Franciscan imagery and vocabulary in the cantos that precede that portrayal. Subsequently, canto 11 itself needs to be read in relation to both literary and visual traditions: to early Franciscan texts and painting and the manuscript illustrations of Dante's St Francis.

The wider political issue of the relationship between evangelical poverty and authority in the Church will then be contextualized in several ways. First, *Paradiso*'s approach to this issue is to be viewed in relation to Dante's own *Monarchia* (which may indeed have been written at about the same time). Finally, the representation of apostolic figures and ideals in the later cantos will be related to the debate about Franciscan poverty and Pope John XXII's actions with regard to it – actions which were making an impact during the years in which the *Paradiso* was taking its final shape and Dante was completing the process of his authorization as poet.

FORERUNNERS OF ST FRANCIS: FOLQUET, ROMIEU, PICCARDA

O insensata cura de' mortali,
quanto son difettivi silogismi
quei che ti fanno in basso batter l'ali!
Chi dietro a *iura* e che ad amforismi
sen giva, e chi seguendo sacerdozio,
e chi regnar per forza o per sofismi,
e chi rubare e chi civil negozio,
chi nel diletto de la carne involto
s'affaticava e chi si dava a l'ozio,
quando, da tutte queste cose sciolto,
con Bëatrice m'era suso in cielo
cotanto glorïosamente accolto.

[Senseless aims of mortals, faulty indeed is the reasoning that leads you to flap your wings towards the ground! Some were pursuing the study of law or medicine; some seeking office in the Church or power by means of force or guile; some exploiting or governing others; some wrapped in the pleasures of the flesh or wholly idle – whilst, freed from all these, I was up there in the heavens with Beatrice and part of such a glorious gathering.] (*Par.* 11. 1–12)

These lines from the opening of the St Francis canto convey the gravitational pull of earthly concerns, including wealth and poverty which continue to be urgent and recurrent issues throughout *Paradiso,* as they have been in the previous two *cantiche.*[1] They serve as a 'prelude to the canto's main theme' (of poverty), and their atmosphere has been characterized as one of 'Franciscan deliverance from worldliness'.[2] They also recall a number of occasions during the cantos and encounters that precede the appearance of St Francis – harking back, for instance, to the descriptions of how false goods can distort the natural upward inclination of the human will (as in *Paradiso* 1. 127–35); to Beatrice's hints about clerical cupidity (5. 76–81); and to Charles Martel's views on avarice and the confusion of religion with worldly power (8. 76–8 and 142–8).[3]

The opening *terzine* of *Paradiso* 11 relate also to the life-histories of three individual figures who have appeared in cantos 3, 6 and 9, and who can be seen as forerunners of Dante's St Francis. These three souls – the poet and bishop Folquet (canto 9), the exile and pilgrim Romieu de Villneuve (canto 6), and the Franciscan nun Piccarda (canto 3) – all carry strong personal significances for Dante, but they can also be seen as prefiguring the St Francis of *Paradiso* 11 in different but quite specific ways. Piccarda reflects – as encounters in *Purgatorio* have done – upon the nature of brotherhood and community. Romieu exemplifies the personal value of poverty; whilst Folquet affirms its political power when he challenges papal authority through a scathing attack on clerical avarice.

1 On avarice and poverty in the *Paradiso*, see also Armour 1994: 20–1 and 23–4.

2 *Par.* 11. 1–12. The lines are described as a 'preludio funzionale al tema centrale del canto' in CL 3: 307. On their 'aura di francescana liberazione dal mondano', see Mineo in Mellone 1992: 264.

3 Since the early commentaries there has continued to be some dispute as to whether Beatrice's reference to *cupidigia* in *Par.* 5. 79 applies to the clergy in particular or the Christian community in general. See, for instance, CL 3: 143–4 for the former view (following Pietro di Dante) against BR 3: 83 for the latter (following Lancia's *Ottimo commento*).

Thus, in the last few *terzine* of canto 9, Folquet, having rebuked the pope for his neglect of the Holy Land, turns to the 'accursed flower' of Florence (the power of the florin), which in his view has diverted both the Christian community and the Papacy from their true goals and has infected the Roman curia and the papal jurists more widely too, turning the 'shepherd' into a 'wolf':[4]

> 'La tua città . . .
> produce e spande il maladetto fiore
> c'ha disvïate le pecore e li agni
> però che fatto ha lupo del pastore
> [. . .]
> Ma Vaticano e l'altre parti elette
> di Roma che son state cimitero
> a la milizia che Pietro seguette
> tosto libero fien de l'avoltero.'
> (*Par.* 9. 127, 130–2, 139–42)

Folquet's vision represents the Vatican and the other sacred sites of Rome as now no more than 'the burial place of that army [of martyrs] who followed St Peter' (140–1). Here, once again, the gravitational pull of greed is apparent: Folquet's vocabulary of clerical avarice finds a number of echoes in the poem. Later on, as we shall see in *Paradiso* 27 (23–7 and 40–60), St Peter himself will develop yet more harshly the implications of what Folquet says here about Rome as the debased cemetery; and that cemetery will become, in his words, a sewer.[5] Much earlier, the encounter with Pope Nicholas III in Malebolge had been prefaced by an apostrophe to simonists which centred upon an image of papal 'adultery' (*Inf.* 19. 55–7) similar to that which concludes Folquet's diatribe in *Paradiso* 9 (142). A significant difference, however, is that the last line of the speech and the canto here – perhaps echoing the prophetic optimism of *Purgatorio* 33 – is able to foretell the deliverance of Rome from Boniface's 'adultery' (*avoltero*, l. 142). It may be the closeness of Folquet's invective against clerical avarice to the celebration of Franciscan poverty in canto 11 that engenders such confidence: just as in life he was a

[4] A lucid summary of Folquet's role in *Par.* 9 and its implications for the Papacy can be found in Balfour 1995: 136–41. For the association of the canonists and decretalists with avarice, see also *Mon.* 3.3, and this chapter, pp. 156–7 below.

[5] St Peter's imagery in *Par.* 27. 22–7 is discussed below, p. 169.

supporter of St Dominic, so here in *Paradiso* he becomes a precursor of St Francis.

Commitment to that ideal of poverty is also reflected in these early cantos through Dante's personal identification with certain specific figures. Folquet himself is one of these; indeed canto 9 has been described as 'one of the most intensely autobiographical in the whole *cantica*'.[6] Another is Peter Lombard, who is described in the next canto as a writer who made offering of his work (*tesoro*) to the Church like the poor widow (*poverella*) of Mark (12: 41–4) and Luke (21: 1–4).[7] Even more striking as an empathetic *exemplum* of poverty is the story of the pilgrim 'Romeo' (Romieu de Villeneuve) which forms the final section of Justinian's narrative in *Paradiso* 6. 127–42, a passage that corresponds precisely in length and positioning to Folquet's later denunciation of avarice.

Dante's story of Romieu in *Paradiso* 6 not only stresses his abjection and poverty but also celebrates him as a pilgrim soul. The recurrent vocabulary of travel in the passage (*cammina*, *peregrina* and *partissi*) reinforces the kinship between him and the *Commedia*'s pilgrim. The identification of Dante with this impoverished wanderer is further strengthened by the concluding lines of this canto:

> 'Indi partissi povero e vetusto;
>   e se 'l mondo sapesse il cor ch'elli ebbe
>   mendicando sua vita a frusto a frusto,
> assai lo loda, e più lo loderebbe.'
>
> ['Thence he departed, impoverished and already stricken in years; and if the world knew what courage was within him as he begged for his livelihood, crust by crust, they would praise him greatly and ought to praise him yet more.'] (*Par.* 6. 139–42)

The discourse of poverty here is consonant with Dante's representation of his own experience, both later and earlier in his writing. It points forward to the imagery of Cacciaguida's well-known speech about the bitterness of his descendant's exile (*Par.* 17. 58–60); and, as several recent commentators have noted, it harks back to Dante's earlier self-image as impoverished wanderer (*peregrino, quasi mendicando*) at the beginning

[6] CL 3: 241 (my translation). [7] *Par.* 10. 106–8.

of the *Convivio*.[8] As in the *Convivio*, there is also a development of the discourse of poverty in *Paradiso* 6, from humiliation to value and honour.[9] Romieu's departure in poverty at the end of the canto leads directly in the next lines to the recognition of the 'courage/heart' that he had and the 'praise' that is due to him. He thus seems well on the way to becoming the kind of 'hero of poverty' that we are soon to encounter in *Paradiso* 11. In a different manner from Folquet, then, Dante's Romieu is not only an *alter ego* and a fellow-mendicant, but also a forerunner for his St Francis.

Engagement with the apostolic ideal in the early cantos of *Paradiso* is reflected, too, on several occasions when souls in these spheres address Dante as 'brother' (*frate*). The often ironic use of the term *frate* (as 'friar') in the *Inferno* has already been discussed; so also has the recovery of the word's apostolic meaning in *Purgatorio*.[10] In most of its occurrences in *Paradiso* use of the term *frate* continues to strengthen the bond of spiritual community between Dante and the souls in the 'cloister' (*chiostro*) that they all now inhabit.[11] Early in the *Paradiso*, most of its occurrences in the cantos preceding the story of St Francis are in speeches directed to the Dante persona. As such, they continue the process of inclusion in a community that has been reflected in *Purgatorio*'s use of this mode of address.[12] Beatrice has used the term already once in the final canto

[8] See esp. Brezzi in Mellone 1992: 126–7 and CL 3: 181. For further discussion of poverty in 'Tre donne' and at the opening of the *Convivio*, see Chapter 1 above, esp. pp. 17 and 19. A few years before Dante characterized Romieu as 'persona umile e peregrina' (*Par.* 6. 135), the exiled Tuscan Spirituals taking refuge in Sicily had portrayed themselves as *peregrini et advene* ('pilgrims and strangers'), citing 1 Peter 2: 11, as St Francis' *Testament* of 1226 had done (see Chapter 1 above, p. 26 and n. 61). See their petition to Frederick III of Sicily, in autumn 1312, in Finke 1908: 2. 664.

[9] On the valuing of poverty in the *Convivio*, see Chapter 1, pp. 22–4 above.

[10] See Chapter 2 above, p. 54 with n. 38, and (on brotherhood in the *Purgatorio*) Chapter 3, pp. 98–104.

[11] Thus, for example, St Benedict in the sphere of the contemplative spirits acknowledges two early hermits as 'li frati miei' and very shortly afterwards uses the same form of address to the Dante persona, to prefigure his inclusion in the community of the *ultima spera* (*Par.* 22. 50 and 61). The last use of the word in the whole *Commedia* is addressed to the founder of the Church himself, St Peter (*Par.* 24. 62); its sense here is, appropriately, the primary apostolic one which Dante and the mendicants of his time were concerned to revive. The 'apostolic' sense of the term is evident in eight of the eleven occurrences of the word in *Paradiso*. The term *chiostro* ('cloister') also metaphorically describes Paradise in *Purg.* 15. 57 and 26. 128–9 and in *Par.* 25. 127.

[12] *Frate* is described as an 'affettuoso vocativo' in BR 3: 55.

of *Purgatorio*, when inviting Dante to question her further about their shared vision of the Church.[13] During the first few cantos of *Paradiso*, she uses it on three more didactic occasions: once when approaching a crucial distinction in the theory of vows and the will (*Par.* 4. 100); and twice when explaining aspects of the doctrine of redemption (*Par.* 7. 58 and 130). It is not, however, Beatrice who is the first soul in Paradise to address Dante in this way. That initial form of welcome comes in the first sphere from the Franciscan nun, Piccarda Donati.

In *Paradiso* 3 Piccarda calls Dante *frate* at the opening of her reply to his question about hierarchy in Heaven and whether the souls in this first sphere might want a higher position or greater closeness to God:

> 'Frate, la nostra volontà quïeta
> virtù di carità, che fa volerne
> sol quel ch'avemo, e d'altro non ci asseta.'
>
> ['The power of love, brother, calms our desire, leading us to want only what we have, and not making us thirst for more.'] (*Par.* 3. 70–2)

This central speech of Piccarda's – affirming the identity of the human with the divine will, and emphasizing harmony rather than hierarchy – thus begins with an unhierarchical form of address and one that in the *Commedia* reflects the fundamental ideal of apostolic community. The personal bond thus implied elides the boundary between Paradise and Purgatory, since Piccarda's brother by blood, Forese, has also twice spoken of the pilgrim as *frate*.[14] Within the context of the encounter, and of Dante's relationship to Piccarda, the term *frate* carries further implications. The speaker has already in the canto identified herself as having been in a more specific sense a 'sister' – that is, a nun: 'I' fui nel mondo vergine *sorella*' (46). The story of Piccarda's entry into a convent, her abduction from this *dolce chiostra* by her brother Corso Donati, and her forced marriage was well known in Dante's time, and he presumably heard about it directly. The convent in question, as Piccarda obliquely acknowledges (97–102), was that of the Poor Clares of Monticelli, near

[13] Beatrice addresses Dante as *frate* in *Purg.* 33. 23 when inviting him to question the meaning of the vision he has just experienced. On this 'brotherhood' with Beatrice and its significance, see Chapter 3 above, p. 110 with nn. 65–6.

[14] *Purg.* 23. 97 and 112.

Florence.[15] There was, of course, a close association between St Clare, the founder of the Order, and St Francis; and Clare's *perfetta vita* (to which Piccarda refers in line 97) was emphatically based on a rigorous observance of poverty.[16] The 'path' (*via*) that Piccarda set out upon but failed to complete (103–5) is thus quite clearly parallel to the one taken by the followers of Lady Poverty and her 'bridegroom' in *Paradiso* 11. Hence, as early as *Paradiso* 3 there is an awareness of the example set by *il poverello*; and these three prominent souls in *Paradiso* 3–9 (Piccarda, Romieu and Folquet) can be seen to prefigure the ideals that are to be affirmed and celebrated in canto 11.

IMAGINING POVERTY IN THE ELEVENTH CANTO OF *PARADISO*: TEXTS AND IMAGES

St Francis in *Paradiso* 11 is primarily a reviver of apostolic ideals rather than an *alter Christus*.[17] Most prominent among such ideals, for Dante, is that of poverty: Lady Poverty in *Paradiso* 11 is at once the saint's inheritance from the crucified Christ and his own legacy to his followers; and he is himself later referred to as 'il poverel di Dio' (*Par.* 13. 33). Yet the St Francis of *Paradiso*, as several modern commentators have emphasized, is not so much the meek *poverello* of tradition as a 'providential hero of poverty'.[18] In the description of his encounter with papal authority (that of Innocent III), he is portrayed not as a supplicant but as a chivalric, even regal figure, whose challenging mission demands recognition:

> regalmente sua dura intenzione
> ad Innocenzio aperse.
>
> [Regally he proclaimed his fixed purpose to Pope Innocent.] (*Par.* 11. 91–2)

Indeed, the portrait that emerges from Dante's *vita* in *Paradiso* 11 minimizes a number of the features that are emphasized in the early Lives

[15] Dante's prominent use of the adjective *chiaro* a few lines earlier (88) perhaps plays upon the saint's name (*Chiara*).

[16] On St Clare's 'love for the Privilege of Poverty' and her resistance to pressures to accept property, see Gennaro in Bornstein and Rusconi 1996: esp. 46–52, n. 33.

[17] BR 3: 176–7.

[18] Da Campagnola 1971: 302; Moleta 1983: 88. The phrase *eroe della povertà* is used by Cosmo 1965: 121. For further discussion of the Dantean figure's 'heroic' qualities, see Ulivi in Mellone 1987: esp. 84 and 90–4.

of St Francis (such as those of Thomas of Celano and Bonaventura). In particular, his role as peacemaker, the various forms of his asceticism, his humility of manner and affection for the created world remain unstressed; and his visions, prophecies and miracles are mostly absent from this account.[19] This is not to say that Dante was unaware of or disregarded the rich tradition of Franciscan hagiography that was available by his time. As this section will show, the narrative in *Paradiso* 11 draws upon both hagiography and early Franciscan painting, in order to dramatize and confirm the saint's apostolic authority. It is, however, the early Franciscan pursuit of Lady Poverty that comes to be the central narrative of this portrayal (in *Par.* 11. 58–117).

Lady Poverty in *Paradiso* 11 is first identified as a mysteriously abject and repellent figure, as 'tal donna . . . a cui, come a la morte, / la porta del piacer nessun diserra' ('the kind of woman whom, like Death, no one willingly entertains', 58–60). Her appearance thus initially recalls the negative portrayals of poverty in Tuscan poetry and particularly the despised and rejected figure of Lady Poverty in the Franciscan *Sacrum commercium.*[20] The description in *Paradiso* 11, however, rapidly modulates into the positive kind of imagery that had characterized Dante's early *canzoni* of exile ('Tre donne' and 'Doglia mi reca').[21] In lines 61–72 the narrative reworks the allusion to Lucan that had celebrated poverty in *Convivio* 4.13.12, combining this with the kind of erotic vocabulary and imagery that had been associated with St Francis in Thomas of Celano's and Bonaventura's Lives, in the *Sacrum commercium* and Ubertino's *Arbor vitae,* as well as in thirteenth- and fourteenth-century Franciscan painting.[22] It then identifies Francis and Poverty explicitly as 'these lovers' ('questi amanti', 74), a couple (*sposo* and *sposa*, 84) who beget a growing 'family' of followers (86, 94), to whom as 'brothers' (*frati*, 112) care of Francis' *donna più cara* is eventually entrusted.[23]

[19] Da Campagnola 1971: 302–3; Moleta 1983: 87; BR 3: 176.

[20] See Chapter 1 above, p. 10 with n. 9; and, for the representation of Lady Poverty as an abject figure in the *Sacrum commercium,* see Brufani 1990: 164 (end of ch. 24).

[21] For discussion of these two *canzoni* of exile, see Chapter 1 above, pp. 18–22.

[22] See, for example: *2 Celano* 55 and 82; Bonaventura, *Legenda maior*, 7. 1 and 6, and 14. 4; *Sacrum commercium,* ed. Brufani 1990: 137, 139–40 and 142; and Ubertino, *Arbor vitae*, ed. Davis 1961: 426a–b.

[23] *Par.* 11. 112–14; see *2 Celano* 216.

In imagining and authorizing poverty here, Dante draws upon the kind of iconography that pervades not only the early Lives of St Francis but also the substantial corpus of early Franciscan art, from Berlinghieri to Giotto. We know from the volume of surviving evidence (mostly in Tuscany and Umbria) that 'the life of St Francis was 'uniquely popular in the thirteenth century', and that during this period 'after Christ and the Virgin no single figure was more frequently depicted'.[24] Of the hundred or so thirteenth-century sequences of paintings that contain images of the saint, fourteen contain two or more narratives from his life, and most of these are dossals or fresco-cycles.[25] Of these, the Bardi Dossal at Santa Croce in Florence (dated variously from the 1240s to the 1270s) is, with its twenty stories, the most ample in its treatment of the saint's life and miracles, and it is also associated with one of the 'schools of the religious' which Dante attended and which probably transmitted to him the radical Franciscanism of Olivi and Ubertino.[26] The Dossal's contribution to the imagining of the wilderness as a setting for the Franciscan legend has already been mentioned in connection with the ascent of the mountain in the *Purgatorio*, but its images of renunciation and commitment also provide specific contexts for two key features of *Paradiso* 11: the friars' barefoot pursuit of Lady Poverty and the 'final seal' of St Francis' mission, the Stigmatization.

In *Paradiso* 11 one of the most vivid gestures of apostolic renunciation and commitment is performed when St Francis' three companions throw off their shoes in order to follow him and Lady Poverty:

> 'l venerabile Bernardo
> si scalzò prima, e dietro a tanta pace
> corse e, correndo, li parve esser tardo.
> Oh ignota ricchezza! oh ben ferace!
> Scalzasi Egidio, scalzasi Silvestro
> dietro a lo sposo, sì la sposa piace.

[24] Cook 1989: 288 and Moleta 1983: 14.

[25] See Cook 1989: 265 and n. 7. The most authoritative survey of early Franciscan images (up to 1320) is now the monograph by Cook (1999).

[26] Recent scholarly dating of the Bardi Dossal varies widely. Frugoni (1988: 43) suggests 1243; Cook (1989: n. 7) 'about 1250'; and Stein (1976: 294) 1254–7; whilst Duffy (1997: 231–2) argues for a date 'later than the publication of Bonaventura's *Legenda* in 1263' and possibly in 'the early 1270s or even later'. Most recently Cook (1999: cat. no. 68) has given the date as 'c. 1245' (p. 98).

[The worthy Bernardo was the first to take off his shoes to run in pursuit of such peace, and even as he ran he thought he had delayed too long. O unknown wealth and bearer of happiness! Then Egidio and then Silvestro cast off their shoes, following the bridegroom for love of the bride.] (*Par.* 11. 79–84)

Casting off shoes, in the Old and New Testaments, can have quite a wide variety of significances – including reverence, renunciation or transfer of ownership, grief or servitude.[27] In this passage, however, the most obviously relevant biblical texts are those which have to do with Christ's instructions to the disciples immediately after the twelve have been chosen for their apostolic mission. Abandonment of possessions, as proponents of *usus pauper* recognized, is most emphatically and explicitly spelled out in Matthew 10: 9–10:

'Nolite possidere aurum, neque argentum, neque pecuniam in zonis vestris: non peram in via, neque duas tunicas, neque *calceamenta*, neque virgam . . .'

['Provide yourselves with no gold or silver, not even with coppers for your purses, with no haversack for the journey or spare tunic or *footwear* or a staff . . .']

Also relevant is a rather more enigmatic passage from Luke 22: 35 which Dante knew well and quoted in *Monarchia* (3.9.5) This is the moment when Christ during the Last Supper reminds the Apostles again of their past and future mission, by asking them: 'Quando misi vos sine sacculo et pera, et calceamentis, numquid aliquid defuit vobis?' ('When I sent you forth without purse or haversack or shoes, did you lack anything?')

Both of these Gospel texts closely associate the abandonment of shoes and other possessions with the assumption of an apostolic mission, and thus they clearly prefigure the scenario in *Paradiso* 11, where St Francis's followers respond to a similar call. In showing the three companions following Francis and Poverty at a run, Dante may also have been influenced by Part 1, chapter 10 of the *Vita prima* of Thomas of Celano, which describes Bernardo da Quintavalle 'running eagerly after the saint' ('post

[27] See, for example: Exodus 3: 5 and Joshua 5: 15; Deuteronomy 25: 9 and (with different significances) Ruth 4: 7–8; Matthew 3: 11, Mark 1: 7, Luke 3: 16 and John 1: 27.

sanctum Dei cucurrit alacriter').[28] In a scene just before this in *1 Celano* (Part 1, ch. 9) St Francis himself has been shown responding directly and energetically to the reading of Christ's instructions to the Apostles in the church at Porziuncola:

> Sed cum die quadam Evangelium, qualiter Dominus miserit discipulos suos ad praedicandum, in eadem ecclesia legeretur, et sanctus Dei assistens ibidem utcumque verba evangelica intellexisset, celebratis missarum solemniis, a sacerdote sibi exponi evangelium suppliciter postulavit. – Qui cum ei cuncta per ordinem enarrasset, audiens sanctus Franciscus Christi discipulos non debere aurum sive argentum seu pecuniam possidere, non peram, non sacculum, non panem, non virgam in via portare, non calceamenta, non duas tunicas habere, sed regnum Dei et poenitentiam praedicare, continuo exsultans in spiritu Dei: 'Hoc est, inquit, quod volo, hoc est quod quaero, hoc totis medullis cordis facere concupisco.'
>
> Festinat proinde pater sanctus, superabundans gaudio, ad impletionem salutaris auditus, nec moram patitur aliquam praeterire quin operari devotus incipiat quod audivit. Solvit protinus calceamenta de pedibus, baculum deponit e manibus et, tunica una contentus, pro corrigia funiculum immutavit.
>
> [But when on a certain day the Gospel was read in church, how the Lord sent his disciples out to preach, the holy man of God, assisting there, understood somewhat the words of the Gospel; after Mass he humbly asked the priest to explain the Gospel to him more fully. When he had set forth for him in order all these things, the holy Francis, hearing that the disciples of Christ should not possess gold or silver or money; nor carry along the way scrip or wallet, or bread, or a staff; that they should not have shoes, or two tunics: but that they should preach the kingdom of God and penance, immediately cried out exultingly: 'This is what I wish, this is what I long to do with all my heart.'
>
> Then the holy father, overflowing with joy, hastened to fulfil that salutary word he had heard, and he did not suffer any delay to intervene before beginning devoutly to perform what he had heard. He immediately put off his shoes from his feet, put aside the staff from his hands, was content with one tunic, and exchanged his leather girdle for a small cord.][29]

[28] BR 3: 187; CL 3: 318.

[29] *1 Celano* 1, ch. 9, tr. in Habig 246–7.

Francis's readiness to answer this call is reflected in the eager, iterative emphases of his speech ('hoc est . . . quod volo, hoc est quod quaero'). It is also evident in his impetuous haste ('Festinat proinde pater sanctus . . . nec moram patitur aliquam praeterire') and in his impulsive actions, beginning with the rapid removal of his shoes ('solvit protinus calceamenta de pedibus').

Neither this scene from Thomas of Celano's *Vita prima* nor the one that seems based upon it in Bonaventura's *Legenda maior* (3. 1, in Habig 646–7) seem yet to have been mentioned in connection with Dante's imagining of the early Franciscan movement in *Paradiso* 11. Yet Thomas in this passage (even more than in the one usually cited by the commentators) clearly evokes the kind of eager response that marks the actions of Dante's friars as they run after the bridegroom and the bride.

Thomas's and (possibly) Bonaventura's narratives of the 'hearing of the Gospel' also provided direct models for the fourth scene of the Bardi Dossal at Santa Croce in Florence (see Fig. 2).[30] This scene forms part of a pattern of five initial images in the sequence: if we read the Dossal downwards from the top left, we follow a narrative that enacts the early development of the Franciscan Order. These first five panels lead the saint from one authority to another: from his release out of his father's control, and on to his and his Order's full acceptance into the Church. The narrative first shows Francis being delivered by his mother from imprisonment at home; secondly, his renunciation of earthly goods and his literal absorption into the Church (as he abandons both parents and is covered by the Bishop of Assisi's robe); thirdly, his choice of a coarse, cruciform garment as a habit to show to the Bishop; fourthly, his response to the reading of the Gospel at Porziuncola (the scene at issue here); and fifthly, the approval of the Rule by Pope Innocent III.[31]

[30] Miller 1961: 50–1, Stein 1976: 279, Frugoni 1988: 16 and n. 31, Goffen 1988: 37 and n. 45 all refer to the version in *1 Celano*. Duffy (1997: 221–2) argues that Bonaventura's more compressed version (in *Legenda maior* 3.1) is closer to 'what we see in the picture', whilst Cook (1999: cat. no. 68) sees only *1 Celano* and oral traditions as sources for the Dossal (see Appendix II for further discussion).

[31] For discussion of all five scenes, see Stein 1976: 277–9, Moleta 1983: 20, Frugoni 1988: 12–17, and Duffy 1997: 218–23. Cook (1999: cat. no. 68, p. 101) notes that '[n]ine stories in the Bardi dossal have no other surviving visual representation (1, 3, 4, 9, 10, 11, 14, 18, 19)'. These include the 'hearing of the Gospel' (scene 4).

Figure 2. St Francis listening to the Gospel and removing his shoes.

The Dossal's fourth scene shows St Francis in the very act of pulling off his footwear. One elegant boot stands empty before him, his left foot is bare, and despite the slightly damaged condition of the panel in this corner, it can clearly be seen that he is beginning to remove the other boot. The text to which he is so vigorously reacting is according to the open book the gospel according to St Luke. Rona Goffen, in her account of the scene, notes how the Saint's action is 'in perfect conformity with his new understanding of apostolic poverty', and she also emphasises the close connection between this scene and the episode in Thomas of Celano's *Vita prima*. 'Celano's audience', she argues, 'would have understood from the context that the text that inspired Francis was Luke 9: 1–5.'[32] However, Luke 9: 1–5 contains no reference of any sort to shoes or sandals; and we can only assume that the painter, like Thomas, is referring only approximately to Christ's instructions to the Apostles (including those in Matthew 10), or that he has in mind one or other of the later passages from Luke's Gospel – such as the instruction in 10: 4 ('Nolite portare sacculum, neque peram, neque calceamenta'), or the question to the Apostles in 22: 35.

[32] Goffen 1988: 37.

Between this scene in the Bardi Dossal and those in Thomas of Celano and Bonaventura there is obviously a strong connection. The Bardi panel is, moreover, the only visual example of this episode that has survived from the period. Its visual images and the voices of Evangelist and saint in Thomas's *Vitae* and Bonaventura's *Legenda* were part of the cultural context for Dante – and a memory of Franciscan Florence – when he came to describe the friars' pursuit of Poverty in *Paradiso* 11.

Why then does Dante focus upon this particular gesture – that of casting off shoes – as one of the very few specific images of Franciscan poverty in the canto? Clothing, or lack of it, clearly formed an important part of the apostolic Franciscan image in the opening sequence of the Bardi Dossal – for instance in the second scene (the 'renunciation of wealth') or the third (the 'adoption of the habit'), as well as in the 'hearing of the Gospel' and the removal of shoes in the fourth.[33] Baring of the feet had also been emphasized by a number of early Franciscan authorities as an essential feature of the apostolic image. The thirteenth-century Franciscan Rule-commentaries and statutes generally specify that shoes are not to be worn except in certain cases of necessity.[34] Sandals (*caligae*) are not specified in either of the early Franciscan Rules (1221 and 1223), but, as the Rule-commentaries point out, they are mentioned in Mark 6: 9, and more detailed provisions about footwear were laid down in the Constitutions of Narbonne in 1260.[35] Even Olivi, the leading spokesman for *usus pauper* in the late thirteenth century, acknowledges that sandals seem to be allowed for in Mark 6: 9 and

[33] A slight problem of iconography in the Dossal is that, unlike many of the thirteenth-century Tuscan paintings, it shows St Francis in most of its scenes (except the central portrait, but including the Stigmatization) wearing sandals. It is, of course, possible that a 'revisionist' painter could have added this detail later, but in any case, according to Miller, the paintings of the period 'reveal no uniform practice in this matter of wearing sandals or not' (1961: 220).

[34] The Rule of 1223 (ch. 2) provides that 'those [friars] who are forced by necessity may wear shoes' (Habig 59). For subsequent views and interpretations, see, for example: the *Expositio quatuor magistrorum*, ed. Oliger 1950: 134–6 (ch. 2); Hugh of Digne, ed. Flood 1979: 110 (ch. 2.3); and the Constitutions of 1260 and 1292 in Little 1917: 56. The English Franciscan John Pecham debated the wearing of shoes and other issues concerning poverty against a Dominican, Robert Kilwardby, at Oxford in 1271/2 (see Burr 1989: 152); and he also wrote the *Epistola de sandalis apostolorum* which was once attributed to Bonaventura (see Douie 1952: 29 and n. 3).

[35] See *AFH* 34 (1941): 43–4.

Acts 12: 8.[36] Yet Olivi still clearly regarded Matthew 10 rather than Mark 6 as the 'counsel of perfection' in this respect: as he puts it, 'the baring of feet always carries the form of humility'; and his follower Ubertino was likewise to insist repeatedly at the Avignon inquiry of 1309–11 that 'non calciari est forma vite nostre' ('being unshod is the sign of our way of life').[37]

Being 'unshod' (*scalzi*) is also clearly a vivid sign of the way of life pursued not only by Dante's early Franciscans in *Paradiso* 11 and the 'primi scalzi poverelli' to whom Bonaventura gestures in *Paradiso* 12. 131, but also by the original Apostles, St Peter and St Paul, as imagined later by Dante's Peter Damian in his vision of the Church's decadence:

> 'Venne Cefàs e venne il gran vasello
> de lo Spirito Santo, *magri e scalzi*,
> prendendo il cibo da qualunque ostello.
> Or voglion quinci e quindi chi rincalzi
> li moderni pastori e chi li meni,
> tanto son gravi, e chi di rietro li alzi.'

> ['Cephas (Peter) and the mighty Vessel of the Holy Spirit (Paul) went on their way, *lean and unshod*, seeking their food from wherever might give it. But now modern Church leaders are so ponderous that they need someone to support them on either side, someone to lead them and someone to prop them up from behind.'](*Par.* 21. 127–32 [my emphasis])

These two *terzine* from near the end of the speech by Peter Damian (the hermit who reluctantly became a cardinal) answer each other: the lightly sketched image of the agile, barefoot Apostles contrasts sharply and harshly with the following portrayal of portly prelates leaning on

36 Olivi notes this in the ninth of his *Questions on Evangelical Perfection*, the 'Quaestio de usu paupere' (written shortly before 1279); see Burr (ed.) 1992: 59, ll. 1868–74.

37 Olivi cites Jerome about Matthew 10 (against Mark 6) as a counsel of perfection in his unpublished *Lectura super Mattheum*; see Bodley MS New College f. 79r a–b. His assertion that 'Denudatio . . . pedum . . . semper ingerit formam humilitatis' is later in the 'Quaestio de Usu Paupere', ed. Burr 1992: 63, ll. 2000–2. For Ubertino's various comments on *calceamenta* and *non calciari*, see his *Sanctitas vestra* (addressed to the Avignon inquiry early in 1310), in *ALKG* 3 (1887), 55, 56, 64, 66, 67 and 78; and his *Rotulus iste* (later 1310), ibid., 94, 101, 104, 109, 114, 125 and 135. In 1312 the exiled Tuscan Spirituals in Sicily asserted that for true Franciscans the wearing of shoes except in cases of dire necessity or infirmity was a mortal sin (Finke 1908: 2. 665).

their attendants. Peter Damian's caricature goes on to describe the thick mantles that cover both these modern *pastori* and their palfreys, so that the humans are metamorphosed into grotesque, four-footed monsters. The scene evoked here plainly aligns itself with and develops the kind of protests which in Dante's time linked elaborate clothing, riding on horseback, and the wearing of shoes as signs of betrayal of the cause that the early Franciscans (like the original Apostles) had followed on foot.[38]

In *Paradiso* 11 the landscape against which this avid pursuit is presented is also partly shaped by early Franciscan texts and paintings. Two features stand out in the otherwise rather sparse scenery of the canto. The first is the description of the side of Monte Subasio above Assisi as the 'fertile slope of the high mountain', from which St Francis literally emerges:

> Intra Tupino e l'acqua che discende
> del colle eletto dal beato Ubaldo,
> fertile costa d'alto monte pende . . .
>
> Di questa costa, là dov' ella frange
> più sua rattezza, nacque al mondo un sole . . .
>
> [Between [the river] Topino and the stream that flows down from the hill chosen by the blessed Ubaldo a fertile slope lies on the side of the high mountain . . . From this slope, at the point where its steepness eases most, a sun was born to the world . . .] (*Par.* 11. 43–50)

The imagery that is to identify St Francis as a sun ascending from Assisi (52–7) is already beginning to emerge from this symbolic landscape.[39] Such introduction of a life through a landscape is not unusual in the narratives of *Paradiso*.[40] It links St Francis not only with his *collega*, St Dominic in the next canto (*Par.* 12. 46–54), but also, once again, with his eremitical predecessor, Peter Damian, whose narrative in *Paradiso* 21 also opens with the same preposition, locating a mountain *between* waters: 'Tra' due liti d'Italia surgon sassi . . .' (*Par.* 21. 106). The mountain

38 For examples in Olivi, see Burr 1989: 110; and in Ubertino, Chapter 2 above, p. 81 and n. 140. Concerns about riding and wearing shoes were also addressed by the Order very close to the probable time of this canto's composition, as part of the general observance of Franciscan *vilitas* at the Assisi Chapter of 1316; see Moorman 1968: 310 and n. 2.

39 For discussion of this symbolism and the use of the term *orïente* in this context, see Chapter 2 above, pp. 86–7 with nn. 162–5.

40 CL 3: 312 compares the geographical settings for the lives of Charles Martel, Cunizza and Folquet (*Par.* 8 and 9).

landscape is envisaged in both passages not only as a challenging location for the life of evangelical poverty, but also (through phrases like 'aqua che discende' and 'fertile costa', in the passage above) as a productive source for its future.

Near the end of the canto, a similar effect derives from the portrayal of La Verna as the scene for the ultimate authorization of Franciscan poverty: the Stigmatization. In Dante's version of this episode, the mountain is – like the 'fertile slope' from which the saint springs – located between waters, as 'the rough rock between the Tiber and the Arno':

> nel crudo sasso intra Tevero e Arno
> da Cristo prese l'ultimo sigillo . . .
> (*Par.* 11. 106–7)

The topography here is precise: La Verna stands on a rocky outcrop below the summit of Monte Penna and is almost equidistant from the upper valley of the Tiber to the east and that of the Arno to the west. Dante was himself directly familiar with this rugged terrain as a refuge for a visionary, since close by in the Casentino ('under the springs of the Arno') he wrote his letters to the Florentines and to Henry VII in March and April 1311.[41] He knew the references to the place in early Franciscan literature – for example, Thomas of Celano's account of the Stigmatization in the *Vita prima* 2.3 (94–5) and, especially, Bonaventura's account of the mountain's remoteness and the harshness of its weather (*Legenda maior* 13.7 and *Legenda minor* 6.5).[42] He would also have encountered the landscape of the Stigmatization frequently in the Franciscan art of his time. A mountain wilderness is the setting for the episode in various forms of Duecento painting; and at a very early stage it can be found in works that survive in parts of Tuscany and Umbria which Dante knew.

The oldest of the surviving Franciscan altarpieces is at Pescia, in the foothills of the Apennines between Pistoia and Lucca (see Fig. 3). It was painted by the Tuscan artist Bonaventura Berlinghieri, and the inscription dates it to 1235, a mere nine years or so after St Francis' death.[43]

[41] Dante, *Epistolae*, ed. Toynbee 1966: 76 and 100. [42] Habig 308–9, 733 and 823–4.

[43] For discussion, see Moleta 1983: 16–20; Cook 1989: 272–6; Frugoni 1993: ch. 8; and Cook 1999: cat. no. 141, pp. 165–8.

Figure 3. The Stigmatization at La Verna (top left), from the panel of scenes from the Life of St Francis in the Church of San Francesco, Pescia.

It is a less ambitious piece than the later Bardi Dossal at Santa Croce, and its six scenes focus quite simply upon St Francis' Christ-like ministry and miracles. Amongst these, on the left of the painting, are the Stigmatization and the Preaching to the Birds, both of which are prominent in their position because of the vivid folds of wild mountain landscape which stand out in contrast to the quite urban-looking ecclesiastical buildings. This contrast is particularly sharp in the Stigmatization panel where the distinctive edge of the La Verna crag directly above him appears to replicate the saint's posture of prayer, particularly his hands. Wilderness seems thus to have become a significant part of the visual vocabulary of the St Francis legend even at this relatively early stage in the thirteenth century.

Again, in the Bardi Dossal at Santa Croce – even closer to Dante's own time and place – we can find some comparable emphases on the wilderness and the pastoral. The Stigmatization scene is not so prominent in the whole composition as it is at Pescia; but the saint's figure here is somewhat more expressive than it is in the older work, and the building (presumably representing his cell) has become absorbed into the hillside, as little more than a cleft.[44] The rocky wilderness continues to form a backdrop to the depictions of the Stigmatization and several other Franciscan legends and miracles in several media during the later thirteenth and early fourteenth centuries.[45] The impact of the new Giottesque

[44] Pastoral features also figure in other panels of the Dossal: in the scene immediately to the left of the Stigmatization (St Francis rescuing a sheep from the goats); in the scene in which the saint gives a new cloak to rescue two lambs on their way to market; and particularly in the 'Nativity at Greccio', where the crib itself rests upon a kind of rocky outcrop with the same colouring as the hillside in the Stigmatization. For further discussion of these particular panels, see: Stein 1976: 280–1 and 283–5; Moleta 1983: 20–2; Frugoni 1988: 17–18; Goffen 1988: 38–40; Frugoni 1993: 365–72; and Cook 1999: cat. no. 68. In the nativity scene, the Bardi painter may, as has been suggested, be echoing Celano's emphasis on the outdoor setting of the Greccio event, with the woodland and 'rocks' (*rupes*) echoing the rejoicing of the crowd (*2 Celano* 1, ch. 30 (85); see also Miller 1961: 58 and n. 34) and may also be seeking to contrast the quite opulent clothing of the celebrant clergy with the impoverishment of the Christ-figure.

[45] The Orte altarpiece, perhaps of around 1260–75, provides the saint with an altar, but the rest of the scene (with hillside and cave) is fairly austere, and a very similar mode of composition can be seen in a French psalter of the same period, now in the Fitzwilliam Museum, Cambridge (see Frugoni 1993: pl. 64 and 13). A dossal of around 1280 or 1290, by a follower of Guido da Siena, again follows the tradition of giving the building prominence in the scene of the Stigmatization; yet in this case the split rocks, the jagged

representations of St Francis in the 1290s and in the early decades of the fourteenth century is also contextually significant for *Paradiso* 11; and important examples are the Stigmatization frescoes in the Upper Church at Assisi and in the Bardi Chapel at Santa Croce.[46] The dating and attribution of the Upper Church frescoes at Assisi continue of course to be fiercely contested.[47] They clearly, however, reflect the new dramatic style of representing events from the St Francis legend – a style that was (whatever particular dates we assign to its products) developing through the thirty or so years of Dante's writing career, and is associated with works that are unquestionably attributed to Giotto, such as the Bardi Chapel frescoes of around 1320.[48] A striking feature of the Assisi and Bardi Chapel frescoes is the prominence given to the craggy landscape of La Verna. A later Trecento commentator, Francesco da Buti, stresses this feature when glossing the phrase *crudo sasso*: he notes that 'there is jutting out from the mountain a very rugged crag which it is impossible to reach without a bridge, and upon this crag St Francis was praying during the night when Christ appeared to him in the form of a seraphim'.[49] The Assisi Stigmatization, like some of the earlier altarpieces, has a few small flowers clinging to the jagged, fissured surface of the rock, and the peak of the crag is clad in trees. Giotto's Bardi Chapel fresco is yet more economical and austere: its outline of the bare-peaked mountain replicates that of the saint's pose; and the pointed dark cleft of the hermitage balances the image of the church door. Through such compositional features, Giotto reinforced for his Florentine mercantile patrons

cave-mouth and the lurking bears all reinforce the wilderness scenario. This latter panel came from the Franciscan church at Colle Val d'Elsa and is now in the Pinacoteca at Siena (for illustration, see Moleta 1983: 30 and Frugoni 1993: pl. 177; and for discussion Miller 1961: 158–72 and Duffy 1997: 233–5). Two other Stigmatizations of this Sienese school (of c. 1270 and c. 1280) are illustrated in Frugoni 1993: pls 72 and 73.

46 For illustrations, see Moleta 1983: 71 and 113; Stubblebine 1985: figs. 19 and 39; and Frugoni 1993: pls. 19 and 21.

47 The Assisi frescoes are usually thought to have been more or less complete by 1307, although Stubblebine argues for a much later date (under the influence of Giotto in the 1330s to early 1340s), and Cook is 'convinced that the frescoes were executed about the year 1292'; whist Lunghi argues that Matteo d'Acquasparta (Minster General from 1287 to 1289) 'was responsible for the iconographic program'. See Stubblebine 1985: 112; Cook 1989: 263–4 and n. 1; and Lunghi (tr. Evans) 1996: 56.

48 For comparison of the Bardi and Upper Assisi Stigmatizations, see Stubblebine 1985: 31–2.

49 Buti (ed. Giannini) 1858–62: 3. 348 (my translation).

the dual status of the saint, as urban missionary and contemplative hermit.[50]

There is thus ample evidence of the *crudo sasso* as background to the Stigmatization in the Franciscan art of Tuscany and Umbria during Dante's time. A related perspective is provided by the work of the *Commedia*'s early illustrators. The Stigmatization, despite (or perhaps because of) its frequent appearance in Franciscan paintings of the period, is not a very prominent subject in the early illustrated manuscripts of the *Paradiso*. A striking exception appears to be one of the historiated initials in a Lombard manuscript of about 1400 (now Florence BN Banco Rari 39); this is the initial 'L' at the start of *Paradiso* 11. 76, which in this manuscript reads: 'La concordia lor e i lor lieti sembianti' (see Fig. 4).[51] The passage of text that is introduced by the initial and enclosed by the decoration and commentary goes on to describe the effects of the union between St Francis and Lady Poverty upon the early followers of the Order (ll. 76–84). The various images compressed within the initial are hard to read, but they appear to point to events further on in the canto: to Francis' appearance before Innocent III (on the left); his preaching before the Sultan (on the right); and the Stigmatization (above). In the latter scene, the *crudo sasso* of La Verna features: the rock rises steeply to the left, and St Francis, attended by a friar (as in the Assisi fresco and several earlier Stigmatizations) kneels on it with his face raised towards the angel. This, then, is an occasion on which an illustrator of the *Paradiso* clearly seems to be working within the tradition of earlier Franciscan painting.

The artist of the BR 39 manuscript, together with some of the other early illustrators, also responded to the asceticism of *Paradiso* 11; and the manuscript also contains a striking miniature that depicts Francis' renunciation of worldly goods (see Fig. 5).[52] A later and better-known approach to the theme is the second of Giovanni di Paolo's illustrations

[50] On the eremitical traditions behind Franciscanism and the liminal status of St Francis, see Chapter 1.iii above.

[51] BN Banco Rari 39, f. 351v. The initial is reproduced in BMS 2: 460b, but the detail of the Stigmatization scene (above left) is not visible in the monochrome reproduction.

[52] BN BR 39 reflects *Paradiso* 11's central concern with poverty and renunciation in its historiation of the initial 'O' of the canto's first line ('O insensata cura de' mortali') on f. 349r. This miniature (Fig. 5) shows a group of monks (or friars) in russet habits outside a church entrance, watching a semi-nude figure who is either taking off or putting on clothing before a bishop on the right. The Brieger and Meiss catalogue describes the scene as St Francis 'don[ning] his monastic habit before the bishop' (BMS: 1. 243). It is more

Figure 4. St Francis before Innocent III (left) and the Sultan (right), with the Stigmatization (top).

likely, however, that the scene represents a quite specific instance of the saint's rejection of the 'insensata cura de' mortali': namely his renunciation of all things, including clothes, that tied him to his family. The garment that the figure is struggling with is pale green, not russet (the colour of the saint's habit in subsequent illustrations), and hence probably represents the life that he is leaving behind, not the one he is embracing (the colour of the garment is clearly visible in the manuscript but not of course in the monochrome reproduction in BMS: 2. 460a). The symbolic renunciation of clothing is a scene that recurs on a number of occasions in Franciscan art, for example in scene 2 of the Bardi Dossal, in scene 5 of Giotto's Bardi Chapel frescoes, and in scene 5 of the frescoes in the Upper Church at Assisi (see Frugoni 1988: 12–13 and pl. 2; Stubblebine 1985: 21–3 and figs. 5 and 30–3). It is also a scene to which Francesco da Buti (whose commentary is included in this manuscript) refers when interpreting the lines about the marriage of St Francis to Lady Poverty (*Par.* 11. 62–3). Buti interprets the lines explicitly and emphatically in terms of the renunciation episode, when Francis 'wedded himself to that lady (namely Poverty), stripping himself naked before the bishop and his father Pietro and rejecting his inheritance . . . [and] after he had rejected this inheritance and stripped himself naked as the day he was born, in front of his father and the bishop, from day to day the love between him and Poverty increased; hence it is said that "he loved her more deeply"' (see Buti (ed. Giannini) 1858–62: 3. 342).

Figure 5. St Francis renouncing worldly goods.

for the canto in BL Yates Thompson 36 (f. 149r), which shows a naked St Francis kneeling for blessing before the bishop in a landscape dominated by the hill-towns of Assisi and Perugia and the mountains in the background.[53] Giovanni painted St Francis on several occasions, notably in the early panel with St Matthew (now in the Metropolitan Museum, New York), in the later Pienza altarpiece, and in the St Nicholas triptych of 1453.[54] His second illustration for *Paradiso* 11 is distinctive not only because it is one of the few to represent St Francis' life directly, but also because the extensive landscape within which he places the naked protagonist, with its mountains and the river flowing from them to the feet of the saint, relates to the initial setting Dante has imagined (*Par.* 11. 43–51) and to the canto's themes of renunciation and commitment: the Franciscan journey through the wilderness. Giovanni di Paolo seems also to have responded to the connections between the asceticism of Dante's St Francis and that of the hermit Peter Damian later on in *Paradiso*: in the second of his illustrations for *Paradiso* 21 he shows Peter Damian as a figure of increasing scale, departing from the kind of plain that had been depicted in the foreground of the St Francis illustration and entering and inhabiting the mountainous contemplative wilderness which Dante's text describes (ll. 106–17).[55] There is thus a certain continuity between the the asceticism of Dante's St Francis and an important later illustrator's representation of the landscape of poverty.

Giovanni di Paolo's programme of illustrations continues to respond to Dante's portrayals of asceticism and apostolic idealism in the later cantos of *Paradiso*. He includes, for example, three scenes from the life of St Benedict in his first illustration for canto 22.[56] In his second illustration for canto 24 he appears to acknowledge Dante's association of St Peter's apostolicism with that of St Francis by turning the circle of light with which the saint here girdles the pilgrim (ll. 152–3) into a cord.[57] And in his elegant rendering of the Celestial Rose in canto 32 he portrays St Francis in a prominent position, grouped with other

[53] See BMS: 1. 274 and 2. 461b; and Pope-Hennessy 1993: 108.

[54] The St Nicholas triptych is now in the Pinacoteca at Siena and shows the Stigmatization in a quadrant.

[55] In Yates Thompson 36 (f. 167r. See BMS: 1. 274 and 2. 487b. For a colour reproduction see Pope-Hennessy 1993: 141.

[56] Yates Thompson 36 f. 168r; BMS 1. 274 and 2. 492a.

[57] Yates Thompson 36 f. 173r; BMS 1. 275 and 2. 497c.

ascetic-looking saints, including (as Dante specifies) John the Baptist, whose entry into the wilderness Giovanni also portrayed in one of his most ambitious projects.[58] Earlier illustrators had also attempted to render the saints in the Celestial Rose of *Paradiso* 32.[59] Giovanni di Paolo's version, however, with its elongated white petals forming, above, five 'panels' for upright figures, comes closest to the kind of altarpieces of the Madonna and saints that Dante would have seen and could have had in mind when imagining the Rose. Such altarpieces (and other paintings), from the thirteenth century on, often include St Francis as one of the saints attending the Virgin.[60] One such example that is very close in time to Dante when he was beginning the *Commedia* is the altarpiece of the Madonna and Child with eight saints by the 'Maestro di Città di Castello' of the first decade of the fourteenth century.[61] This portrays St Francis as one of the four larger figures: prominently positioned to the left of the Virgin, next to St John the Evangelist and below the smaller busts of St Augustine, St Peter, Christ, the Baptist and the Magdalen in the five triangular niches that crown the structure. Hollow-faced, in an earth-coloured robe that reveals the wound in his side, he stands out particularly in contrast to the healthier-looking figures of St Lawrence and St Clare on the right. Together with the Madonna, then, the altarpiece includes five of the saints who are placed in Dante's Celestial Rose; and the proximity of Francis to the Evangelist and Peter reinforces

[58] Yates Thompson 36 f. 187r; BMS 1. 111 and 275, and 2. 516a. Giovanni's painting of John the Baptist entering the wilderness is the first of six panels (possibly composing a reliquary for the saint's arm, acquired by Siena cathedral in the early 1460s), now in the Reyerson Collection in the Art Institute of Chicago (inventory no. 1010-15; see also Pope-Hennessy 1938: 84).

[59] Examples of other renderings of the Rose are those in London BL Egerton 943 f. 181v; Bodley, Holkham misc. 48 p. 145; and Florence Laurenziana Plut. 40.1 f. 328v. See also BMS 1. 111, 230, 257 and 268, and 2. 511a–b and 515a–b.

[60] For early examples, see Miller 1961: 108–9; also Cook 1999: cat. nos. 42, 43, 78, 79, 88, 127, 150, etc.

[61] This is now, with other works attributed to the same painter, in the Pinacoteca in Siena (inventory no. 33). It was originally in the convent of Clares at San Lorenzo, Siena (hence the appearance of Lawrence and Clare as the two larger figures on the right of the Virgin and Child). For a description and illustration of the St Francis image (only), see Cook 1999: cat. no. 182, pp. 212–13. It is not suggested here that Dante might have seen this particular image (unlikely in view of its original location), but that he would have seen similar collocations of St Francis with other saints and the Virgin (see note 60 to this chapter, above).

(as *Paradiso* does) his 'angelic', prophetic and apostolic role.[62] Compositions like this may, as Giovanni di Paolo's later illustration suggests, have been among the visual sources that contributed both to Dante's imagining of the Rose and to his final celebration of the Franciscan ideal in the *Paradiso*.[63]

As its proliferation and survival suggests, orthodox opinion in the Church would not have had any problem with such visual imagery – nor would it necessarily have questioned the representation of evangelical poverty in *Paradiso* 11. Yet, as we shall see, the writing of the middle cantos of the *Paradiso* coincided with the arrival (in 1316) of a pope who thought that obedience rather than poverty was the prime virtue to be celebrated. In the context of John XXII's immediate and active hostility to the Franciscan rigorists, to dramatize the marriage to Lady Poverty so intensely – and to evoke so fiercely the founding principles and passions of the Order – was to enter highly contested territory, as the problems identified in *Paradiso* 12 will also show.

FRANCISCAN FAILURES: *PARADISO* 12

Celebration of Franciscan and apostolic ideals in the *Paradiso* is coupled with an acute sense of their failures in contemporary practice. This discrepancy is poignantly apparent in the histories of St Francis and St Dominic (*Par.* 11 and 12), and awareness of it continues to be registered during Dante's ascent through the higher circles of Paradise. In both these cantos praise for the energies of one Order's founder is immediately followed by a lament for the other's decline.[64] This symmetry is reinforced in a number of other ways: the *cortesia* whereby Aquinas

[62] The five saints that *Par.* 32 and the altarpiece have in common are: the Baptist (*Par.* 32. 31–3), Francis and Augustine (35), Peter (124–6) and John the Evangelist (127–30). Cook points out that 'John the Evangelist prophesied Francis as the angel bearing the seal of the living God [Rev. 7:2]' and that '[t]he likely presence of Peter [as a smaller bust] above Francis suggests that just as Peter was prince of the apostles, Francis is the leader of the new band of apostolic men' (1999: cat. no. 182, pp. 212–13). Other visual analogues for Francis's appearance in the Rose of *Paradiso* include contemporary mosaics (see n. 158 to this chapter, below).

[63] For other suggestions about visual and literary sources, see CL 3. 849; also Apollonio in *ED* 1. 786–7, and Di Scipio in *DE* 881–3.

[64] For description of *Par.* 11 and 12 in terms of 'chiasmus', see Mineo in Mellone 1992: 247–8 and 262–3.

becomes (as narrator) a Franciscan and Bonaventura a Dominican is stressed at several points in *Paradiso* 12 (34–6, 109–11, 142–5); and the balancing metaphors of steering the ship of St Peter (*Par.* 11. 118–20) and of driving the chariot of the Church (*Par.* 12. 106–8) confirm the complementary role of the two saints. Such ideal complementarity is also reflected in a number of contemporary sources, yet Dante would also have been aware of tensions and rivalry between the two Orders.[65] His choice of Aquinas to celebrate the mystical marriage of St Francis with Lady Poverty is imbued with a certain irony, in view of Aquinas' relatively low rating of poverty as 'the least of the three principal instruments of perfection'.[66] This kind of revisionism, however, is by no means uncommon in the *Commedia* (witness Aquinas' own 'reconciliation' with Siger of Brabant at the end of the previous canto); and in the context of *Paradiso* 11 and 12 it seems particularly appropriate.

Each of the narrators (Aquinas and Bonaventura) acknowledges the problems within his own Order once he has celebrated the founding ideals of the other, and it is at this point in each of the cantos that the imagery of decadence emerges. Hence, whereas the ills of St Dominic's later 'flock' are defined by Aquinas as worldliness (straying in search of 'new pasture', *Par.* 11. 124–39), the dysfunctionality of St Francis's modern 'family' is described by Bonaventura in terms of contrary and eventually conflicting movement (*Par.* 12. 112–26). The latter's concern with internal faction recalls the difficult conditions under which the historical Bonaventura became Minister General in 1257 and his careful negotiation of the doctrine of poverty and the observance of the Franciscan Rule.[67]

At the end of *Paradiso* 12, the manner in which Bonaventura addresses the disputes within the Franciscan Order is considerably more uneasy and potentially ambiguous than Aquinas' relatively straightforward

65 Francis' and Dominic's shared mission is emphasized in, for example, the joint encyclical by the Ministers General of the two Orders in 1255 (see Reeves 1969: 146); by Salimbene (*Cronica*, ed. Scalia 1966: 28–9, tr. in *FF* 2106); and by Ubertino in Bk 5, ch. 3 of the *Arbor vitae* (tr. in *FF* 1688). Dante's underlying awareness of 'bickering and . . . mutual acrimony' between the two Orders is suggested by Kirkpatrick 1978: 32.

66 *S Th.* 2a 2ae, q. 188, a. 7, referred to in Burr 1989: 47–8 and n. 36. On controversies between Dominicans and Franciscans about poverty see also Lawrence 1994: 61–2, and Jones (ed.) 1999: 1–18.

67 On Bonaventura's views on poverty and his handling of faction within the Order, see Moorman 1968: 141–54, Burr 1989: 24–7, and Lawrence 1994: 57–60.

account of Dominican problems at the corresponding point in *Paradiso* 11 (124–32). Unlike Aquinas, he goes so far as to name names but does so in a rather allusive and laconic way:

> 'Ben dico, chi cercasse a foglio a foglio
> nostro volume, ancor troveria carta
> u'leggerebbe "I' mi son quel ch'i' soglio";
> ma non fia da Casal né d'Acquasparta,
> là onde vegnon tali a la scrittura,
> ch'uno la fugge e altro la coarta.'

> ['Indeed, those who pore over our volume a leaf at a time may still find pages they could read as saying: "I still am as I once was." But it will not be by means of [Ubertino of] Casale or [Matteo of] Acquasparta that such people will come to understand the [Franciscan] Rule, for the one abandons it while the other constricts it.'] (*Par.* 12. 121–6)

He then immediately changes the subject; and his terse, allusive manner reflects Dante's awareness of how fiercely contentious these issues were at the time of the poem's composition.[68] The choice here of Ubertino da Casale (leading voice of the Spiritual Franciscans) and Matteo of Acquasparta (a Paris-trained theologian, Minister General and ally of Boniface VIII) to represent conflicting tendencies in the Order is logical enough: both were politically active around the fictional date of the *Commedia*; both wrote Apocalypse commentaries of very different kinds; both would have been known to the *Commedia*'s Florentine readers and could even have been encountered personally by Dante himself.[69] Ubertino had been at Santa Croce from 1285–9 and was possibly there again in 1298–1302; and he was, as we have seen, a major participant at several phases of the dispute about Franciscan poverty.[70] Matteo of Acquasparta, as Minister General of the Franciscan Order (from 1287–9) and a cardinal (from 1288), came in the view of the Florentine Bianchi to be associated more with the authority of the Papacy than with that of

[68] See Mineo in Mellone 1992: 227–45; also Chapter 2 above, pp. 73–81 and pp. 159–75 of this chapter below.

[69] For Matteo of Acquasparta's *Expositio super apocalypsim* as an example of 'respectable apocalyptic', see Burr 1993: 45 (with n. 73) and (for contrast with Olivi) 119.

[70] On Ubertino's role in the debate about Franciscan poverty, see especially Chapter 1 above, p. 36 with nn. 109–12, and Chapter 2 above, pp. 75–81 with nn. 111–40. On his movements from 1298 to 1302, see Callaey 1911: 19 (n. 1) and 43; Mineo 1993: 561 and n. 41; and Chapter 1 above, n. 102.

poverty. Dino Compagni represents him as a tool of Boniface VIII's policy and of the Pope's Florentine bankers (the Spini, Mozzi and Chiarenti) when describing his mission to adjudicate between the factions during Dante's priorate, in June 1300.[71]

The relevance of line 126 to these two Franciscans' observance of their Rule ('one abandons it [*la fugge*] while the other constricts it [*la coarta*]') is at first not entirely clear, especially in view of Bonaventura's abrupt change of subject directly afterwards. If we were to date the composition of the canto at 1317 or later, *fugge* could refer to Ubertino's departure from the Order in that year; and *coarta* might conceivably refer to Matteo as an 'authoritarian' figure. However, Matteo's Generalship was relatively brief and does not seem to have been notably constrictive; indeed, he presided over a chapter-general which accepted Olivi's exposition of his doctrines on *usus pauper* and sent him to teach at Santa Croce.[72] It seems more likely that *fugge* refers (chiastically) to Matteo and to his 'departure' through resigning as Minister General and becoming more closely associated with the *sinistra cura* of Boniface VIII's policies.[73]

Similarly, the verb *coarta* is, in the end, much more likely to apply to Ubertino as the spokesman for the Franciscan 'rigorist' interpretation of the doctrine of poverty, for example at Clement V's Avignon inquiry of 1309–12. Indeed, the Latin verb *artare,* along with the related adjective (*ar*[*c*]*tus*), adverb (*arte*) and noun (*artitudo*) figure frequently in discussions of the strict observance of Franciscan poverty, from Hugh of Digne through Bonaventura to Ubertino's mentor, Olivi.[74] Ubertino

[71] See Compagni, *Cronica* 1.21, Luzzato 1968: 49–52 and notes on ll. 1–4, 11 and 54–5. As compensation for having had a crossbow-bolt shot at a window of his residence, the Commune offered the cardinal a silver cup filled with 2000 florins, which (says Compagni) 'he gazed at for a long time, but did not take' (Luzzato 1968: 53, ll. 54–5).

[72] See Manselli 1973: 326; Burr 1989: 107; and Lambert 1998: 167 (with n. 33) and 175.

[73] The term *sinistra cura* is used by Bonaventura a few lines later (*Par.* 12. 129) to refer generally to temporal affairs, with an implicit rebuke to Matteo's careerism. For a broadly similar approach to Matteo's gradual abandonment of Franciscan values during the pontificate of Boniface VIII, see Cosmo 1965: 153–4 and Mineo 1993: 559–60. For the argument that while Dante might have seen Ubertino as a divisive elitist, he regarded Matteo as 'a politician whose career supported the realization of worldly papal ambitions that . . . had caused the church's ruin', see Davis 1990: 249.

[74] Hugh of Digne's *Disputatio inter zelatorem paupertatis et inimicum domesticum eius* (in Sisto 1971: 347) cites Matthew 7: 14 in connection with the signs of poverty: '*arcta* est via que ducit ad vitam'. Bonaventura uses the terms *artare* and *artitudo usus* in his discussion of the doctrine in the *Apologia pauperum*, in Quaracchi edn 1882–92: 8. cap. 7 and 12,

himself used this vocabulary in his submissions to the Avignon inquiry of 1309–12, and the question implied by Dante's Bonaventura here – whether Franciscans are obliged by their vow to observe 'strict and poor use' – was also addressed by the Bull (*Exivi de Paradiso*) which emerged from that inquiry, when it asserted that 'fratres Minores . . . specialiter obligantur ad *arctos usus* seu pauperes'.[75] Towards the end of *Sanctitati apostolicae*, his fourth submission to the inquiry, Ubertino had accused his opponents in the Franciscan Community of 'fostering laxity and oppressing those who are devoted to the Rule' ('relaxationes nutriunt et . . . in amatores regule tyranizant'); and this kind of assertion – as well as his own use of terms like *arctus* and *artare* – provides a precedent for Dante's unique use of the verb *coartare* to imagine the Spirituals' extreme and beleaguered attitude towards the Franciscan Rule and the ideal of evangelical poverty.[76]

Paradiso 12 thus implies a political context for its imagining of Franciscan dispute about the Order's founding ideals – a context that includes both the recent disputes of the Avignon inquiry and the writings of Ubertino and his predecessors. The role of the Papacy in the debate about Franciscan poverty is not spelled out by Dante's Bonaventura, although he explicitly deplores current papal attitudes towards poverty in general here (ll. 88–90). The popes who were involved (Boniface, Clement and particularly John XXII) will, however, be named and challenged by others later in the *Paradiso.* To provide a political frame of reference for that challenge, we can draw upon a contemporary text which addresses the relationship between papal authority and evangelical poverty and which at points converges with the ideals affirmed in *Paradiso* 11 and 12: the third book of Dante's own *Monarchia*.

e.g. pp. 272 and 322–3. Olivi uses all four words in his ninth *Quaestio* and throughout the *Tractatus de usu paupere*, ed. Burr 1992: e.g. 34 (l. 1060), 99 (l. 308), 103 (l. 460) and 113 (ll. 792 and 799).

75 For instance Ubertino uses expressions such as 'artante conscientia'; 'usus pauperis moderati vel arti'; 'usum pauperem . . . non tamen ad sic arctum'; and 'regule artitudinem' in his *Sanctitati apostolicae*, submitted to the Avignon inquiry in June 1311; see *ALKG* 2: 386 (l. 29), 387 (ll. 2 and 12) and 400 (l. 13). For the phrase as used in the Bull, see *BF* 85a and above, p. 77.

76 See *ALKG* 2: 415 (ll. 31–2). Mineo (1993: 577–80) suggests that the chief forms of *artitudo* that Dante disapproved of in Ubertino and the Spirituals were their hostility to intellectual life and institutionalized preaching and their objection to residence in large convents.

POPES AND POVERTY: *MONARCHIA* 3

The dating of the *Monarchia* is problematic, but a number of recent commentators assign it to the period during which Dante was also composing the *Paradiso*.[77] The concern in its third book with the abuses of papal power may thus reflect Dante's concern not only about Boniface VIII (1294–1303) and Clement V (1305–14) but also about the last pope of his lifetime, John XXII (1316–34), who, as we shall see, is also referred to twice in the later cantos of *Paradiso* (18 and 27). If the *Monarchia* is contemporary with these cantos and with this pope, then its preoccupation with *cupiditas* and its location of evangelical poverty at the core of the Church's authority take on an added degree of urgency in the light of John XXII's confrontations with the Franciscan Spirituals (which will be the subject of this chapter's next section).[78] Yet, whatever date we assign to the *Monarchia*, its concerns with ecclesiastical *cupiditas* – with the origins and problems of the Church's wealth, and with the Papacy's claims to temporal power – still remain relevant to the politics of papal authority and evangelical poverty, as played out in the later cantos of the *Paradiso*.

'Greed' (*cupiditas*) has been described as 'the most insistent and powerful of all [the *Monarchia*'s] recurring themes'.[79] The earliest references to it in Book 1 represent it as the force that compromises and contradicts justice (1.11.6 and 11) and is opposed to the 'rightly directed love' that should govern the actions of the ideal ruler (1.11.13–14). It also informs *Monarchia*'s view of the mythic origin of the temporal power and wealth of the Church and Papacy: the Donation of Constantine.[80] The text's

[77] For example, the main entry on *De Monarchia* in the *Dante Encyclopedia* begins by placing it 'sometime during the last seven years of [Dante's] life'; and one of the recent English translators suggests that it could belong 'to the very last years of its author's life' (see Cassell in *DE* 616, Shaw [ed.] 1996: xxxiii, and Bemrose 2000: 199). This brings it very close to or even within the period over which the first half of the *Paradiso* was composed: autumn 1316 to some time in 1318, according to Petrocchi (see *ED* 5. 46–7).

[78] Additionally, the attack on canon lawyers ('quos decretalistas vocant') in *Mon.* 3.3.9 could, in view of John's professional origins, be somewhat subversive of the respect that Dante's treatise has expressed for the *summus Pontifex* (*Mon.* 3.3.7).

[79] Shaw 1996: xxxi.

[80] The 'Donation of Constantine' (*Constitutum Constantini*), which had been forged by a Roman cleric around 760 and purported to transfer 'all provinces, palaces and districts of the city of Rome and Italy and of the regions of the West' to the pope, had been put to various uses, first in Frankish canon law and then in Rome (see *CHMPT*, 230–1,

first reference to the Donation, at the end of Book 1, represents it in terms which recall the symbolism of *Purgatorio* 32 (112–29). It is here described as the rending of the unity of the Empire by 'the talon of greed' ('cupiditatis ungue', *Mon.* 1.16.3); and subsequent references (*Mon.* 2.11.8 and 3.10.1) confirm this impression. Both here and in the *Commedia* Dante appears to have envisaged the Donation as a kind of second Fall.[81] Early in the *Paradiso*, for instance, it forms, for Justinian, part of an unnatural reversal of Aeneas' journey; and it is seen by Constantine himself as a well-intentioned act which bore 'evil fruit' for the whole world.[82]

If Rome in the *Monarchia* and *Commedia* unwittingly infects the Papacy with greed, it also, especially in Book 2 of the former, provides it with positive examples of voluntary poverty. In *Monarchia* 2 Dante's account of those republican Romans, such as Cincinnatus, Fabricius, Camillus and Cato, who served the state 'with toil, with poverty, with exile' serves not only as validation of the Roman right to rule but also as a model for the ideal Emperor and as a contrast to those clerical and papal opponents of Empire who are said to have abused the wealth donated by Constantine.[83] In the emphasis on the Roman heroes' endurance of both *paupertas* and *exilium* (*Mon.* 2.5.8) there seems to be a degree of personal identification on Dante's part – as in the portrayal of the 'umile e peregrina' figure of Romieu de Villeneuve in *Paradiso* 6 (127–42). Like the lean and barefoot Apostles of *Paradiso* 21 (127–9), or the early Franciscans of *Paradiso* 11 (73–84), the austere Romans in *Monarchia* 2.5 possess an authority imparted by poverty. Books 1 and 2 of the *Monarchia* thus carry some powerful implications for ecclesiastical *cupiditas*.

Book 3 of the treatise addresses that very issue. Dante's prologue to his discussion of papal and imperial power (*Mon.* 3.1) expresses a

Ullmann 1974: 118, 133, and 152 and *CHMPT*, 281). For discussion of the origins of the legend and a translation of the text, see Tierney 1980: 18–19 and 21–2.

81 For this view and discussion of previous opinions on the subject, see Nardi 1944: 153–7.

82 *Par.* 6.1–6 (Justinian) and 20. 55–60 (Constantine).

83 On the austerity of Cincinnatus, Fabricius *et al.*, see *Mon.* 2.5.5, and 2.5.8–12, and 17. Dante also reverts to the example of Fabricius (the republican consul who resisted avarice and rejected offers of wealth from the Samnites and Pyrrhus) in *Conv.* 4.5.13 and in *Purg.* 20. 25–7. Dante's contemporary, the Florentine Dominican Tolomeo da Lucca, had also (c. 1300) cited Fabricius, Curius and others as examples of incorruptibility in the service of the state; see his continuation of the *De regimine principum*: 2.8.3, 3.4. 5 and 4.15. 4–7. On the classical and patristic sources for the eulogies of Roman heroes (including Fabricius), see Davis 1984: 262–9.

mixture of confident quasi-prophetic authority and a certain degree of apprehension, as the author prepares to enter the subject's main 'arena' (or 'lions' den') of contention.[84] The opponents for whom his arguments may cause 'shame' (*rubor*) or 'resentment' (*indignatio*) must include those clerics whose misuse of ecclesiastical wealth has already been condemned (2.10.1–3) as well as those unspecified 'sons of the Church' whose resistance to the 'light of reason' is later in this Book said to be governed by *cupiditas* (3.3.8). The 'sons of wickedness' whose enslavement to *cupiditas* is deplored at the end of *Mon.* 3.3 are also probably clerics. They are said to 'prostitute their mother' the Church, and to 'drive out their brothers' – which may allude to (amongst other things) the persecution of the Franciscan rigorists from Boniface VIII onwards. Their refusal to accept a 'judge' is also expressed in similar terms to those describing the clerics of *Mon.* 2.10 and their denial of imperial authority.[85] These 'sons of wickedness', finally, are said to be not only enslaved by greed but also 'incapable of seeing first principles' ('principia non viderent').

Founding principles – those governing the authority both of the Church and the Empire – become central to the argument of *Monarchia*'s third book. Having (in chs. 4–9) reviewed the hierocratic interpretations of the 'two great lights' of Genesis 1: 16, the keys of Matthew 16: 19 and the two swords of Luke 22: 38 (all images brandished by the papal apologists of the thirteenth century) – Dante now turns once again to deal with the Donation of Constantine.[86] Reaching the core of his argument in chapter 10, he begins by confronting the canonists' claim that the Donation shows that 'one authority [that of the Empire] was dependent

84 A perceptive account of the implications of Dante's Daniel-like stance at the start of *Mon.* 3 is in Hawkins 1999:20–3.

85 On the other hand, see Vinay 1950: 208–9 and n. 2, for the argument that these may be 'lay authorities'.

86 Papal apologists in opposition to secular rulers in the thirteenth and fourteenth centuries continued to deploy images, allegories and texts that Dante was to confront in the *Monarchia*: not only the 'two swords' of Luke 22: 38, but also the 'keys' of Matthew 16: 19, the two 'great lights' of Genesis 1: 16, and the body requiring a single head. On the 'two swords' see Tierney 1980: 118, 120, 122–4, 148–9, 156–7, 161, 183, 187–8, 198, 200, and Watt 1964: 200–11; on the 'keys', see Tierney 1980: 117, 132–3, 135, 144, 147, 151; on the 'two lights', see Tierney 1980: 156, Maccarrone 1955: 33–5, Ullmann 1974: 224, and *Mon.*, tr. Shaw (ed.) 1996: xxiv. On the head and body, see Tierney 1980: 185 and 188, and *CHMPT*, 382.

on the other [the Church]'. Subsequently, in order to demonstrate his main thesis (that 'Constantine was not in a position to give away the privileges of empire, nor was the church in a position to accept them'), Dante turns first to the Emperor's duty to maintain the Empire's unity (recalling his first reference to the Donation at the end of Book 1), and then to the concept of the 'foundation' or 'founding principle' (*fundamentum*, 3.10.7–8). The founding principle of the Empire is said to be 'human right' (*ius humanum*, 3.10.7). That of the Church, on the other hand – that against which it must not act (3.10.8) – is said to be Christ as 'the rock upon which the Church is built' (3.10.7). An intrinsic part of this latter principle is said to be the initial commandment not to carry money (Matthew 10: 9–10), which therefore renders it 'utterly unsuited to receiving temporal things' ('omnino indisposita . . . ad temporalia recipienda', *Mon.* 3.10.14).

Monarchia 3.10, like the later cantos of *Paradiso*, thus seems to be placing evangelical poverty at the very core of the Church's authority.[87] It acknowledges the 'relaxation' (*relaxationem*) in Luke 22:35–6 of the strict rule in Matthew 10, and it concedes that although Constantine could not give full ownership of wealth (*temporalia*) to the Church, he could still (with a view to the apostolic model of Acts 4: 34–7) have consigned wealth to its guardianship ('in patrocinium', *Mon.* 3.10.16). At the same time it stresses that such a relaxation does not apply 'to the possession of gold and silver' ('ad possessionem . . . auri et argenti', 3.10.14); and the chapter concludes by emphasizing that the Pope's 'guardianship' is to be exercised 'for the Church and for Christ's poor' ('pro Ecclesia pro Christi pauperibus', 3.10.17). The latter point was commonplace among the canonists as a justification for the retention of ecclesiastical wealth and temporal power, but it had also formed part of Dante's criticism of contemporary clerics earlier in the *Monarchia* (2.10.2).[88]

[87] See pp. 159–80 of this chapter below. Similar points about the crucial importance of *Mon.* 3.10 for Dante's thinking about the Church are also made by Mineo (1993: 563–8).

[88] On the Church's 'guardianship' of its patrimony for the poor (including the voluntary poor) see the argument of Gerhoh of Reichersberg, summarized in *CHMPT* 620 (with n. 49). Other discussions of the subject can be found in: Gratian (*Decretum* 2.12, q.1, a.3); Aquinas (*S Th* 2 2ae, q.87, a.4 and *In octo libros politicorum expositio* 1.1); Tolomeo da Lucca (*De regimine principum* 3.10.8, citing John 21: 15–17); and John of Paris (*De potestate regia et papali*, ch. 6).

Dante's definition of the Church's authority here – in terms of the strictness or otherwise of the original commandments on evangelical poverty and of its role as guardian rather than owner of property – finds parallels in the contemporary debates about the Franciscans' strict or relaxed observance of their founder's various rules and injunctions and about their use of material resources.[89] In this context, it is also relevant that during the whole of Dante's lifetime the Papacy (following the arrangements of Gregory IX, Innocent IV and Nicholas III) remained officially the holder of property used by the Franciscans, since this 'legal fiction' was not revoked until a year after his death.[90] *Monarchia* 3 thus addresses issues that, as Dante would have known, closely concerned the Franciscans at this time, even if it does not adopt quite the same approach towards them.[91]

The *Monarchia*'s ideas about ecclesiastical poverty and clerical *cupiditas* can moreover be seen as reflecting collisions between the Franciscan ideal and papal practice in other writers of the period and in Dante's own work. For instance, Marsilius of Padua in the *Defensor pacis* (1324) adopted a yet more radical approach to papal authority, and like Dante he extended the ideal of ecclesiastical poverty well beyond the Franciscan context.[92] Later, in the 1330s (following the breach between John XXII and Michael of Cesena), the claims of the Papacy to temporal lordship were subjected to even more thoroughgoing demolition by the Franciscan William of Ockham, for instance in chapter 93 of his

89 On the relationship of the Franciscans' situation to the Roman law theory of ownership and use, see Coleman's concise discussion in *CHMPT*, 611–12 and 631–7.

90 John XXII formally cancelled papal dominion over Franciscan goods in the bull *Ad conditorem canonum*, issued on 8 December 1322 (see *BF* 5. 235–7 and Lambert 1961 (repr. 1998): 247–52.

91 Dante does not here argue about ecclesiastical *dominium* and *usus* in the manner of the Franciscan Petrus Iohannis Olivi or the Dominican John of Paris; and the *Monarchia* is at this point, as Davis suggests, 'closer to certain rhetorical passages in Dante's letters or his *Commedia* than to a legalistic Franciscan treatise' (Davis 1990: 254). Davis here considers that 'the closest resemblances in genre . . . language and . . . substance' to Dante's way of arguing here can be found in Frederick II's letter of 1246 to the princes of Europe following his deposition by Innocent IV; for a translation of the letter, see Tierney 1980: 147.

92 Coleman (*CHMPT*, 644) argues that Marsilius '[took] the Franciscan example and universalized it regarding the whole church and its relationship to temporal goods'. On Dante's extension of evangelical poverty to the whole Church and not just the elite of the Franciscan Order, see Chapter 3 above, p. 121 with n. 110. On the ways in which Marsilius 'put the axe to the root of hierocratic logic', see Watt in *CHMPT*, 415–21.

Opus nonaginta dierum.[93] In Dante's own work the closing argument in *Monarchia* 3.10, about the need for the Papacy to follow apostolic example in its guardianship of wealth 'for the Church and Christ's poor', is not only paralleled by the earlier attack on clerical adversaries (*Mon.* 2.10.1–3); it also finds an echo from a major Franciscan voice in *Paradiso* 12. In that canto the notion of guardianship *pro Christi pauperibus* also forms the basis for an accusation levelled against the current pope (Boniface) by St Bonaventura, when praising an idealistic mendicant, St Dominic:

> E a la sedia che fu già benigna
> più a' poveri giusti, non per lei,
> ma per colui che siede, che traligna . . .
> non *decimas, quae sunt pauperum Dei*
> addimandò . . .

> [And before the throne which used to be more benevolent to the worthy poor than it is now, not because of (fault in) itself, but because of the straying of the one who now occupies it, it was not the 'tithes that are due to Christ's poor' that he requested.] (*Par.* 12.88–94)

Thus, although Dante ultimately has a broader concept of ecclesiastical poverty than did the Spirituals (or even the Franciscans as a whole), he acknowledges through passages like this the significant contribution to its theory and practice that had been made and continued to be made by the mendicant Orders. Bonaventura, as spokesman for the voluntary poor and the author of the *Apologia pauperum*, here confronts an abuse of authority by those whose responsibility is to the poor in general; and he addresses the Papacy with the authority of poverty. The Franciscan's words about St Dominic not only converge with the argument of *Monarchia* 3; they also set the tone for speaking about and to the Papacy in the later cantos of the *Paradiso.*

POPES AND APOSTLES: *PARADISO* 18 AND 27

Throughout the later cantos of the *Paradiso* various challenging voices redefine the apostolic ideal in relation to the present state of the Church and its leadership. Founding principles – reiterated by figures such as

[93] Tr. in Ockham (ed. McGrade and Kilcullen) 1995: 72–115.

Peter Damian, St Benedict and, above all, the Apostle Peter – here collide with reminders about present 'unprincipled pastors'. Amongst the latter, the usual suspects, Boniface VIII and Clement V, are hauled in for final condemnation by St Peter in *Paradiso* 27 and by Beatrice at the end of *Paradiso* 30. Along with them, however, there appears a new figure to complete the *Commedia*'s own *vaticinia de summis pontificibus.* In cantos 18 and 27 attention also turns to the second of the Avignon popes and the last of Dante's lifetime: John XXII (1316–34).

Well over seventy when elected pope in August 1316, the historical John XXII (Jacques Duèse) was a canon lawyer and administrator of long experience. As pope, he has been described as 'a first-class organizer . . . able to reduce everything to system', a centralizer who 'had supreme confidence in the benefits of his own control'.[94] It has also been claimed that the status achieved by the Avignon curia during his pontificate 'was the closest that the later medieval papacy came to emulating the universality of an earlier epoch'.[95] During the early years of his rule John began as he meant to go on, by making moves to suppress the dissident elements within the Franciscan Order: the Spirituals and their followers among the laity. He also instigated an inquiry into the apocalyptic doctrines of the Spiritual master Petrus Johannis Olivi (d. 1298), and initiated a process of re-examining the whole question of Franciscan poverty.[96] The former inquiry resulted in a commission to examine Olivi's *Lectura*; and this duly condemned the work in 1319, the same year in which the Franciscan general chapter at Marseilles also did so.[97] The latter process was eventually to culminate in John's bull *Cum inter nonnullos* (12 November 1323), in which he condemned as 'erroneous and heretical' the Franciscan assertions that Christ and the apostles

[94] Barraclough 1968: 148.

[95] Leff 1966: 26. Lambert (1972–3: 126) describes John as 'the true creator of the Avignonese Papacy'.

[96] For recent accounts of John XXII's motives in his dealings with the Spiritual Franciscans and the Franciscan community, see Tierney 1972: 171–204; Lambert 1972–3: 123–43; Heft 1986 esp. 22–32; Turley 1989: 74–88; and Burr 2001: esp. 200–4. John paid close attention to texts that were hostile to the Spirituals, such as the *Liber de paupertate Christi et apostolorum* by the Dominican Master General Hervaeus Natalis (d. 1323); see Lambert 1972–3: 135 and Jones 1999: 8 and n. 33.

[97] On the process of condemning Olivi's work, see: Burr 1993: 203–6; Pásztor 1970: 82–111; and Lambert 1972–3: esp. pp. 124–5 and 132–5. For the issues addressed and the articles in Olivi's *Lectura* that were singled out as heretical by the inquiry, see Mansi 1761: 2. 258–72.

possessed nothing, either individually or in common, and that they had no right of using or disposing of property.[98] For the pope and his allies there was a clear perceived relationship between these issues: between Olivi's eschatology and *usus pauper* (the strict Franciscan interpretation of poverty). On both fronts they recognized that they were facing a threat to good order in the Church and a challenge to papal authority.[99]

During part of this highly contentious period, from about 1317 until the year of his death (1321), Dante was probably working on the later cantos of the *Paradiso*.[100] It is in these later cantos, as most modern commentators agree, that John XXII is obliquely but recognizably represented as an enemy to the apostolic ideal: first in *Paradiso* 18 (130–6), and then rather more explicitly in *Paradiso* 27 (58–9).[101] The representation of John XXII in *Paradiso* 18 and 27 can therefore be seen in the light of two different but closely contemporaneous processes: the completion of Dante's *poema sacro* and the initial stages of the pope's campaign (as he himself put it) to 'obliterate', 'extirpate' and 'exterminate' the Spiritual Franciscans and their followers.[102]

Seen in this context, *Paradiso*'s initial portrayal of John XXII (in canto 18) also serves to illustrate further how the *Commedia* continues to appropriate discourses of Franciscanism as a way of addressing papal authority. In *Paradiso* 11 the 'regal' authority of Franciscan poverty had been shown confronting and commanding that of the Papacy (91–3);

98 See *BF* no. 518, 256–9.

99 See Burr 1993: 210–11. Leff (1967: 161) notes John's awareness of 'the full subversive nature of the doctrine of absolute poverty'. Lambert contends that 'his place in Franciscan history [is] a more honourable one than he has usually been assigned'; that he 'simply saw the dangers [of Spiritual heresy] more clearly than others, and acted more vigorously'; and that his approach to the problem 'offered realism' and 'a possible reform in the early fourteenth-century doctrine of poverty' (Lambert 1972–3: 125, 132 [n. 29] and 137).

100 Manselli (1965: 126) also stresses the significance of this contemporaneity: 'Precisely when Dante was writing the *Commedia* thousands of *beguins* in the Midi were being pursued and struck down by the Inquisition, and dozens of them were mounting the pyre' (my translation). On the composition of *Paradiso* (probably begun in 1316), see *ED* 2. 82a, and Vallone 1965: 18.

101 See, for example, the article on 'Giovanni XXII Papa' in *ED* 3. 190a. Among the Trecento commentators, Benvenuto da Imola explicitly identifies John XXII as one of the popes referred to in *Paradiso* 27. 58–59; see his *Comentum*, ed. Lacaita 1887: 5. 392–93. The account of Dante's John XXII that follows here is based on my previously published article 'The Blood of the Apostles' (Havely 1997).

102 Typical terms in the pope's mission statements are *exterminatio* (*BF* 5.133a), *abolere* and *extirpare* (*BF* 5. 135b).

and in the following canto, as we have seen, Dante's Bonaventura had spoken out against the pope's neglect of the poor (12. 88–90). Well before that (as we have also seen) many of the poem's representations of popes had explicitly or implicitly involved questions and terms relating to the Franciscan Order and its apostolic mission – one obvious example being the contrast between the roles of Boniface VIII and St Francis in the drama of Guido da Montefeltro's damnation (*Inf.* 27). Less obviously, encounters with and references to popes throughout the *Commedia* reinforce the links between Franciscan traditions and issues and those relating to papal authority – particularly the authority of the Avignon Papacy, which was in power during the whole period of the poem's composition.[103] Hence, when reading the two cantos that refer to John XXII (*Par.* 18 and 27), it will be necessary to consider what is known from contemporary documents about this pope's attitudes towards the Franciscan Spirituals, and about what they (as well as Dante) thought of him.

Dante's first allusion to John XXII occurs during the apostrophe that concludes *Paradiso* 18:

> O milizia del ciel cu' io contemplo,
> adora per color che sono in terra
> tutti svïati dietro al malo essemplo!
> Già si solea con le spade far guerra;
> ma or si fa togliendo or qui or quivi
> lo pan che 'l pïo Padre a nessun serra.
> *Ma tu che sol per cancellare scrivi,*
> *pensa che Pietro e Paulo, che moriro*
> *per la vigna che guasti, ancor son vivi.*
> *Ben puoi tu dire: "I' ho fermo 'l disiro*
> *sì a colui che volle viver solo*
> *e che per salti fu tratto al martiro*
> *ch'io non conosco il pescator né Polo".*

> [Powers of Heaven who now fill my gaze, pray for those on earth who have been so much misled by following bad leaders. Once holy wars were waged with swords, but now that is done by depriving one place or another of the bread that the loving Father withholds from no one. *But you who write only in order to erase, remember that Peter and Paul,*

[103] See Chapter 2 above, pp. 70–87.

who died for the sake of the vineyard you are ravaging, are still alive. Well may you say 'I have set my heart so firmly upon (the image of) *him who was brought to martyrdom by means of dance-steps that I am not aware of either the Fisherman or St Paul'.*] (*Par.* 18. 124–36 [my emphases])

This passage concludes the initial description of the Eagle of justice in the heaven of Jupiter. It is the third of three apostrophes which increasingly contrast the imagined order represented by that Eagle with actual disorder upon earth and particularly in the Church. The authority of the current corrupt leadership of the Church (the Avignon Papacy) is thus contrasted twice here (ll. 131 and 136) with the still vital examples of St Peter ('il pescator') and St Paul ('Polo'), the two apostles who are most associated with the Church's foundation and who, at several points in the later cantos of *Paradiso*, embody its apostolic ideals.[104] It is on this sharp note of contrast that the canto ends.

In the first line of the passage, the precise reference of the phrase 'tu che sol per cancellare scrivi' (l. 130) is problematic and has exercised a number of commentators from the Trecento onwards.[105] Within the context of the canto, however, the phrase assumes a considerably wider significance. From its mid-point, where Dante and Beatrice ascend to the heaven of Jupiter, the canto has literally been concerned with justice in the form of *writing*. Jupiter's Eagle is formed from the last 'm' of the phrase *DILIGITE IUSTITIAM QUI IUDICATIS TERRAM*, words which in turn have been 'written' by the souls in this sphere (88–111).

[104] Both Apostles are mentioned together again in *Par.* 21. 127–9 (as examples of evangelical poverty) and in 24. 62–3 (as regenerators of Rome).

[105] The two main alternative readings of *cancellare* are with reference (a) to the revoking of excommunications for a fee, and (b) to dealings in benefices. The Trecento commentators, such as Pietro Alighieri (ed. Nannucci) 1845: 674, Andrea Lancia ('l'Ottimo', ed. Torri) 1829: 3. 425, Benvenuto de Imola (ed. Lacaita) 1887: 5. 227, and Buti (ed. Giannini) 1862: 3. 531–32, all appear to favour the first interpretation, and so do a number of modern editors, such as BR 3. 309 and CL 3. 518. On the other hand, Accame Bobbio (1971: 655), argues that the *terzina* alludes to a wider range of papal cancellations; and Gmelin (1954–7: 3.348) suggests it refers to John's cancellation of benefices granted by his predecessor, in order to re-sell them.

One possibility that has not yet (to my knowledge) been suggested is that Dante may be ironically referring to John XXII's previous career as a successful secular administrator – a career in which he achieved the positions of chancellor of the University of Avignon in 1298 and of the Kingdom of Sicily during 1308–9 (see Heft 1986: 3). The latter appointment was certainly well known to Villani and may also have been to Dante (see Villani, *Nuova Cronica*, ed. Porta 1990–91: 2. 286 [Book 10, ch. 81]).

The discrepancy between the order of the heavenly circle and the disorder of the earthly state (particularly that of the earthly Church) is thus heightened by the contrast between the images of creative and destructive writing: between that which embodies and affirms justice (the Eagle as the final 'm' of the motto) and that of which the aim is to erase or obliterate (*cancellare* as in the description of John XXII's purposes in writing). There is, moreover, evidence for this view of 'writing to erase' in some of the documents that were actually being written by and on behalf of the pope at this time (around 1317–18).

Various political considerations may have contributed to the animus of Dante's phrase in *Paradiso* 18. 130.[106] Yet it was in particular the confrontation between John XXII and the Spirituals that drew forth some of his most decisively 'destructive' writing. Before the start of his pontificate the controversy at Clement V's Avignon inquiry had, as we have seen, focused particularly upon the interpretation and observance of the Franciscan Rule (particularly as it concerned poverty); the orthodoxy of the apocalyptic and other writings and teachings of the Spiritual master Petrus Johannis Olivi; and the persecution of Spirituals and their followers by the authorities of the Franciscan community.[107] However, the Spirituals – particularly the *beguins* of Provence and the *fraticelli* of central and southern Italy – had continued since Avignon to challenge the authority of the community and the Pope; and very soon after he was elected in 1316 John XXII began to move decisively against both groups. His actions over the next two years were 'concerned not so much with eliciting the facts as with establishing correctly the true ground for condemning one side, the Spirituals'.[108] He proceeded to deal briskly and harshly with the Spirituals from Provence and Italy, some of whom appeared before him at Avignon on

[106] Some time ago Parodi drew attention to John's excommunication of Cangrande della Scala, very close to the time when Dante was writing this canto, as a possible specific reason for the hostility behind this phrase; see *Bull.* (n.s.) 18 (1911), 72–73, and for further details, see Accame Bobbio 1971: 654. The date given by Parodi for the excommunication is 1317, but this has been corrected to 6 April 1318 (when the bull was published); see Mineo in Mellone 1992: 238 and n. 53.

[107] These issues had been the subject of the inquiry instituted by John XXII's predecessor, Clement V, and they were meant to have been resolved by Clement's bull *Exivi de Paradiso* (6 May 1312). See Chapter 2 above, pp. 73–4 with nn. 102–4.

[108] Lambert 1972–3: 128.

22 May 1317.[109] During late 1317 and early 1318 he issued three bulls: demanding that the Spirituals obey their superiors; denouncing the *fraticelli* and the *beguins*; and condemning specifically a number of their doctrines.[110] In October 1317 he arranged for Ubertino da Casale, the most articulate of the surviving Tuscan Spirituals and the one who had stood up to him at the meeting of 22 May, to be transferred to the Benedictine Order at Gembloux, for his own 'greater personal quiet' ('pro maiori personae quiete'), as the document puts it.[111] Shortly afterwards (by May 1318) he had also instituted the inquiry into the apocalyptic doctrines of Petrus Johannis Olivi, whose work had by now become a powerful influence, especially among the *beguins* of Provence.[112] Over these years the pope's energetic pursuit of the Franciscan dissidents in Provence and Italy is reflected not only through major declarations in bulls, but also in letters to secular and religious authorities and in specific instructions to inquisitors. Thus, in March and April 1317, he wrote to Frederick III of Sicily, asking him to arrest and hand over to their superiors the Tuscan Spirituals who had fled to the island; in April it became officially known that he had decided in favour of the Franciscan community against the Spirituals in Provence; and on 6 November he authorized Michel Le Moine, Franciscan Inquisitor in Provence, to proceed against twenty-five Provençal Spirituals, whom he describes as devious and mendacious pseudo-Franciscans ('pseudo-Minorum ordinis fratres, solo nomine professores').[113] Of these twenty-five, four were eventually condemned and burnt as heretics at Marseilles on 7 May

109 There is a graphic account of the pope's style of proceeding in Angelo Clareno's *Historia septem tribulationum*: see F. Ehrle's partial edition in *ALKG* 2 (1886), 106–64 and 256–327, especially pp. 143 and 146. For a summary of one of the episodes in English, see Douie 1932: 18–19; and for a more recent (parallel-text) edition of Angelo's account, see Boccali and Bigaroni 1999: esp. 720–43.

110 The bulls were: *Quorumdam exigit* (7 Oct. 1317; *BF* 5, no. 289, pp. 128–30); *Sancta Romana* (30 Dec. 1317; *BF* 5, no. 297, pp. 134–35); and *Gloriosam ecclesiam* (23 Jan. 1318; *BF* 5, no. 302, pp. 137–42).

111 *BF* 5, no. 287, p. 127.

112 See also above, n. 97 to this chapter. On the various stages of the inquiry into Olivi's doctrines, see Burr 1993: 202–20; and Burr 2001: 207–12. On Olivi's posthumous cult and influence in Provence, see Manselli 1959: especially 35 and n.1, 154–55, 173–76, 181, and 195–205; Leff 1966: 197–9, 212–15; Nimmo 1987: 181–90; Burr 1989: 124–27 and n. 83; Burr 1993: 198ff.; and Burr 2001: 173–4.

113 *BF* 5, nos 256 (pp. 110–11) and 293 (pp. 132–33); and for discussion of these letters to Frederick of Sicily, see also Burr 2001: 179–81.

1318, and a number of similar executions took place in Provence and Languedoc over the next few years.[114]

The four Spirituals burnt in 1318 were soon accorded the status of 'martyrs and saints', as the subsequent *beguin* trial records show.[115] The executions and their implications did not go unnoticed by the Pope's opponents in Italy; Angelo Clareno recorded it in his *Historia septem tribulationum* (completed c. 1325?).[116] The earliest manuscript (dated 1334) of the vernacular translation of Angelo's *Historia* further reflects the effect of the martyrdom upon the minds of the Italian *fraticelli*: one of its illustrations shows the four Marseilles Spirituals, each of them bearing a flame in his right hand.[117] Angelo himself was in Avignon (under the protection of Cardinal Giacomo Colonna) at the time of the burnings; so, probably, was Ubertino da Casale. They may both have suspected that the Italian dissidents would be the next target, and they would not have been wrong to do so.[118] The longest and most specific of the pope's three anti-Spiritual bulls of 1317–18, *Gloriosam ecclesiam*, is known to have been formally published by the Bishop of Florence on 13 July 1318, and it focuses particularly upon the Italian *fraticelli*.[119] On 3 December 1319 Michel Le Moine (the Inquisitor responsible for

[114] The sentence against the four Spirituals singles out particularly their obduracy with regard to clothing and other aspects of *usus pauper*, as well as their continuing adherence to the 'errors and heresies' which 'processerunt sive originem habuerunt à venenato fonte doctrinae immo verius seductrinae quam frater Petrus Johannis Olivi Biterrensis diocesis super Apocalypsi & in quibusdam eius / opusculis contra honorem sanctae Romanae Ecclesie & auctoritatem eiusdem temere scriptavit' (transcribed in Mansi 1761–4: 2. 249–50). For further discussion of the execution and its effects see Manselli 1959: 152–53 and 194; Lambert 1992: 210–11; and von Auw 1979: 153 and n. 16.

[115] See the sentences in the Toulouse heresy trials of c. 1318–24, in *Historia Inquisitionis cui subiungitur Liber sententiarum Inquisitionis Tholosanae*, ed. Limborch 1692: 299, 302, 315, 321 and 323 (references are to the *Liber sententiarum*, which is paginated separately). There is also an account of the same beliefs in the survey 'De erroribus bequinorum' (completed about 1324) by Bernard Gui, Inquisitor of Toulouse: see Mollat 1926: 1. 126–29, 130, 132–34, and 142.

[116] See Ehrle in *ALKG*, 2 (1886), 146–7.

[117] The manuscript (Rome, Biblioteca Nazionale Vittorio Emanuele 1167) is described in some detail by von Auw (1979: 218–19), and she suggests it could be attributable to a *fraticello* of Central Italy. The illustration (one of fourteen in the manuscript) is on fol. 75.

[118] Von Auw 1979: 136–37, and (on Ubertino) Douie 1932: 128–30.

[119] See Ini 1973: 305–77, especially 357–8. For more recent discussion (and summary) of the contents of *Gloriosam ecclesiam*, see Burr 2001: 199–200.

the condemnation of the Marseilles Spirituals) instructed the Franciscan Provincial of Tuscany to search out and imprison the group of Spirituals who had absconded from Provence after promising to submit themselves to their superiors; and on 9 June 1321 James II of Aragon wrote to his brother, Frederick III of Sicily, warning him of the grave consequences of disobeying the pope by continuing to shelter the group of exiled Tuscan *fraticelli* led by Henry of Ceva.[120]

By 1318, then, the ruthlessness of John XXII's approach to the Spiritual notions of strict observance would have been abundantly clear to Dante's contemporaries, in Italy as well as in Provence. Meanwhile, Dante himself, in exile at Verona or Ravenna, was in the midst of composing a *cantica* which expresses recurrent concern about the Papacy and Franciscan ideals, and refers specifically to both John XXII and Ubertino da Casale. It seems, therefore, highly unlikely that events at Avignon were passing unnoticed by the poet.[121] His concern with the apostolic ideals of and divisions within the Franciscan Order had by this time been implied in *Inferno* 19 and 27 and were being explicitly articulated in *Paradiso* 11 and 12. The representation of John XXII as writing to 'erase' (*cancellare*) in *Paradiso* 18 effectively characterizes the pope's actions with regard to the whole Spiritual movement – actions which, in John's bulls and letters, are accompanied not only by descriptions of the Spirituals as 'pestiferous men', 'disseminators of error', and 'ravening wolves', but also by verbs such as *abolere*, *extirpare* and *exterminare*.[122]

At the point in *Paradiso* 18 where the Church is described as a vineyard laid waste by the depredations of the Papacy ('la vigna che tu guasti'), Dante's language even seems to answer that of John XXII's letter of 6 November 1317, instructing the Inquisitor of Provence (Michel Le Moine) to proceed against twenty-five of the Provençal Spirituals who had appeared before him earlier in the year.[123] Both texts (Dante's canto and John's letter) draw upon the traditional anti-heretical interpretation

120 Ini 1973: 359 (items 45 and 46). Parts of James's letter are also in Finke 1908: 673–4.

121 On the question of Dante's whereabouts during 1318, see Petrocchi 1994: 88–103, especially 101ff.; also BR 3. 279–80 and 289–90 (notes on *Par.* 17. 71 and 76); also Mineo in Mellone 1992: 230–1 and Bemrose 2000: 206.

122 For the last three terms, see *Gloriosam ecclesiam* in *BF* 5. 141a ('pestiferi homines'); 141b ('seminatores errorum'); and 142a ('lupos rapaces'). For the last three terms as part of John's vocabulary and mission statement, see *BF* 5. 133a and 135b.

123 *BF* 5, no. 293, pp. 132–3.

of the Church as the vineyard described in Isaiah (5: 2 and 27: 2) and Jeremiah (2: 21) and particularly the vineyard threatened by the foxes that spoil the vines (Song of Songs 2: 15).[124] John's letter to the Inquisitor expresses the hope that the vineyard of the Franciscan Order will bear 'the fruit of Catholic purity once the little foxes who dare to ravage it with their poisonous gnawing have been exterminated' ('exterminatis vulpeculis quae illum venosis morsibus demoliri praesumunt'). *Paradiso* 18. 132 thus appears to be turning against the pope himself the kind of rhetoric that he was using to denounce the Spirituals.

Later, in *Paradiso* 27, it is the voice of the founder of the Papacy that Dante turns against the pope; and in doing so, he addresses some of the themes and deploys some of the discourse of the dissidents who, at the time of writing, were ranged against John XXII. St Peter's invective in this canto encompasses a series of violent spatial and temporal contrasts: between the founding Apostle and the pope who, in 1300, usurps his place ('il luogo mio') at the head of the Church (ll. 21–2); between Lucifer's states, 'up here' and 'down there' (26–7); between a 'good beginning' and a 'wretched end' (59–60); between the circles of Paradise and the stormy sea of avarice (121–3 and 144–8); and between Dante's present visionary exaltation and his imminent return to earth 'because of the burden of mortality' (64). To 'look downwards' in this canto, then (as Dante is invited to do in ll. 77–8) is, for the pilgrim and the reader, to grasp all at once the scale of the discrepancies with which the *Paradiso* in general and this episode in particular are concerned.

St Peter's denunciation of the current Papacy here has (as noted above) compressed within itself some of the most wide-ranging and violent contrasts: between founding Apostle and corrupt pope; angel and devil; Heaven and Hell:

> 'Quelli ch'usurpa in terra il luogo mio,
>   il luogo mio, il luogo mio che vaca
>   ne la presenza del Figliuol di Dio,
> fatt'ha del cimitero mio cloaca
>   del sangue e de la puzza; onde 'l perverso
>   che cadde di qua sù, là giù si placa.'

[124] As Manselli points out in the *ED* (3. 190a), in commentary from the twelfth century to the fourteenth the 'little foxes' were commonly identified as heretics.

['He who usurps my place upon earth – my place, my place which now in the view of God's Son lies vacant – has turned my burial place into a bloody, stinking sewer; and that delights the renegade who fell from this height, as he lies down there.'] (*Par.* 27. 22–7)

The pattern of descent traced here parallels the repeated papal recession that had previously been imagined in the third *bolgia* of the *Inferno.* There Nicholas III had foretold how he would sink deeper into the rock with the advent of Boniface VIII and Clement V (*Inf.* 19. 73–84). Indeed, soon after St Peter's denunciation in *Paradiso* 27, Beatrice will prophesy how (in that same travesty of apostolic succession) Clement will thrust Boniface 'più giuso' (*Par.* 30. 146–8). But the rapid and vivid sequence of contrasts here in *Paradiso* 27 also generates other, more immediate effects, some of which are potentially (and constructively) confusing. The 'right' identification of 'quelli ch'usurpa' (l. 22) within the fictional time-scheme of the *Commedia* is, of course, as Boniface VIII, the pope at the moment of Dante's imagined journey. But there is also a 'wrong' interpretation which Dante's earliest readers or hearers (at least up until 1334) might initially have entertained: the identification of this usurper not with Boniface, but with their *present* pope, John XXII.[125] Such an extension of the invective to the current 'usurper' of St Peter's 'place' would be a quite understandable consequence of the temporal and spatial leaps that are taking place at this point in *Paradiso*, in St Peter's speech and the pilgrim's mind.

Very shortly after this, the apostolic outburst encompasses events that fall beyond the *Commedia*'s fictional date; and, through explicit allusions to the Gascon Clement V and the Cahorsin John XXII, St Peter now brings papal history down to the moment of the poem's composition:

'Non fu nostra intenzion ch'a destra mano
  d'i nostri successor parte sedesse,
  parte da l'altra del popol cristiano;
né che le chiavi che mi fuor concesse,
  divenisser signaculo in vessillo
  che contra battezzati combattesse;
né ch'io fossi figura di sigillo
  a privilegi venduti e mendaci,

[125] A similar ambiguity is noted in Ferrante 1984: 95.

ond'io sovente arrosso e disfavillo.
In vesta di pastor lupi rapaci
si veggion di qua sù per tutti i paschi:
o difesa di Dio, perché pur giaci?
Del sangue nostro Caorsini e Guaschi
s'apparecchian di bere: o buon principio,
a che vil fine convien che tu caschi!'

['It was not our purpose that one faction of Christendom should be sat at our successors' right hand and another on the left; nor that the keys that were entrusted to me should become a device on the banner borne against those who are baptized; nor that I myself should be made the image on the seals of false privileges dispensed for cash – which makes me redden and flash with fire. From up here we can see across all our pastures ravening wolves in the guise of shepherds; why then has God's justice still not arisen? Those from Cahors and Gascony are now about to drink our blood. Noble foundation, to what sad ruin have you fallen!'] (*Par.* 27. 46–60)

The terms applied to the Papacy in this passage show marked affinities with those used earlier in the poem and with the language of Spiritual dissidents such as Jacopone da Todi and Ubertino da Casale. St Peter's view of contemporary popes fostering division ('parte', 47–8) and waging war against the baptized (49–51) recalls, for instance, the portrayal of John XXII waging war with the pen against part of the Christian community (*Par.* 18. 127–32). His earlier description of the Church as the 'sposa di Cristo', the bride abused by the contemporary Papacy (40–2), recalls the reference to Boniface VIII's treatment of the same 'bella donna' (*Inf.* 19. 55–7), as well as Jacopone's attacks on Boniface and complaints about the state of the Church.[126]

Imagining popes such as Clement V and John XXII preparing to drink 'our blood' – the blood of the apostles – provides the climactic metaphor of St Peter's prophecy – and one that suggests a further convergence between Dante's representation of the current Papacy and the history and rhetoric of the Spiritual Franciscans. This strikingly vivid image combines the canto's previous associations of blood with violence

[126] See, for example, Jacopone in Mancini 1974: nos. 83 ('O Papa Bonifazio') and 35 ('Plange la Eclesia').

and defilement (ll. 25–6) as well as martyrdom and nourishment (40–1 and 45). In lines 58–9 it clearly alludes to the apocalyptic scenario in Revelation 17: 6, where the Whore of Babylon is described as 'the woman drunk with the blood of saints and with the blood of Christ's martyrs' ('mulierem ebriam de sanguine sanctorum, et de sanguine martyrum Iesu').[127] Such a correspondence is consistent with the apocalyptic tone of the whole passage and with its subsequent appeal for Dante to witness and judge in a prophetic role (64–66). It harks back to the more explicit allusion to Revelation 17 (vv. 1–3) in *Inferno* 19. 106–11, where the corrupt leadership of the Church had been envisaged (by the Dante *persona*) as a combination of the Whore of Babylon and the beast upon which she sits:

> 'Di voi pastor s'accorse il Vangelista,
>   quando colei che siede sopra l'acque.
>   puttaneggiar coi regi a lui fu vista . . .
> quella che con le sette teste nacque,
>   e da le diece corna ebbe argomento,
>   fin che virtute al suo marito piacque.'
>
> ['It was you, [false] shepherds, whom the Evangelist beheld when the woman sitting upon the waters and whoring with kings was revealed to him . . . she who was born with seven heads and had the power of ten horns as long as her spouse was devoted to virtue.']

The metaphor also recalls Dante's reinvention of the *meretrix magna* of Revelation 17 as the 'puttana sciolta' on the chariot of the Church, during the final scene of its transformation and degradation, in *Purgatorio* 32.[128] It has long been recognized that, in both *Purgatorio* 32 and *Inferno* 19, Dante's identification of the corrupt Church with the Whore of Babylon bears affinities with the rhetoric of the Spiritual Franciscans, as well as with the language of some thirteenth- and fourteenth-century

[127] The correspondence with Revelation 17: 6 does not appear to be noted by any of the Trecento or modern commentators that I have consulted so far, although a number of them (such as Buti, Casini and Barbi, Porena, Sapegno, Montanari, Giacalone, and Bosco and Reggio) recognize the link between the image here (l. 58) and that of the blood of martyrs (40–5). Davis 1957: 227 and n. 61 compares the imagery of blood, persecution and martyrdom in ll. 25–26 and 40–45 with the linking of 'the sufferings of the past [and] the degradation of the present' in Olivi's Apocalypse commentary.

[128] See Chapter 3 above, pp. 114 and 115–17 with nn. 79–80 and 88–93.

Apocalypse commentary.[129] In particular, as we have seen, Olivi's *Lectura super Apocalypsim* in the 1290s had identified Revelation's *meretrix* as 'the multitude of the reprobate who assault and blaspheme against the pilgrim church through unjust acts'; as a persecutory authority 'striking fear into many and fornicating with this world'; and as a figure 'stained with the blood or the slaughter of souls and the impious persecution of the spirit and spiritual persons'.[130] Shortly after this, in his *Lectura,* Olivi turns to the description of the Whore as *ebriam de sanguine sanctorum*; and he interprets the verse at some length – a full column of text in the Rome (Angelica 382) manuscript – with reference to the apocalyptic persecutions of the dawning sixth period which, in his view, include attacks on Franciscan poverty.[131] Olivi's *meretrix* has already been said to stand 'for the Roman people and Empire, both as it once was in its most pagan state and *as it subsequently was through the Christian faith.*'[132] Here, when explaining how she comes to be 'drunk with the blood of saints', Olivi argues that the persecuting Church of the sixth age inherits and re-enacts the blood guilt of its pagan Roman ancestors, citing in support Christ's prophetic denunciation of the Pharisees in Matthew 23: 35: 'ut veniat super vos omnis sanguis iustus qui effusus est a sanguine abel iusti etc.' ('so you will draw down on yourselves the blood of every upright person that has been shed on earth, from the blood of Abel the just').[133]

Olivi's ideas were highly influential upon the *beguins* of Provence during the first two decades of the fourteenth century. It has been emphasized that 'an Olivi cult was gaining enormous momentum between 1300 and 1318 among the laity in the areas around Narbonne, Béziers and Carcassonne' and that 'the most influential of Olivi's writings by far was

[129] Important earlier accounts are Tocco 1902: 23–5; and Davis 1957: 226–27 and 229. Manselli (1965: 124–5) refers to Olivi and Ubertino in this context, 'non come fonti di Dante, ma come elementi paralleli di confronto' ('not as sources for Dante but as parallel material for comparison').

[130] Olivi, *Lectura* in Rome Bibl. Ang. 3MS 382, f. 103rb. See Chapter 3 above, pp. 116–17 with nn. 90–2.

[131] Olivi, *Lectura*, f. 103vb–104ra. See also the transcript from Florence Laur. conv. soppressi MS 397, f. 193v in Tocco 1903: 42. On Olivi's concept of 'the dawning sixth period' of Church history (which would see persecutions of spiritual men, the destruction of the carnal Church and the advent of the Antichrist), see Burr 1993: 76, chs. 5 and 6, and 166.

[132] See Chapter 3 above, p. 116 with n. 90.

[133] *Lectura super Apocalypsim*, in Rome Bibl. Ang. MS 382, f. 104ra; also in Tocco 1903: 42.

a vernacular version of his Revelation commentary' – a text that is mentioned frequently in the *beguin* trial records.[134] The records themselves provide further significant evidence of convergence between the discourse of Olivi's followers and Dante's representation of John XXII and the Avignon Papacy in *Paradiso.* Many of the *beguins* were tried before Bernard Gui, the Dominican Inquisitor of Toulouse, between 1318 and 1324.[135] A number of them are said to have read or heard read Olivi's Apocalypse commentary 'translated into the vernacular' ('transposit[a] in vulgari'), and to have drawn from it the belief that the 'carnal Church' or (in several cases) the 'Roman Church' was to be identified with the 'Great Whore' (*meretrix magna*) of Revelation 17.[136] Olivi himself in the 1290s (and Ubertino at Avignon in 1311) had sought to avoid identifying the *meretrix magna* too closely with the instititutional Church or the Papacy.[137] His *beguin* followers, according to Gui, appear to have had no such qualms, and a number of them are said to have alluded to the blood of saints and martyrs (Revelation 17: 6) in a way that refers directly to John XXII's persecution of the Spirituals. Thus, for example, at least four of the *beguins* sentenced at Toulouse in the early 1320s are said to have regarded the Spirituals burnt at Marseilles in 1318 as martyrs and to have identified the 'carnal' or Roman Church with the Apocalypse's 'meretrix magna . . . *ebria de sanguine martirum*'.[138]

Further evidence for this dissident reading of Revelation 17:6 – for its attribution to Olivi and its application to the persecution of the Spirituals – can be found in Bernard Gui's general survey *De erroribus seu opinionibus bequinorum moderni temporis* ('Of the errors or opinions of the *beguins* of the present time') in the treatise that he completed about

[134] Lerner in Biller and Hudson 1994: 186–204, especially 196–98. On Olivi's cult and influence, see above, n. 112.

[135] For details of Gui's life and career, see Mollat 1926: vi–vii, and Leff 1966: 196.

[136] For the use of the term *meretrix magna*, see the *Liber sententiarum Inquisitionis Tholosanae* (above n. 25), 301, 304, 306, etc., and for the identification with the 'ecclesia Romana', see 302, 311, 316, etc.

[137] See Chapter 2 above, p. 80 with n. 138, and Chapter 3, pp. 115–16 with n. 89. However, Olivi does appear to have envisaged such an identification at certain points in history; see Burr 1993: 94–5.

[138] The *Liber sententiarum* records both assertions as having been made by Petrus de Maseriis of Beaupuy (p. 302), Guilielmus Ruffi of Cintegabelle (pp. 315–16), Raymundus Stephani de Cruce (pp. 321–2), and Petrus Tort of Montréal (pp. 327 and 330). On the last of these (a Franciscan tertiary whose confession probably dates from May 1322), see Burr 2001: 221–8.

1323–4.[139] In this account of the *beguins*, Olivi figures as a canonical writer for the Spirituals and their supporters and as (literally) a cult-figure in Provence.[140] Gui refers a number of times to the use of Olivi's work 'in vulgari' by the *beguins*, and in particular to their appropriation of his Revelation commentary.[141] At one point in his account of their 'errors', he reports that

> informati seu potius deformati ex doctrina quam auriunt ex postilla prefati Petri Johannis super Apocalipsim, dicunt ecclesiam carnalem, per quam intelligunt Romanam ecclesiam, [. . .] esse illam Babilonem meretricem magnam de qua loquitur Johannes in Apocalipsi; et de ipsa exponunt et intelligunt mala que leguntur ibidem, *videlicet quod ipsa est ebria de sanguine martirum Jhesu Christi* . . .
>
> [informed, or rather *de*formed by the doctrine they draw from the commentary on the Apocalypse by the said Peter of John [Olivi], they claim that the "carnal church", by which they mean the Roman Church [. . .] is that great Whore of Babylon of whom John speaks in Revelation; and it is to her [i.e. the Roman Church] that they relate and attribute the evils that are described there, *namely, that she is drunk with the blood of martyrs for Christ* . . .][142]

Gui then immediately proceeds to explain that the *beguins* were applying Olivi's words to the martyrdom of the four Spiritual Franciscans burnt in May 1318 and to their *beguin* supporters who had subsequently been condemned and executed:

> et exponunt de sanguine illorum quatuor fratrum Minorum qui fuerunt apud Massiliam condempnati ut heretici et combusti et de sanguine Bequinorum de tertio ordine qui fuerunt in istis retro annis tanquam heretici condempnati et combusti in provincia Narbonensi [. . .] quos asserunt esse martires Jhesu Christi.
>
> [and they interpret this as the blood of those four Franciscans who were condemned as heretics and burnt at Marseilles, and as the blood of the

[139] See Mollat 1926: I. 108–54.

[140] Mollat 1926: I. 112, 130 and (on the cult of Olivi and his tomb) 190–3.

[141] Mollat 1926: I. 110, 140, and 142.

[142] Mollat 1926: I. 142. Gui's own language seems to be influenced here by that of the sentence against the Marseilles Spirituals (7 May 1318), which attributes their errors and heresies to Olivi's 'venenato fonte doctrinae immo verius seductrinae' (see n. 114 to this chapter, above).

> *beguins* of the third Order who in recent years have been condemned as heretics and burnt in the province of Narbonne [. . .] whom they claim to be martyrs for Christ.][143]

He also goes on to show how the *beguins* laid the guilt for this persecution directly at John XXII's door, identifying him with (amongst other things) the Antichrist, Caiaphas, Herod and Nero.[144] Here again (although Gui does not say so) the *beguins* show themselves to be assiduous readers of Olivi, who had quite specifically likened the 'mystical Antichrist' to Caiaphas and Herod and the 'great Antichrist' to Nero.[145]

In these ways, therefore, during the early years of John's pontificate (around 1318–20), the Spiritual Franciscans and Dante were invoking similar kinds of apocalyptic imagery in order to characterize the pope's actions. There are, it is true, marked textual and ideological differences between the exegesis of Revelation 17 that Gui attributes to the *beguins* of Provence and the apocalyptic vision with which Dante endows St Peter (and subsequently Beatrice) in *Paradiso* 27. Nevertheless, the degree of convergence here suggests that Dante is appropriating elements of the current dissident Franciscan discourse, in order to convey his own sense of the contrasts between the 'carnal' and the 'spiritual' Churches. Olivi, in his commentary on Revelation 17, had linked the sufferings of the past with the degradation of the present through the image of martyrs' blood and the blood of guilt; and he had linked the *meretrix magna* at least with the 'ecclesia[m] a christo meretricat[a]'.[146] But it was both Dante, the vernacular poet, and the readers of Olivi's commentary *in vulgari* who were to claim that the Papacy of their time was drinking the blood of the Apostles.

It does not, of course, follow that we can therefore conscript Dante as a crypto-*beguin* or pseudo-*fraticello*. Such parallels, however, strengthen the case that he knew or knew of the Spirituals' apocalyptic ideas (and quite possibly those of Olivi and Ubertino) in some detail; and, more importantly, that the *Paradiso* assimilates such discourse when portraying the power of the Avignon Papacy under John XXII, and placing it within an apocalyptic vision of the Church's history.

143 Mollat 1926: I. 142. 144 Mollat 1926: I. 148, 152, and 172.

145 On Olivi's view of the relationship between Caiaphas, Nero and the two Antichrists, see Burr 1993: 149 (with n. 56), and Chapter 3 above, p. 116 with n. 91.

146 See Davis 1957: 227 and n. 61, and Tocco 1902: 39–53, especially 40–3 and 51.

POVERTY, AUTHORITY AND THE POET: CANTOS 24–32

How, finally, does this view of John XXII and the Avignon Papacy in *Paradiso* 27 relate to the representation of apostolic ideals in the later cantos of the *Paradiso* and to the imagined role of the *cantica*'s poet? By this stage *Paradiso* has at several points shown cupidity diverting the Papacy from the *buon principio* of its founding apostolic ideals.[147] It has also on a number of occasions represented those primitive apostolic ideals in terms of the Franciscan ones. Thus, for example, the Apostles Peter and Paul have appeared in *Paradiso* 21 as 'impoverished, barefoot' mendicants (ll. 127–9); and St Peter's own evangelical poverty ('sanz' oro e sanz' argento', 'povero e digiuno') as founder of the Church has been emphasized in two further cantos.[148] In *Paradiso* 24 also the *Commedia*'s final use of the word *frate* has characterized these two early Apostles.[149]

At the very end of the Dante persona's encounter with St Peter, the Apostle signifies his approval of what the pilgrim-poet has said on the subject of faith:

> così, benedicendomi cantando,
>   tre volte cinse me, sì com' io tacqui,
>   l'appostolico lume al cui comando
> io avea detto: sì nel dir li piacqui!
>
> [thus, blessing me and singing, the apostolic light at whose behest I had been speaking circled me three times as I fell silent, so greatly did my speech please him!] (*Par.* 24. 151–4)

The ritual here in some ways recalls that which Virgil performed on Cato's instructions at the entrance to Purgatory: the girding with the reed at the end of *Purgatorio* 1.[150] Yet St Peter's threefold encircling of the pilgrim is, like the acceptance of Dante as *frate* by souls in *Purgatorio* and *Paradiso* – a rather more inclusive gesture.[151] The verb that expresses this inclusion (*cignere*) has been used in the *Inferno* to describe the

147 For example, in *Par.* 9. 127–42 and 21. 127–42; for discussion, see this chapter above, p. 126 with n. 4, and p. 139 with n. 38.
148 *Par.* 22. 88 and 24. 109–11.
149 For the mendicant and Franciscan resonances of the term (*frate*) in the *Commedia* (and for reference to discussion in earlier chapters), see nn. 10–12 to this chapter above.
150 For discussion of this episode, see Chapter 3 above, p. 93 with n. 20.
151 See nn. 10–12 to this chapter above.

adoption of the insignia of Franciscanism, the cord; and on several other occasions it carries Franciscan or apostolic connotations.[152] Guido da Montefeltro had meant, as he neared the end of his journey, to make amends by becoming girded 'with that cord which used to make those who wore it grow more lean' ('quel capestro / che solea fare i suoi cinti più macri').[153] Unlike Guido, Dante – as narrator and poet nearing the end of his journey and his vision – is authoritatively 'girded' (*cinto*) at the close of *Paradiso* 24; and he has indeed become, as the opening of the next canto will claim, ascetically 'lean' (*macro*).[154] By the start of *Paradiso* 25, therefore, the pilgrim of *Paradiso* has taken on yet more qualities of the 'persona umile e peregrina' that had earlier been attributed to Romieu (*Par.* 6. 135) – and is adopting again the role that the exile had envisaged for himself at the beginning of the *Convivio* (1.3.4), as 'peregrino . . . mendicando'.

Soon after this, during his encounter with St Peter in *Paradiso* 27, Dante's prophetic and poetic voice receives its last explicit authorization.[155] St Peter, having condemned the present leadership of the Church and looked to some future providential revival, ends his speech by addressing Dante as the 'son' who will pass on this prophecy in its entirety:

> 'e tu, figliuol, che per lo mortal pondo
> ancor giù tornerai, apri la bocca,
> e non asconder quel ch'io non ascondo.'
>
> ['and you, my son, who because of the burden of mortality must return to earth, raise your voice; do not hide the things I have not hidden.'] (*Par.* 27. 64–6)

In such ways the authorizing of the impoverished exile's voice towards the end of the *Commedia* converges with the poem's ultimate vision of evangelical poverty and its implications for the Church.

A further *implicit* authorization for the pilgrim-poet's vision accompanies the portrayal of Apostles, at the end of the poem's penultimate canto. Here, in St Bernard's description of the Celestial Rose, Dante's

152 The verb conveys such significance in *Inf.* 27. 68 as well as 93 and again in *Purg.* 1. 133.

153 *Inf.* 27. 92–3; see Chapter 2 above, pp. 65–6 and nn. 79–82.

154 *Par.* 25. 3.

155 CL 3. 751 (note on *Par.* 27.64–6) compares the language of similar adjurations by Beatrice (*Purg.* 32. 103–5 and 33. 52–4) and by Cacciaguida (*Par.* 17. 124–5).

St Francis makes his final appearance, alongside John the Baptist, as prophet of the desert, and Benedict and Augustine as fathers of the Church and sources of rules for the religious. Here also, St Peter appears for the last time, alongside St John the Evangelist, as the founder of the Church:

> 'dal destro vedi quel padre vetusto
> di Santa Chiesa a cui Cristo le chiavi
> raccomandò di questo fior venusto.
> E quei che vide tutti i tempi gravi,
> pria che morisse, de la bella sposa
> che s'acquistò con la lancia e coi clavi,
> siede lungh'esso . . .'
>
> ['on her [the Virgin's] right you see that ancient father of Holy Church, to whom Christ entrusted the keys to this lovely flower. And seated beside him is he who saw, before he died, all the afflictions of that fair bride who was won with the lance and the nails'] (*Par.* 32. 124–30)

Once again, as in *Paradiso* 27, the vision concisely surveys a vast range of historical contrasts. St Bernard's words here require the reader to look both up, to the centre of 'questo fior venusto', and (as so often in the *Paradiso*) down, to the ongoing earthly tribulations of 'la bella sposa'. Describing the ideal Church as *bella sposa* here also invites retrospection along paths that the *Commedia* has traced: from the *bella donna* abused by Boniface VIII to the ideal *sposa* wooed by St Francis; and from the betrayed *sposa di Cristo* of St Peter's diatribe to the souls who are exalted in the Rose as 'la milizia santa / che nel suo sangue Cristo fece *sposa*' ('those holy forces / which Christ through his blood made his bride').[156] As in the invective of *Paradiso* 27 – but in a more quietly articulated form – there is a contrast here once again between the beginning instituted by St Peter and the end foreseen (according to Dante) by St John in Revelation. The authority of St John's apocalyptic prophecy has been invoked on several crucial occasions in the *Commedia*: in the pilgrim's denunciation of corrupt popes in *Inferno* 19; in his vision of the Church in *Purgatorio* 32; and in the revelation that he has been urged to pass on in *Paradiso* 27.[157] There is thus, in this final appearance of these

[156] See *Inf.* 19. 57; *Par.* 11. 58–62 and 84; *Par.* 27. 40; and *Par.* 31. 2–3.
[157] On Dante, St John and authority, see Hawkins 1999: esp. 66–71.

apostolic figures (John the Baptist, Peter, John the Evangelist, Francis), an alignment of their vision with that of Dante's pilgrim and a further conjunction between the authority of poverty and that of the prophetic poem.[158]

In the *Paradiso*, therefore, the figure of Francis, the traditions of early Franciscanism and the idea of evangelical poverty form an integral part of the poem's impetus towards papal and apostolic renewal. As in the *Purgatorio*, they also help to shape the identity of the pilgrim-poet and to convey the gathering significance of his ascent and vision. Throughout these two *cantiche* the imagining of 'poverty in spirit' and brotherhood has been set against the recognition of avarice and the abuses of power. Such developments had been foreshadowed in the *Inferno* through that *cantica*'s recurrent concern with clerical avarice (including the 'avarice of high position') and through its dramatization of encounters between Franciscan ideals and papal power which is implicit in the representation of the simonist Nicholas III (*Inf.* 19) and fully explicit in the later scene which pits a Franciscan and St Francis against a pope and a devil (*Inf.* 27).

Various popes have been identified and mentioned thoughout the *Commedia*; but there are only three with whom the pilgrim comes into contact and actually exchanges words. These are Nicholas III (*Inf.* 19), Hadrian V (*Purg.* 19) and St Peter in the later cantos of the *Paradiso.* It is not only the words of such popes that have a bearing upon the Dante persona and through him on the relationshp between poverty and the papacy in the poem; it is also their gestures. In response to the gestures of the three popes, the body of 'Dante' can be seen to undergo three significant changes of posture which are all consistent with his role as a kind of new 'mendicant wayfarer', addressing and assessing the state of the Papacy. In *Inferno* 19 he had been the tentatively prophetic satririst of avarice who stands 'like a friar' over the flailing feet of Nicholas III. The corresponding scene in *Purgatorio* 19 showed the visionary 'brother'

[158] In the context of *Par.* 32 it is also worth noting that several contemporary mosaics which could have been seen by Dante also show St Francis among the *milizia santa.* At Rome, Jacopo Torriti's 'Coronation of the Virgin' in the apse of S. Maria Maggiore (dated 1291–5) places Francis in the company of four apostles: John the Baptist, Peter, Paul and John the Evangelist (see Cook 1999: cat. no. 156, pp. 186–7); and the Last Judgement in the dome of the Baptistery in Florence (a section dated c. 1250 and possibly by the painter of the Bardi Dossal) portrays him as one of a group of saints in between Christ and the gate of Heaven (Cook 1999: cat. no. 72, p. 104).

being urged to go higher by a pope who is still prostrated on the floor of the fifth terrace. Finally, as we have seen, the 'son' of the original barefoot mendicant and first pope is, at the end of his encounter with St Peter (*Par.* 24), received into the paradisal community by being girdled with 'apostolic light'.

The authorizing of the Dante persona as poet and prophet has thus taken 'almost the entire length' of the *Commedia* to complete.[159] The authorizing of poverty has continued through all three *cantiche* to contribute to that process; and the voice that addresses the Papacy in *Paradiso* still has recognizable affinities with the one that was raised against the Avignon cardinals in the letter of 1314 or against the *avari* of 'Doglia mi reca' during the earlier years of Dante's exile. To the end, the *Commedia* continues to draw upon the discourses of Franciscanism as a means of making its vision of the Church's history manifest and of constructing the pilgrim-poet's identity as prophetic wayfarer. This identity is partly that of the 'lowly wandering mendicant' (*Conv.* 1.3.4 and *Par.* 6. 135 and 141), but the voice is also one which, when raised, will 'strike hardest at the highest peaks' (*Par.* 17. 134). Dante's own authorization of poverty will thus enable him, as he nears the end of the whole poem (*Par.* 25.1–9), to express hope of reward from a work which has made him 'per molti anni macro', 'over long years lean'.

[159] On this process of 'authorization' see Hawkins 1999: 31.

Epilogue

The dispute about Franciscan poverty and the influence of the Spirituals' polemic were to last well beyond the end of *Paradiso* and its poet's death in 1321. Soon afterwards the Franciscans found the decisive weight of papal authority brought down on them by John XXII's two bulls *Ad conditorem* (1322) and *Cum inter nonnullos* (1323). In these the pope not only disposed of the Spirituals' case but in doing so also dismissed the distinction between ownership and use (as enshrined in Nicholas III's *Exiit qui seminat* of 1279), and thus challenged the basis of even the Conventuals' doctrine of poverty.[1] Protests were quickly voiced by various elements in the Order; and its more radical members and associates in the 1330s went so far as to describe John as a heretic, a 'pseudo-pope' or not a pope at all.[2] For the Spirituals, John XXII continued after his death to be the apocalyptic persecutory figure that the Provençal *beguins* (according to Bernard Gui) had compared to Antichrist, Caiaphas, Herod and Nero.[3] In the second set of *Vaticinia de summis pontificibus* (produced by Florentine *fraticelli* shortly before

[1] On the motives and context for John's re-examination of Franciscan poverty (leading up to *Cum inter nonnullos*), see Chapter 4 above, pp. 160–1 with nn. 96–9.

[2] For the Franciscan 'Michaelist' view of John XXII as heretic and pseudo-pope because of his declarations on poverty, see William of Ockham's *Letter to the Friars Minor* (Pentecost 1334) ed. McGrade and Kilcullen 1995: esp. 8–9 and 12–15; and the anonymous public letter from the Italian 'poveri servi di Yhesu Christo' later in the 1330s, in Zambrini 1865: esp. 8–9. Also relevant are the repeated assertions of the *fraticello* Francesco di Vanne of Assisi (at his trial before the Inquisition in Rieti in February/March 1334) that he had heard the *fraticelli* affirm that 'dom. papa Johannes non est papa'; see *ALKG* 2. 9 (lines 3–4), 10 (line 33), 12 (lines 10–11), and 13 (line 25). Around 1340–2 an Italian *fraticello* writing a treatise on evangelical poverty attacked John XXII as the 'regem locustarum qui Christi vitam exterminavit'; see Bihl 1939: 411, also 279 and 292.

[3] See Chapter 4 above, p. 175 with n. 144.

1356) John is represented as a bloodstained beast devouring the apostolic dove.[4]

During the fourteenth century the *Commedia* itself came to be appropriated for this purpose. In 1361 an apocalyptic poem by Fra' Giovanni of Florence (possibly a *fraticello*) alludes to Dante and describes 'new Pharisees' drinking the *sangue povero*, the blood of the Church. The same friar may have been the author of another apocalyptic poem which describes *pellegrina Italia* by echoing Beatrice's words about humanity as starving child (*Par.* 30. 141); which foresees shipwreck in the sea of *cupidigia*; and which ends with an exact quotation of the apocalyptic last line from *Paradiso* 27.[5] The convergence of discourses between Dante and the Spiritual Franciscans thus continues some way beyond the poet's lifetime.

The Italian *fraticelli*, vocal as they were, became increasingly marginalized during the fourteenth century, and their role as rigorists within the Order was eventually taken over by the Observants, who gradually gained official recognition.[6] But the Franciscan doctrine of poverty developed by other means into a powerful ideological weapon for those who were challenging various forms of clerical dominion.[7] This development is reflected in the work of some of the century's most influential thinkers. In part 2 of the *Defensor pacis* (completed 1324) Marsilius of Padua, who may have known Dante, presses yet further the *Monarchia*'s argument against the temporal wealth and power of the Papacy. Marsilius thus moves from the assertion that 'the preacher's office does not befit the ruler' into an extended defence and eventually a celebration of voluntary or 'meritorious' poverty as the true path of

[4] On the second series of *Vaticinia* and the argument for a date shortly before 1356, see Reeves 1969: 214–15 and 412–14.

[5] The poems are quoted and described in Reeves 1969: 216–17. The 'frottola' *O pellegrina Italia* is printed in Renier (ed.) 1883: 191–210. According to Renier (p. ccclvii), it is attributed to Fra' Giovanni in two of the later manuscripts: Magliabechiano cl. VII.1081, f. 7r, and cl. XXV.344, f. 17v. The lines cited here are ll. 3 (p. 191), 14–27 (p. 192) and 390 (the final line of the poem on p. 210). Other possible allusions to Dante are in ll. 63–5 (p. 194), 95–6 (p. 196), and 235–6 (p. 202).

[6] On the fortunes of the *fraticelli* and other Spirituals in Italy during the course of the fourteenth century, see Douie 1932: 210–13 and Reeves 1969: 210–25. For an account of the *fraticelli* in Florence in the fourteenth century and their survival into the fifteenth, see Stephens 1972: 33–41 and 42–53. On the growth of the Observant movement, see Moorman 1968: 369–73.

[7] On the significance for lay culture of this development, see Vallone 1988: 47–8.

perfection for the apostolic 'wayfarer'.[8] In the middle of the century, the Franciscan apocalyptic visionary John de Rupescissa (Roquetaillade) prophesied the regeneration of the world through those who observed strict Franciscan poverty: the 'little cords' who would 'expel all corrupt, lustful, and avaricious priests from the temple'.[9] From a very different standpoint in the 1350s, Richard Fitzralph (championing the secular clergy) was to turn the Franciscan doctrine against the friars in general by developing an 'antifraternal account of evangelical poverty, which endorsed renunciation of civil dominion but rejected voluntary mendicancy'.[10] Later in the century, Wyclif's views were to converge at some points with those of the Franciscan Spirituals, for example when he denounced clerical avarice as 'the most dangerous of all heresies' and looked back to the early Apostles' total commitment to humility and poverty.[11] In view of such developments and convergences, and their consequences for the Church and for lay culture, it is not surprising that sixteenth-century Reformation polemicists (from Flacius and Foxe onwards) were so ready to enlist Dante along with Marsilius, John de Rupescissa, FitzRalph, Wyclif and others as prophets of Protestantism.[12]

[8] See *Defensor pacis* 2. 11–14, and esp. 13, paras. 14, 22–3, 25, 33 and 37–9. For a suggestion that Dante and Marsilius 'knew of each other and of each other's ideas', see Ferrante 1984: 37 and n. 67.

[9] The standard study of John de Rupescissa (of Roquetaillade) is Bignami-Odier 1952. For outlines of his ideas in English, see Reeves 1969: 225–8 and Kerby-Fulton 1990: 188–91. For the quotation here (from the 'Twelfth Instruction' of his *Vade mecum in tribulatione*), see McGinn 1998: 232.

[10] Scase 1989: 56. On Fitzralph's 'refashioning' of the Franciscan theory of poverty, see also Scase's discussion in 49–56, and Dawson 1983.

[11] Wyclif, *De civili dominio* 1. 59 and *De veritate sacre scripture* 1. 70, quoted in Leff 1967: 527–8. Leff also argues that while Wyclif shared the Spirituals' 'conception of the apostolic tradition' and his doctrine of poverty in *De civili dominio* 'closely followed' that sustained by Michael of Cesena and his colleagues against John XXII, he did not formulate a notion of *usus pauper* and tended to rate 'spiritual poverty' (humility) higher than material poverty (Leff 1967:, 527, 529 and 530 (and n. 8)).

[12] See Flacius 1556: 815 (Marsilius, Ockham, Dante and others); 846–9 (Wyclif); 868 (Dante); 897 (John de Rupescissa). In Foxe 1570, see 485–6 (Marsilius, Ockham, Dante) 486 (John de Rupescissa and Wyclif); 523–52 (Wyclif). For further Protestant references to John of Rupescissa alongside Dante, see Boswell 1999: 182, 199, and 209. The Protestant polemicists (and sometimes their Catholic opponents) also frequently link Dante with Marsilius (see Boswell 1999: e.g. 27, 29–30, 40–1, 72, 123–4, 133, 139); unfortunately these references do not appear in Boswell's index. On reception of Marsilius in the Reformation period, see Piaia 1977.

It has not been the purpose of this study to bind the *Commedia* with the Franciscan cord, still less to conscript Dante as a proto-Protestant. The exact location of his anti-papal stance, however, remains problematic, as does the precise genesis of the *Commedia*'s radical vision of Church history.[13] It is resoundingly obvious that (as several Counter-Reformation defenders of the poem's orthodoxy were already asserting) attacking the vices of individual popes does not necessarily constitute a challenge to the institutional authority of the Papacy; and the *Commedia* itself acknowledges that distinction on several occasions.[14] Yet even in Dante's time new political theories – as well as concern about the claims and practices of a pope such as Boniface VIII – were beginning to erode the ancient distinction between the papal office and the person of the pope, and thus to raise questions about the basis of the institution's authority.[15] And, as we have seen, with the *Commedia*'s reinvention of the *meretrix magna* (Revelation 17), shows Dante, like Olivi before him, venturing into dangerous ideological border-country. Denouncing popes as a group (as Dante clearly does in *Inferno* 19 and *Paradiso* 27) still does not negate the authority of the institution, but it can be and was seen as a serious challenge to that institution.

What, then, was the actual nature of that challenge? Dante's way of speaking to popes (as characterized in the previous chapters) can, I suggest, be seen as contributing not to the sixteenth-century Reformation but rather to the fourteenth-century tradition of 'reformist apocalypticism'.[16] Among the concerns that were shared by late medieval writers in this tradition were those relating especially to the role of religious orders (especially the Franciscans), the leadership of the Church, and 'a desire to return the clergy to the rigorous discipline of early monastic

[13] On the development of 'apocalyptic religious radicalism' in Dante's later life as 'perhaps the most mysterious part of his spiritual biography', see Holmes 1980: 37.

[14] See, for example, 'John Clare' (1630) in Boswell 1999: 191. See also Holmes 1997: 53–5, arguing that there is 'no evidence that Dante ever questioned the spiritual authority of the papacy' and that 'criticism of papal conduct does not imply any disbelief in the spiritual power of the papacy'.

[15] Ullmann 1974: 270 argues that at the turn of the thirteenth and fourteenth centuries 'this crucial papal distinction between office and person . . . was beginning to be reversed'. See also pp. 268, 277, 284.

[16] 'Reformist apocalypticism' is the term proposed by Kerby-Fulton (1990: 3) 'to denote the medieval "school" of alternative apocalypticism which is concerned primarily with clerical reform'.

founders or of the early apostolic Church itself, with particular emphasis on poverty and simplicity of life'.[17] The idea of 'repristination' of the Church was not itself new, but the call for the clergy to revert *ad pristinum statum* was renewed with particular intensity by apocalyptic writers of the thirteenth and fourteenth centuries. In the Joachimist texts of the earlier thirteenth century the proposed renewal of the Church involved radical measures on the part of the Papacy: as Marjorie Reeves summarizes it, 'a violent gesture, either by the papacy itself or by others towards it, begins to appear in the expected programme. Peter must cast off his coat and plunge naked into the waves.'[18] Dante's idea of a new order in the Church and world differs in form and means (as has been recently noted) from the monastic utopia of Joachimism.[19] Nonetheless, renunciation of temporal power and property and return to apostolic founding principles is envisaged for the Papacy in Book 3 of the *Monarchia* and increasingly in the *Commedia.* In the *Paradiso,* as we have seen, the Franciscan pursuit of poverty provides the model for the repristination that is, later in the *cantica*, called for by Peter Damian, St Benedict and St Peter himself – the 'lean and barefoot' apostle who, it has been noted, is the only exemplary pope to be given prominence in the *Paradiso.*[20] The call for the Church and Papacy to return *ad pristinum statum* intensifies among apocalyptic writers during the middle and later fourteenth century. Bridget of Sweden and John de Rupescissa have been mentioned as examples; and a 'Franciscan impetus', including the continuing influence of Olivi, is discernible behind it.[21]

Both Dante and Olivi were subject to official condemnation in the late 1320s. In 1328 or 1329 Cardinal Pouget, John XXII's legate in Emilia

[17] Kerby-Fulton 1990: 9. On earlier (twelfth-century) ideas about the *ecclesia primitiva*, see Olsen 1969.

[18] Reeves 1969: 397.

[19] See Mineo 1998: 29–30, where the similarity between Dante and the Spirituals in their diagnoses of corruption and cupidity is recognized, along with the differences in their concepts of the means that would be required. Once again, Dante's commitment to some kind of imperial ideal distances him from the Spirituals.

[20] Agapetus (pope from 535–6) is said to have led Justinian back to orthodoxy (*Par.* 6. 16–18); and John XXI (1276–7) is referred to in his previous role as a scholar (as *Pietro Spano* in *Par.* 12. 134–5); but, as Ferrante (1984: 256) points out, 'The absence of popes as popes is one of the most striking features of Dante's Paradise.'

[21] Kerby-Fulton 1990: 187 and (for reference to Olivi's influence) 189.

Romagna, condemned both the *Monarchia* and its author's body to be burnt; and some time between 1327 and 1334 (and perhaps as a justification) the Dominican Guido Vernani of Rimini delivered his *De reprobatione 'Monarchiae'*.[22] Those in the Church hierarchy who condemned this text may not only have been responding to its obvious political use, as a weapon in the dispute between John XXII and Ludwig of Bavaria. They may also have been aware of the more insidious vernacular voice raised against papal 'pastors' in certain passages from the *Commedia* that would later be officially expurgated.[23] Certainly Vernani, if not Pouget, recognizes the dangerous power of Dante's poetic *volgare* when, at the opening of his attack, he characterizes the writer of the *Commedia* as a deceptively poisonous vessel whose attractive and eloquent appearance, poetic illusions and fictions, and 'sweet siren songs' were likely to lead souls astray.[24]

The *Commedia*'s use of the *volgare* has been compared in its strategy and goals with the vernacular texts disseminated by the Spirituals in Dante's own time.[25] Recent work has also emphasized the poet's wider indebtedness to the educative and popularizing work of both of the major mendicant Orders, the Dominicans as well as the Franciscans; and the parallels between Dante's project and the mission of the mendicants have been emphasized.[26] The mendicant orders continued to respond to one of the chief impulses of religious culture in the fourteenth century:

[22] On the process of condemnation, see Ferrante 1984: 127–30, and Comollo 1990: 41–54. For the text of *De reprobatione*, see Matteini 1958: 93–118; and for translation of part of Vernani's argument about the 'true' (papal) monarch, see Caesar 1989: 112–13.

[23] Certain passages from the *Commedia* (including the address to the popes in *Inf.* 19. 48–117 and the attack on the papal 'wolf' in *Par.* 9. 136–42) were placed on the *Index expurgatorius* in the seventeenth century (see Toynbee 1921: 111–12; Martinelli 1966: 75; and Caesar 1989: 31). There is, however, also evidence of an official attempt at censorship very soon after the condemnation of the *Monarchia* (by the Florentine Dominicans in 1335; see Matteini 1958: 36 and n. 13).

[24] Matteini 1958: 93 (ll. 7–23). Vernani also mentions (l. 24) 'other works of his [Dante's]' only to dismiss them 'with contempt'. His addressee, Graziolo de' Bambaglioli, chancellor of the Commune of Bologna, had himself written a commentary on the *Inferno* (1324) in which he defended the poet's orthodoxy, so he would have known what Vernani was referring to.

[25] For comparison between the Spirituals' project and Dante's, see Manselli 1982: 59–60. On the vernacular texts of Olivi's followers, see Lerner 1994.

[26] On Dante's broader indebtedness to the mendicant orders, see Davis 1984: 154–65 and Botterill's article in *DE* 606–8. For the comparison of his 'project' with theirs (and some subsequent distinctions), see Hawkins 1999: 28–30.

the laity's demand for involvement in the Church, a demand that was reflected in the growth of lay orders and the audience for preaching and devotional texts.[27] But the laity's own new authors had their agenda too, one which Dante helped to set. Beatrice's satirical attack on vain preachers towards the end of the *Paradiso* can be seen as reflecting the *Commedia*'s successful bid to rival the mendicants for the ear (and the eye) of the educated and literate laity.[28] This rivalry was also to be reflected in different ways by later lay writers of the fourteenth century, such as Boccaccio and Chaucer, both of whom looked back to Dante as the new vernacular author.[29]

[27] On the laity and the Church in Trecento Italy, see Pullan 1973: 62. More generally on the clergy and laity, see Swanson 1995: 62–91, 102–16 and (on 'lay aspirations') 221–4.

[28] On Dante's role in the 'laicization of culture', see Paparelli 1975: 25.

[29] On Chaucer, Boccaccio and the mendicant orders see Havely 1983, and more recently Georgianna 2000.

Appendix 1: The *Sacrum commercium*: manuscripts and date of composition

When considering the parallels between the *Purgatorio* and the *Sacrum commercium sancti Francisci cum domina Paupertate*, we must take into account the problematic and controversial aspects of the Franciscan text. Of these the questions of dating and authorship are particularly important, since they affect the position of the *Sacrum commercium* as part of the Franciscan context for Dante's *Commedia*.

There are fifteen extant manuscripts of the *Sacrum commercium*, and a further two are known to have been in the convent library at Assisi, according to a catalogue of 1381.[1] Of the extant witnesses, two are assigned by the most recent editor (Stefano Brufani) to the thirteenth or fourteenth century, two to the fourteenth, two to the fourteenth or fifteenth, and the rest to the fifteenth century or later.[2] Six of the manuscripts give the year of composition as 1227 (the year after the death of St Francis). This date was accepted by the Quaracchi editors and by a number of other scholars, although it does not appear in the two earliest manuscripts, and modern opinion has placed the composition of the work anywhere between 1227 and 1270.[3] There is no certainty, either, about the text's authorship. The late fourteenth-century *Chronicle of the Twenty-Four Generals* and two of the fifteenth-century manuscripts attribute it to

[1] For descriptions of all the known manuscripts and a full account of the relationships between them see Brufani's edition (1990), pp. 59–125. This largely supersedes the survey on pp. 16–19 of the 1929 Quaracchi edition, but on the two lost Assisi mss, see ibid., p. 20 and nn. 1–3.

[2] See Brufani 1990: 59–62. One of the manuscripts assigned by him to the 'sec. xv' (Oxford, Bodley, Canon. misc. 263) appears, on closer examination, to be of an even later date: its script is of the fifteenth-century or later, but the watermark design (visible on ff. 7, 8, 16, 17 and 18) indicates that the paper cannot be earlier than c. 1500 and could well date from around 1520–30 (for evidence see Piccard 1978: 219–34 and figs. v. 222–347).

[3] On the dating of the *Sacrum commercium*, see especially Brufani (ed.) 1990: 36–42 (relating it to the first phase of the conflict between mendicants and seculars at Paris, 1250–68). See also (arguing for a much earlier date) Esser 1964: 3–7. For a general review of the question, see Mellone 1987: 71 and nn. 364–6; and for a recent argument for a very early date, see below, n. 9.

John of Parma, though this would make a date of 1227 somewhat too early, since John was born in 1208 and did not even enter the Order till around 1232–3.[4] Two of the manuscripts (one of the late fourteenth, the other of the early sixteenth century) name St Anthony of Padua as the author, but this ascription seems unlikely on stylistic and thematic grounds.[5] Two early Ministers General of the Order, John Parenti (1227–32) and Crescentius of Iesi (1244–7), have also at various times been proposed as authors.[6] One of the recent translators of the text has emphasized the verbal similarities between it and Thomas of Celano's *Vita prima* of 1228–9 and the *Vita secunda* of 1246–7, and suggested common authorship.[7] The *Vita secunda* also speaks at length of Francis' pursuit of Poverty in terms of love and marriage (55), but, as Kajetan Esser has pointed out, such resemblances could indicate influence either way.[8] The most recent candidate for authorship (proposed by M. Cusato) is Caesar of Speyer, the first Franciscan Provincial in Germany, who had assisted Francis in the preparation of the 1221 Rule and who was in Italy from 1223.[9]

There is no decisive evidence to align the text's representation of poverty or avarice with Spiritual Franciscan polemic; indeed, it has been argued that Lady Poverty's denunciation of her rival (Avarice) in paragraphs 38–52 (Brufani [ed.]: 154–66) is attacking 'not lax friars, but the old monastic orders'.[10] Yet some features of the polemic here could clearly have been read in relation to the developing debate about evangelical poverty and the *usus pauper*.[11]

[4] The two manuscripts that ascribe authorship to John of Parma are Barcelona, Biblioteca Central de la Diputació de Catalunya, 665, and Ravenna, Biblioteca Comunale Classense, 25. See Brufani 1990: 10 with n. 22, and 50–1 with nn. 129–34; and Esser 1964: 4–5.

[5] The two manuscripts that ascribe authorship to Anthony of Padua are Oxford, Bodley, Canon. misc. 525, and Dorsten, Franziskanerkloster (unnumbered). See Brufani 1990: 10 (n. 22) and 50 (with n. 130) and Esser 1964: 5.

[6] Brufani 1990:, 4–5, the Quaracchi edn, 30 and 32, and Brufani 1990: 10, n. 22.

[7] See Habig 1535–9.

[8] Esser 1964: 9.

[9] The date of composition thus proposed is very early: the mid-1230s. For supporting arguments, see the discussion of *SC* in the new collection of early Franciscan documents: Armstrong, Hellmann and Short 1999–2002: I. 525–7.

[10] See Brooke 1959: 9, n. 2.

[11] For further discussion, see Havely 1996: 231 with nn. 13–18. It has also been argued that, while the writer of *SC* may have had monastic corruption in mind, he could also have 'intended to use this generic image of corruption [the portrayal of Lady Avarice] to draw attention to the specific problems that faced the Franciscan order in the wake of its founder's death' (Wolf 2003: 34).

Appendix II: The Bardi Dossal: landscape and ideology

Amongst contemporary Franciscan paintingst the Bardi Dossal at Santa Croce in Florence is the Franciscan image that can be located closest to Dante, at least before his exile, and the background to several of the episodes is rugged or mountainous. Its version of the Stigmatization, for instance, makes the saint's cell, in terms of structure and coloration, little more than a cleft in the hillside, a feature comparable to the narrow entrance of the cave-hermitage in Giotto's later fresco, also in the Bardi Chapel.[1] Mountains or rocky outcrops also appear in three of the Dossal's other scenes from St Francis' life: his rescue of a sheep from the goats; his sacrifice of a cloak to redeem two lambs; and his staging of the Nativity at Greccio.[2]

A number of critics have argued that the Dossal may reflect the thinking of the Franciscan rigorists; and its wilderness settings could thus perhaps be read as ways of harking back to the initial landscapes inhabited by the Order and its early *zelanti.*[3] Such a view may, however, overstress the dependence of the iconography upon the Celano *Vitae.* In a recent account of the Dossal's programme Eamon Duffy argues that it represents, rather, 'a rich and eclectic reading of Francis and his legend, drawing on the writings of Celano, Bonaventure and perhaps others' and the tradition of Franciscan panel-painting up to the 1260s.[4] Duffy's interpretation would of course require a dating for the Dossal of later than 1263 (when Bonaventura's *Legenda* was published); hence he suggests that it could have been painted in the early 1270s or later.[5] Other recent critics – such as Stein, Goffen, Frugoni and Cook – assign a much

[1] See Frugoni 1988: 26–8 and pl. 12. On Giotto's version, see Goffen 1988: 60–3 and pl. 2; also Stubblebine 1985: 31–3 and pl. 39.

[2] See Frugoni 1988: pls. 6, 9 and 10.

[3] On the Bardi Dossal and the Franciscan Spirituals, see Stein 1976: 294–5; Goffen 1988: 29–30, 47–8 and 59; and Frugoni 1993: 357–98.

[4] See Duffy 1997: 231. [5] Ibid., 232.

earlier date: the 1250s or even the 1240s.[6] Even if it were to be accepted, Duffy's argument would not, however, exclude from the work the kind of rigorist concerns that made Santa Croce in the 1280s a suitable platform for the likes of Ubertino and Olivi; indeed it would bring the painting closer to the milieu of the Spirituals and to Dante's early years.

[6] Cook 1999: 101 rejects Duffy's argument, asserting that 'there is in fact no narrative material in the dossal from any written source other than 1 *Celano*'. See Chapter 4 above, p. 135 with n. 30.

Bibliography

Accame Bobbio, A. (1971), 'Canto XVIII', in *Lectura Dantis Scaligera: Paradiso*, ed. S. Pasquazi (Florence: Le Monnier), pp. 627–62.

Adamo, Salimbene de: *see* Holder-Egger.

Ageno, F. (ed.) (1953): *see* Iacopone da Todi.

Alighieri, Dante: *see* Dante Alighieri.

Alighieri, Pietro (ed. V. Nannucci) (1845 and 1846), *Petri Allegherii super Dantis ipsius genitoris Comoediam commentarium* (Florence: Piatti).

Angiolieri, Cecco: *see* Cavalli, G.; Lanza, A.

Armour, P. (1983), *The Door of Purgatory: A Study of Multiple Symbolism in Dante's 'Purgatorio'* (Oxford: Clarendon Press).

Armour, P. (1989), *Dante's Griffin and the History of the World: A Study of the Earthly Paradise (Purgatorio XXIX–XXXIII)* (Oxford: Clarendon Press).

Armour, P. (1991), 'Comedy and the Origins of Italian Theatre around the Time of Dante', in *Writers and Peformers in Italian Drama from the Time of Dante to Pirandello*, ed. J. R. Dashwood and J. E. Everson (Lewiston, New York, Queenston, Ontario, and Lampeter: Edwin Mellen Press), pp. 1–31.

Armour, P. (1994), 'Gold, Silver, and True Treasure: Economic Imagery in Dante', *Romance Studies* 23, 7–30.

Armstrong, R. J., Hellmann, J. A. W. and Short, W. J. (1999–2002), *Francis of Assisi: Early Documents* (4 vols. with index) (New York, London, Manila: New City Press).

Auw, L. von (1979), *Angelo Clareno et les spirituels italiens* (Rome: Edizioni di storia e letteratura).

Auw, L. von (1980), *Angeli Clareni opera: 1, Epistole* (Rome: Istituto storico per il medio evo).

Balfour, M. (1995), '[*Paradiso*] IX', *Lectura Dantis* 16–17, 131–45.

Barański, Z. G. (1994), 'Dante, commentatore e commentato: riflessioni sullo studio dell'*iter* ideologico di Dante', *Letture classensi* 23, 135–58.

Barber, M. (1978, repr. 1993), *The Trial of the Templars* (Cambridge University Press).

Barberino, Francesco da: *see* Egidi, F.

Barnes, J. C. (1986), 'Dante, Cimabue and Giotto', *Strathclyde Modern Language Studies* 6, 5–27.

Barr, H. (1993), *The Piers Plowman Tradition* (London: Dent).
Barraclough, G. (1968), *The Medieval Papacy* (London: Thames & Hudson).
Bartoli, M. (1999), 'Olivi et le pouvoir du Pape', in Boureau and Piron (1999), pp. 173–91.
Belting, H. (1977), *Die Oberkirche von San Francesco in Assisi* (Berlin: Mann).
Bemrose, S. (2000), *Dante: A New Life* (Exeter: University of Exeter Press).
Bettarini, R. (1969), *Jacopone e il Laudario Urbinate* (Florence: Sansoni).
Bignami-Odier, J. (1952), *Etudes sur Jean de Roquetaillade (Johannes de Rupescissa)* (Paris: Vrin).
Bihl, P. M. (1939), 'Fraticelli cuiusdam *Decalogus Evangelicae Paupertatis* An. 1340–1342 conscriptus', *AFH* 32, pp. 279–411.
Bihl, P. M. (1941), 'Statuta generalia ordinis edita in capitulis celebratis Narbonae an. 1260, Assisii an. 1279 atque Parisiis an. 1292 (editio critica et synoptica)', *AFH* 34, pp. 13–94.
Boase, T. S. R. (1933), *Boniface VIII* (London: Constable).
Boccali, G and Bigaroni, M. (1999), *Liber chronicarum sive tribulationum ordinis minorum di Frate Angelo Clareno* (Santa Maria degli Angeli: Edizioni Porziuncola).
Boehmer, H. (1904), *Analekten zur Geschichte des Franciscus* (Tübingen; 2nd edn. F. Wiegand, 1930).
Bolton, B. M. (1975), 'The Poverty of the Humiliati', in Flood (ed.) 1975.
Bonaventura (ed. PP Collegii S. Bonaventurae) (1882–1902), *Opera omnia* (10 vols; Quaracchi: Typographia Collegii S. Bonaventurae).
Bornstein, D. E. and Rusconi, R. (eds.) (1996), *Women and Religion in Medieval and Renaissance Italy* (Chicago: University of Chicago Press).
Bosco, U. (1966), *Dante vicino* (Caltanisetta and Rome: Sciascia).
Bosco, U. (1977), 'Dante e il teatro medievale', in *Studi filologici, letterari e storici in memoria di Guido Favati*, ed. G. Varanini and P. Pinagli (Padua: Antenore).
Boswell, J. C. (1999), *Dante's Fame in England: References in Printed British Books 1477–1640* (Newark, Del. and London: University of Delaware Press and Associated University Presses).
Botterill, S. (1994), *Dante and the Mystical Tradition: St Bernard of Clairvaux in the 'Commedia'* (Cambridge: Cambridge University Press).
Boureau, A. and Piron, S. (1999), *Pierre de Jean Olivi (1248–1298): Pensée scolastique, dissidence spirituelle et société*. Actes du Colloque de Narbonne (mars 1998) (Paris: Vrin).
Boyde, P. (2000), *Human Vices and Human Worth in Dante's 'Comedy'* (Cambridge University Press).
Brand, C. P. and Pertile, L. (1996), *The Cambridge History of Italian Literature* (Cambridge University Press).
Brandi, C. (1983), *Giotto* (Milan, Mondadori).
Brooke, R. B. (1959), *Early Franciscan Government: Elias to Bonaventure* (Cambridge: University Press).
Brooke, R. B. (1970), *Scripta Leonis, Rufini et Angeli, Sociorum S. Francisci: The Writings of Leo, Rufino and Angelo, Companions of St Francis* (Oxford: Clarendon Press).

Brufani, S. (1990): *see Sacrum commercium.*

Bughetti, B. (1926), 'Vita e miracoli di S. Francesco nelle tavole istoriate dei secoli XIII e XIV', *AFH* 19, pp. 636–72 and 936–45.

Burr, D. (1981), 'Olivi's Apocalyptic Timetable', *Journal of Medieval and Renaissance Studies* 11, 237–60.

Burr, D. (1989), *Olivi and Franciscan Poverty: The Origins of the 'Usus Pauper' Controversy* (Philadelphia: University of Pennsylvania Press).

Burr, D. (1992), *Petrus Iohannis Olivi, 'De Usu Paupere': The 'Quaestio' and the 'Tractatus'* (Florence and Perth: Olschki and University of Western Australia Press).

Burr, D. (1993), *Olivi's Peaceable Kingdom: A Reading of the Apocalypse Commentary* (Philadelphia: University of Pennsylvania Press).

Burr, D. (2001), *The Spiritual Franciscans: From Protest to Persecution in the Century After St Francis* (University Park, Pa.: Pennsylvania State University Press).

Buti, Francesco da (ed. C. Giannini) (1858–62), *Commento sopra la 'Divina Commedia' di Dante Allighieri* (3 vols.) (Pisa: Nistri).

Cachey, T. J. (1995), *Dante Now: Current Trends in Dante Studies* (Notre Dame, Indiana and London: University of Notre Dame Press).

Caesar, M. (1989), *Dante: The Critical Heritage* (London and New York: Routledge).

Callaey, F. (1911), *L'idéalisme franciscain spirituel au XIVe siècle: Ubertin de Casale* (Louvain: Bureau du Receuil).

Callaey, F. (1921), 'L'influence et la diffusion de l'*Arbor vitae* d'Ubertin de Casale', *Revue d'Histoire Ecclésiastique* 17.

Campagnola, S. da (1971), *L'Angelo del Sesto Sigillo e l'"Alter Christus": Genesi e sviluppo di due temi francescani nei secoli XIII–XIV* (Rome: Ed. Laurentianum/ Ed. Antonianum).

Capitani, O. (1965): *see* dei Girolami, Remigio.

Carlini, A. (1911), 'Constitutiones Generales Ordinis Fratrum Minorum Anno 1316 Assisii Conditae', *AFH* 4, pp. 269–302.

Casale, Ubertino da: *see* Ubertino da Casale.

Cavalca, Domenico (1763), *Esposizione del simbolo degli Apostoli* (Rome).

Cavalli, G. (ed.) (1975), *Cecco Angiolieri: Rime* (Milan: Rizzoli).

Cioffari, V.: *see* Guido da Pisa.

Cirino, A. and Raischl, J. (eds.) (1995), *Franciscan Solitude* (St Bonaventure, New York: The Franciscan Institute).

Civezza, M. da, and Domenichelli, T.: *see* Serravalle, Giovanni da.

Clareno, Angelo (ed. L. Oliger), *Expositio regulae* (Quaracchi: PP S. Bonaventurae).

Clareno, Angelo: *see also* Auw, L. von.

Clareno, Angelo: *see also* Boccali, G. and Bigaroni, M.

Coleman, J. (1987), 'The Two Jurisdictions: Theological and Legal Justifications of Church Property in the Thirteenth Century', *SCH* 24, 75–110.

Comollo, A. (1990), *Il dissenso religioso in Dante* (Florence: Olschki).

Compagni, D. (ed. G. Luzzatto) (1968), *Cronica* (Turin: Einaudi).

Compagni, D. (ed. and tr. D. E. Bornstein) (1986), *Dino Compagni's Chronicle of Florence* (Philadelphia: University of Pennsylvania Press).

Contini, G. (1960), *Poeti del Duecento* (2 vols.) (Milan and Naples: Ricciardi).
Contini, G. (1965), 'La questione del *Fiore*', *Cultura e scuola* 13/14, 768–73.
Contini, G. (ed.) (1970a): *see* Dante Alighieri.
Contini, G. (1970b), 'Il *Fiore*' in *ED* vol. 2, pp. 895–901.
Contini, G. (1973), 'Un nodo della cultura medievale: la serie *Roman de la Rose – Il Fiore – Divina Commedia*', *Lettere italiane* 25, 162–89.
Contini (1984): *see* Dante Alighieri.
Cook, W. R. (1989), 'Fraternal and Lay Images of St Francis in the Thirteenth Century', in *Popes, Teachers and Canon Law in the Middle Ages*, ed. J. R. Sweeney and S. Chodorow (Ithaca, New York: Cornell University Press), pp. 263–89.
Cook, W. R. (1999), *Images of St Francis of Assisi . . . from the Earliest Images to 1320 in Italy* (Florence: Olschki and Perth: University of Western Australia).
Corti, M. (1983), *La felicità mentale: nuove prospettive per Cavalcanti e Dante* (Turin: Einaudi).
Cosmo, U. (1898), 'Le mistiche nozze di Frate Francesco con Madonna Povertà', *Giornale dantesco* 6, 49–82 and 97–117.
Cosmo, U. (1965), *L'ultima ascesa* (new edn.; Florence: La Nuova Italia).
Da Alençon, E. (1925), 'Il colore dell'abito dei Frati Minori', *Miscellanea Francescana* 25.1, pp. 3–12.
Daniel, E. R. (1973), 'Spirituality and Poverty: Angelo da Clareno and Ubertino da Casale', *Medievalia et Humanistica* (new series) 4, 89–98.
Daniel, E. R. (1992), *The Franciscan Concept of Mission in the High Middle Ages* (rev. edn; New York: Franciscan Institute).
Dante Alighieri (1947), *La Divina Commedia*, ed. M. Porena (3 vols.) (Bologna: Zanichelli).
Dante Alighieri (1950), *Monarchia*, ed. G. Vinay (Florence: Sansoni).
Dante Alighieri (1954–7), *Dante: Die Göttliche Komödie: Kommentar*, ed. H. Gmelin (3 vols.) (Stuttgart: Klett).
Dante Alighieri (1966), *Dantis Alagherii Epistolae: The Letters of Dante*, ed. P. Toynbee (2nd edn, Oxford: Clarendon Press).
Dante Alighieri (1966–7), '*La Commedia*': *secondo l'antica vulgata*, ed. G. Petrocchi (3 vols.) (Milan: Mondadori).
Dante Alighieri (1970), *Rime*, ed. G. Contini (Turin: Einaudi).
Dante Alighieri (1984), *Il Fiore e Il Detto d'Amore attribuibili a Dante Alighieri*, ed. G. Contini (Milan and Naples: Ricciardi).
Dante Alighieri (1986): *Purgatorio*, ed. A. Vallone and L. Scorrano. (Naples: Ferraro).
Dante Alighieri (1988), *Dante Alighieri: Convivio*, ed. C. Vasoli and D. De Robertis in *Dante Alighieri: Opere minori* (Milan and Naples: Ricciardi).
Dante Alighieri (1996), *Dante: il Fiore, Detto d'Amore*, ed. L. Rossi (Milan: Mondadori).
Dante Alighieri (1996), *Dante, 'Monarchy'*, ed. and tr. P. Shaw in *Cambridge Texts in the History of Political Thought* (Cambridge University Press).
Dante Alighieri (2003), *The Divine Comedy of Dante Alighieri*, vol. 2: *Purgatorio*, ed. and tr. R. M. Durling, Introduction and Notes by R. Martinez and R. M. Durling (New York: Oxford University Press).

D'Arcais, F. (1978), 'Miniature del Ricc. 1005', *Storia dell'arte* 33, 107–11.

Dashwood, J. R. and Everson, J. E. (1991): *see* Armour, P. (1991).

Davidsohn, R. (1900–8), *Forschungen zur älteren Geschichte von Florenz* (vols. 2 and 4; Berlin: Mittler).

Davidsohn, R. (1927), *Geschichte von Florenz* (Berlin: Mittler), vol. 4.3.

Davis, C. T. (1957), *Dante and the Idea of Rome* (Oxford: Clarendon Press).

Davis, C. T. (1961): *see* Ubertino da Casale.

Davis, C. T. (1963), 'The Early Collection of Books of S. Croce in Florence', *Proceedings of the American Philosophical Society* 107(5), 399–414.

Davis, C. T. (1981), 'Ubertino da Casale and his Conception of *altissima paupertas*', *Studi medievali* (3a serie) 22 (1), 1–56.

Davis, C. T. (1984), *Dante's Italy and Other Essays* (Philadelphia: University of Pennsylvania Press).

Davis, C. T. (1990), 'Dante and Ecclesiastical Property', in *Law in Medieval Life and Thought*, ed. E. B. King and S. J. Ridyard (Sewanee, Tennessee: The Press of the University of the South), pp. 244–57.

D'Avray, D. (1985), *The Preaching of the Friars: Sermons Diffused from Paris before 1300* (Oxford: Clarendon Press).

D'Avray, D. (1995), 'Philosophy in Preaching: The Case of a Franciscan based in Thirteenth-Century Florence (Servasanto da Faenza)', in *Literature and Religion in the Later Middle Ages: Philological Studies in Honour of Siegfried Wenzel*, ed. R. G. Newhauser and J. A. Alford (Binghamton, New York: MARTS), pp. 263–73.

Dawson, J. D. (1983), 'Richard Fitzralph and Fourteenth-Century Poverty Controversies', *JEH* 34, 315–44.

De Matteis (1977): *see* dei Girolami, Remigio.

Delcorno, C. (1974), *Giordano da Pisa: quaresimale fiorentino 1305–6* (Florence: Sansoni).

Delcorno, C. (1975), *Giordano da Pisa e l'antica predicazione in volgare* (Florence: Olschki).

Delcorno, C. (1996), 'Dante e il linguaggio dei predicatori', *Letture classensi* 25, 51–74.

Demski, A. (1903), *Papst Nikolaus III: eine Mongraphie* (Münster: Schöningh).

Denifle, H. (1889), 'Die Denkschrift der Colonna gegen Bonifaz VIII', *ALKG* 5, 509–15.

Douie, D. (1932), *The Nature and the Effect of the Heresy of the Fraticelli* (Manchester University Press).

Douie, D. (1952), *Archbishop Pecham* (Oxford: Clarendon Press).

Duffy, E. (1997), 'Finding St Francis: Early Images, Early Lives', in *Medieval Theology and the Natural Body*, ed. P. Biller and A. Minnis (York and Woodbridge: York Medieval Press and Boydell), pp. 193–236.

Egidi, F. (ed.) (1905–27), *Francesco da Barberino: Documenti d'Amore* (4 vols.) (Rome: Società filologica romana).

Emmerson, R. K. and Herzman, R. B. (1980), 'Antichrist, Simon Magus and Dante's *Inferno* XIX', *Traditio* 36, 157–73.

Emmerson, R. K. and Herzman, R. B. (1992), *The Apocalyptic Imagination in the Middle Ages* (Philadelphia: University of Pennsylvania Press).

Emmerson, R. K. and McGinn B. (1992), *The Apocalypse in the Middle Ages* (Ithaca, N.Y.: Cornell University Press).

Esser, K. (1964), 'Untersuchungen zum "Sacrum Commercium Beati Francisci cum Domina Paupertate"', in *Miscellanea Melchor de Pobladura* (Rome: Biblioteca Seraphico-Capuccina 23), pp. 1–33.

Eubel, C. (1898), *Bullarium Franciscanum*, vol. 5 (Rome: Typis Vaticanis).

Faccioli, E. (1975), *Il teatro italiano I: dalle origini al Quattrocento* (Turin: Einaudi).

Faral, E. and Bastin, J. (eds.) (1959–60), *Œuvres complètes de Rutebeuf* (2 vols.) (Paris: Picard).

Ferrante, J. (1984), *The Political Vision of the "Divine Comedy"* (Princeton, N.J.: Princeton University Press).

Ferretti, G. (1909), 'Ancora di Marzucco Scornigiani', *Bull.* 16, 54–60.

Finke, H. (1908), *Acta Aragonensia* (2 vols.; Berlin and Leipzig: Rothschild).

Flacius, M. (1556), *Catalogus testium veritatis qui ante nostrum aetatem reclamarunt Papae* (Basel: Oporinus).

Fleming, J. V. (1977), *An Introduction to the Franciscan Literature of the Middle Ages* (Chicago: Franciscan Herald Press).

Flood, D. (1972), *Olivi's Rule Commentary* (Wiesbaden: Steiner).

Flood, D. (1975), *Poverty in the Middle Ages* (Werl, Westf.: Coelde).

Flood, D. (1979), *Hugh of Digne's Rule Commentary* (Grottaferrata: Editiones Collegii S. Bonaventurae Ad Claras Aquas).

Flood, D. (1999), 'Poverty as Virtue, Poverty as Warning', in Boureau and Piron (1999), pp. 157–72.

Flood, D. (2000), 'Recent Study on Peter Olivi', *Franciscan Studies* 58, 111–19.

Fortini, A. (1961), *La lauda in Assisi e le origini del teatro italiano* (Assisi: Edizioni Assisi).

Foster, K. (1957), *God's Tree: Essays on Dante and Other Matters* (London: Blackfriars).

Foster, K. (1969), 'The Canto of the Damned Popes: *Inferno* XIX', *DS* 87, 47–68.

Foxe, J. (1570), *The ecclesiastical history contayning the actes and monumentes. Newly recognised and inlarged* (London: Day).

Freccero, J. (1961), 'Dante's Pilgrim in a Gyre', *PMLA* 76 (1961), 168–81.

Frugoni, A. (1969), 'Dante tra due conclavi: la lettera ai cardinali italiani', *Letture classensi* 2, 71–91.

Frugoni, C. (1988), *Francesco: un'altra storia* (Genoa: Marietti).

Frugoni, C. (1993), *Francesco e l'invenzione delle Stimmate: una storia per parole e immagini fino a Bonaventura e Giotto* (Turin: Einaudi).

Fussenegger, G. (1957), 'Relatio commisionis in concilio Viennensi institutae ad decretalem *Exivi de paradiso* praeparandum' *AFH* 50, 145–77.

Gardner, E. G. (1926), 'St Francis and Dante', in *St Francis of Assisi 1226–1926: Essays in Commemoration*, ed. W. W. Seton (London: University of London Press), pp. 65–93.

Gay, J. (1898–1916), *Les régistres de Nicolas III* (5 vols.) (Paris: Fontemoing).

Gennaro, C. (1996), 'Clare, Agnes and Their Earliest Followers', in Bornstein, D. E. and Rusconi, R. (1996), pp. 39–55.

Georgianna, L. (2000), 'Anticlericalism in Boccaccio and Chaucer: The Bark and the Bite', in *The 'Decameron' and the 'Canterbury Tales': New Essays on an Old Question*, ed. L. M. Koff and B. D. Schildgen (Madison and London: Fairleigh Dickinson University Press and Associated University Presses).
Geremek, B. (tr. A. Kolakowska) (1997), *Poverty: A History* (Oxford: Blackwell).
Giamboni, Bono (ed. C. Segre) (1968), *Il libro de' vizi e delle virtudi* (Turin: Einaudi).
Girolami, Remigio dei (ed. O. Capitani) (1965), 'Il *De Peccato Usure* di Remigio de' Girolami', *Studi medievali* (3a serie) 6 (2), 537–662.
Girolami, Remigio dei (ed. M. C. Matteis) (1977), *La teologia politica comunale di Remigio de' Girolami* (Bologna: Pàtron).
Girotto, S. (1952), *Corrado di Sassonia predicatore e mariologo del sec. xiii* (Florence: Studi francescani).
Gmelin, H.: *see* Dante Alighieri.
Goffen, R. (1988), *Spirituality in Conflict: Saint Francis and Giotto's Bardi Chapel* (University Park and London: The Pennsylvania State University Press).
Gorra, E. (1917), 'Dante e Clemente V', *GSLI* 69 (1917), 193–216.
Grundmann, H. (1932), 'Dante und Joachim von Fiore', *DDJb* 14, 210–56.
Grundmann, H. (1977), *Ausgewählte Aufsätze* (Stuttgart: Hiersemann).
Guerri, D. (1908), *Di alcuni versi dotti della 'Divina Commedia: ricerche sul sapere grammaticale di Dante* (Città di Castello: Lapi).
Guido da Pisa (ed. V. Cioffari) (1974), *Expositiones et Glose super Comediam Dantis* (Albany, N.Y.: State University of New York Press).
Guillemain, B. (1966), *La Cour pontificale d'Avignon: étude d'une société* (Paris: De Boccard).
Gurevich, A. (1985), *Categories of Medieval Culture* (London: Routledge).
Gurevich, A. (1990), *Medieval Popular Culture* (Cambridge University Press and Editions de la Maison des Sciences de l'Homme).
Habig, M. A. (1973), *St Francis of Assisi: Writings and Early Biographies. An English Omnibus of the Sources for the Life of St Francis* (Chicago: University of Chicago Press).
Hagman, E. (1988), 'Dante's Vision of God: The End of the *Itinerarium Mentis*', *DS* 106, 1–20.
Havely, N. R. (1983), 'Chaucer, Boccaccio and the Friars', in *Chaucer and the Italian Trecento*, ed. P. Boitani (Cambridge University Press), pp. 249–68.
Havely, N. R. (1986), 'The Self-Consuming City: The Body Politic in Dante's *Commedia*', *DDJb* 61, 99–113.
Havely, N. R. (1996), 'Poverty in Purgatory: From *Commercium* to *Commedia*', *DS* 104, pp. 229–43.
Havely, N. R. (1997), 'The Blood of the Apostles: Dante, the Franciscans and Pope John XXII', *Italian Studies* 52, 38–50.
Hawkins, P. (1999), *Dante's Testaments: Essays in Scriptural Imagination* (Stanford, Ca.: Stanford University Press).
Heft, J. (1986), *John XXII and Papal Teaching Authority* (Lewiston, N.Y. and Queenston, Ont.: Edwin Mellen).

Herde, P. (1981), *Cölestin V (Peter vom Morrone) Der Engelpapst* (Stuttgart: Hiersemann).
Hervaeus Natalis (ed. and tr. J. D. Jones) (1999), *The Poverty of Christ and the Apostles* (Toronto: Pontifical Institute of Medieval Studies).
Herzman, R. (1982), 'Dante and Francis', *Franciscan Studies* 42, 96–114.
Herzman, R. (1992), 'Dante and the Apocalypse', in Emmerson and McGinn (eds.) (1992), pp. 398–413.
Herzman, R. and Stephany, W. A. (1978), '"O miseri seguaci": Sacramental Inversion in *Inferno* XIX', *DS* 96, 39–65.
Holder-Egger, O. (1905–13), *Salinbene, Chronica, MGH Scriptores* 32 (Hanover: Hahn).
Holmes, G. A. (1980), 'Dante and the Popes', in *The World of Dante: Essays on Dante and his Times*, ed. C. Grayson (Oxford: Clarendon Press), pp. 18–43.
Holmes, G. A. (1986), *Florence, Rome and the Origins of the Renaissance* (Oxford: Clarendon Press).
Holmes, G. A. (1997), '*Monarchia* and Dante's Attitude to the Popes', in *Dante and Governance*, ed. J. R. Woodhouse (Oxford: Clarendon Press), pp. 46–57.
Hudson, A. (1978), 'A Neglected Wyclifite Text', *JEH* 29, 257–79.
Hudson, A. (1988), 'The Legacy of *Piers Plowman*', in *A Companion to 'Piers Plowman'*, ed. J. A. Alford (Berkeley: University of California Press), pp. 251–66.
Hugh of Digne: *see* Flood, D. and Sisto, A.
Iacopone da Todi (ed. F. Ageno) (1953), *Laudi, Trattato e Detti* (Florence: Le Monnier).
Iacopone da Todi (ed. F. Mancini) (1974), *Laude* (Rome and Bari: Laterza).
Illiano, A. (1997), *Sulle sponde del Prepurgatorio: poesia e arte narrativa nel preludio all'ascesa* (Fiesole: Edizioni Cadmo).
Imola, Benvenuto da (ed. J. P. Lacaita) (1887), *Comentum super Dantis Aldigherii Comoediam* (5 vols.) (Florence: Barbera).
Ini, A. M. (1973), 'Nuovi documenti sugli spirituali di Toscana', *AFH* 66, 305–77.
James, M. R. (1924), *The Apocryphal New Testament* (Oxford: Clarendon Press).
Jenaro-MacLennan, L. (1974), *The Trecento Commentaries on the 'Divina Commedia'* (Oxford University Press).
John of Paris (ed. and tr. A. P. Moynihan) (1974), *John of Paris on Royal and Papal Power* (New York and London: Columbia University Press).
Jones, J. D. (1999): *see* Hervaeus Natalis.
Kaske, R. E. (1961), 'Dante's "DXV" and "Veltro"', *Traditio* 17, 185–254.
Kaske, R. E. (1971), '"Sí si conserva il seme d'ogne giusto" (*Purg.* XXXIII, 48)', *DS* 89, 49–54.
Kaske, R. E. (1973–4), 'Dante's *Purgatorio* XXXII and XXXIII: A Survey of Christian History', *University of Toronto Quarterly* 43, 193–214.
Kaske, R. E. (1983), 'The Seven *Status Ecclesiae* in *Purgatorio* XXXII and XXXIII', in *Dante, Petrarch, Boccaccio: Studies in the Italian Trecento in Honor of Charles Singleton*, ed. A. S. Bernardo and A. L. Pellegrini (Binghamton, N.Y.: MARTS), pp. 89–113.
Kaye, J. (1998), *Economy and Nature in the Fourteenth Century: Money, Market Exchange, and the Emergence of Scientific Thought* (Cambridge University Press).
Keen, C. M. (2000), 'Images of Exile: Distance and Memory in the Poetry of Cino da Pistoia', *Italian Studies* 55, 21–36.

Kerby-Fulton, K. (1990), *Reformist Apocalypticism and 'Piers Plowman'* (Cambridge University Press).

Kirkpatrick, R. (1978), *Dante's 'Paradiso' and the Limitations of Modern Criticism* (Cambridge University Press).

Lacaita, J. P.: *see* Imola, Benvenuto da.

Lambert, M. D. (1961, repr. 1998), *Franciscan Poverty: The Doctrine of the Absolute Poverty of Christ and the Apostles in the Franciscan Order 1210–1323* (rev. edn, New York: The Franciscan Institute).

Lambert, M. D. (1972–3), 'The Franciscan Crisis under John XXII', *Franciscan Studies* 32, 123–43.

Lambert, M. D. (1992), *Medieval Heresy: Popular Movements from the Gregorian Reform to the Reformation* (2nd edn, Oxford: Blackwell).

Lambertini, R. (1990), *Apologia e crescita dell'identità francescana (1255–1279)* (Rome: Istituto storico italiano per il Medio Evo).

Lambertini, R. (1999), 'La difesa dell'ordine francescano' in Boureau and Piron (1999), pp. 193–205.

Lambertini, R. (2000), *La povertà pensata: evoluzione storica della definizione dell' identità minoritica da Bonaventura ad Ockham* (Modena: Mucchi).

Lancia, Andrea (ed. A. Torri) (1827–9), *L'ottimo commento della Divina Commedia* (3 vols.) (Pisa: Capurro).

Langlois, E. (1914–24), *Le Roman de la Rose* (5 vols.) (Paris: SATF).

Lansing, C. (1991), *The Florentine Magnates: Lineage and Faction in a Medieval Commune* (Princeton, N.J.: Princeton University Press).

Lanza, A. (1990), *Cecco Angiolieri: Le Rime* (Rome: Izzi).

Lanza, A. (1991), 'Il *Fiore e il Detto d'Amore:* Ser Durante, non Dante Alighieri. Storia d'un miraggio' in *idem, Primi secoli: Saggi di letteratura italiana antica* (Rome: Izzi).

Latini, Brunetto (ed. F. J. Carmody) (1948), *Li Livres dou Tresor* (Berkeley and Los Angeles: University of California Press).

Lawrence, C. H. (1994), *The Friars: The Impact of the Early Mendicant Movement on Western Society* (London and New York: Longman).

Lee, H. E., Reeves, M., and Sillano, G. (1989), *Western Mediterranean Prophecy: the School of Joachim of Fiore and the Fourteenth-Century Breviloquium* (Toronto: Pontifical Institute of Medieval Studies).

Leff, G. (1966), *Heresy in the Later Middle Ages: The Relation of Heterodoxy to Dissent, c.1250–c.1450* (2 vols., continuously paginated) Manchester University Press).

Leff, G. (1968), *Paris and Oxford Universities in the Thirteenth and Fourteenth Centuries: An Institutional and Intellectual History* (New York, London, Sydney: John Wiley & Sons).

Le Goff, J. (tr. A. Goldhammer) (1984), *The Birth of Purgatory* (Chicago: University of Chicago Press).

Lerner, R. (1988), 'On the Origins of the Earliest Latin Pope Prophecies: A Reconsideration', in *MGH Scriptores* 33.5, pp. 611–35.

Lerner, R. (1994), 'Writing and Resistance among Beguins of Languedoc and Catalonia', in *Heresy and Literacy 1000–1530*, ed. P. Biller and A. Hudson (Cambridge University Press), pp. 186–204.

Lesnick, D. R. (1977–8), 'Dominican Preaching and the Creation of Capitalist Ideology in Late-Medieval Florence', *Memorie domenicane* (n.s.) 8–9, 199–247.

Lesnick, D. R. (1989), *Preaching in Florence: The Social World of Franciscan and Dominican Spirituality* (Athens, Ga. and London: University of Georgia Press).

Levasti, A. (1960), *Mistici del Duecento e del Trecento* (Milan: Rizzoli).

Lewis, W. (1972), 'Peter John Olivi OFM (1248–1298): Prophet of the Year 2000 – Ecclesiology and Eschatology in the *Lectura super Apocalipsim* (1297)' (PhD dissertation, Eberhard-Karls-Universität, Tübingen).

Lewis, W. (1999), 'Peter John Olivi, Author of the *Lectura super Apocalipsim*: Was He Heretical?', in Boureau and Piron (1999), pp. 135–56.

Limborch, P. (1692), *Historia Inquisitionis cui subiungitur Liber sententiarum Inqusitionis Tholosanae* (Amsterdam: Wetstenius).

Little, A. G. (1917), *Studies in English Franciscan History* (Manchester and London: Manchester University Press and Longman).

Little, L. K. (1971), 'Pride Goes before Avarice: Social Changes and the Vices in Latin Christendom', *American Historical Review* 76, 16–49.

Little, L. K. (1975), 'Evangelical Poverty, the New Money Economy and Violence', in Flood (1975), pp. 11–26.

Little, L. K. (1978), *Religious Poverty and the Profit Economy in Medieval Europe* (London: Paul Elek).

Luiso, F. P. (1907), 'Per una allusione della *Divina Commedia*', *Bull.* 14, 44–78.

Lunghi, E. (tr. C. Evans) (1996), *The Basilica of St Francis in Assisi* (Florence: Scala).

Maccarone, M. (1955), 'Il terzo libro della *Monarchia*', *Studi danteschi* 33, 5–142.

Mancini, F. (1974): *see* Iacopone da Todi.

Mandelbaum, A., Oldcorn, A., and Ross, C. (1998), *Lectura Dantis: Inferno* (Berkeley, Ca.: University of California Press).

Manselli, R. (1959), *Spirituali e beghini in Provenza* (Rome: Istituto storico per il medio evo).

Manselli, R. (1965a), 'Dante e l'*Ecclesia Spiritualis*', in *Dante e Roma: Atti del convegno di studi*, a cura della 'Casa di Dante' (Florence: Le Monnier).

Manselli, R. (1965b), 'Pietro di Giovanni Olivi ed. Ubertino da Casale', *Studi medievali* (ser. 3) 6, 95–122.

Manselli, R. (1971), 'San Francesco e San Domenico nei canti del *Paradiso*', *Frate Francesco* 38, 143–54.

Manselli, R. (1973), 'Firenze nel Trecento: Santa Croce e la cultura francescana', *Clio* 9, 325–42.

Manselli, R. (1975), 'A proposito del cristianesimo di Dante: Gioacchino da Fiore, gioachimismo, spiritualismo francescano', in *Letteratura e critica: Studi in onore di Natalino Sapegno*, ed. W. Binni *et al.* (Rome: Bulzoni), vol. 2, pp. 163–92.

Manselli, R. (1976), 'La resurrezione di san Francesco dalla teologia di Pietro di Giovanni Olivi ad una testimonianza di pietà popolare', *Collectanea Franciscana* 46, 309–20.

Manselli, R. (1982) 'Dante e gli Spirituali francescani', *Lettture classensi* 11, 47–61.
Mansi, J. D. (1761–4), *Stephani Baluzii Tutelensis Miscellanea: novo ordine digesta et non paucis ineditis monumentis opportunisque animadversionibus aucta* (Lucae: V. Iunctinius, sumptibus J. Riccomini [Paris]).
Marsilius of Padua (ed. and tr. A. Gewirth) (1980), *Defensor Pacis* (repr. Toronto: University of Toronto Press).
Marti, B. M. (1952), 'A Crux in Dante's *Inferno*', *Speculum* 27, 67–70.
Marti, M. (1957), 'Il canto VII dell' *Inferno*', in *Lectura Dantis romana* (Turin, Genoa: Società editrice internazionale).
Martinelli, L. (1966), *Dante* (Palermo: Palumbo).
Martines, L. (1972), *Violence and Disorder in Italian Cities* (Berkeley, Ca.: University of California Press).
Martines, L. (1983), *Power and Imagination: City States in Renaissance Italy* (Harmondsworth: Peregrine Books).
Matteini, N. (1958), *Il piú antico oppositore politico di Dante: Guido Vernani da Rimini: testo critico del 'De reprobatione monarchiae'* (Padua: CEDAM).
Mazzotta, G. (1979), *Dante, Poet of the Desert* (Princeton, N.J.: Princeton University Press).
McGinn, B. (1978), 'Angel Pope and Papal Antichrist', *Church History* 47, 155–73.
McGinn, B. (1998), *Visions of the End: Apocalyptic Traditions in the Middle Ages* (rev. edn, New York: Columbia University Press).
Mellone, A. (1987), *Lectura Dantis Metelliana: Dante e il Francescanesimo* (Cava dei Tirreni: Avagliano).
Mellone, A. (1992), *Lectura Dantis Metelliana: I primi undici canti del 'Paradiso'* (Rome: Bulzoni).
Menache, S. (1998), *Clement V* (Cambridge University Press).
Menchenni, P. S. (1909), 'Constitutiones Generales Ordinis Fratrum Minorum a Capitulo Perpiniani Anno 1331 celebrato editae', *AFH* 2, 269–92.
Menestò, E. (1977), *Le vite antiche di Jacopone da Todi* (Florence: La Nuova Italia).
Miller, W. B. (1961), 'The Franciscan Legend in Italian Painting in the Thirteenth Century' (PhD dissertation, Columbia University).
Mineo, N. (1968), *Profetismo e apocalittica in Dante* (Catania: Università di Catania).
Mineo, N. (1992), 'Il canto XI del *Paradiso*', in *Lectura Dantis Metelliana: I primi undici canti del 'Paradiso'*, ed. A. Mellone (Rome: Bulzoni), pp. 221–320.
Mineo, N. (1993), 'Ancora su *Paradiso* XII 106–45', in *Miscellanea di studi danteschi in memoria di Silvio Pasquazi*, ed. A. Paolella, V. Placella and G. Turco (Naples: Federico and Ardia), vol. 2, pp. 551–88.
Mineo, N. (1998), 'Gli Spirituali francescani e l'"Apocalisse" di Dante', *La Rassegna della letteratura italiana* 102, 26–46.
Minnis, A. (1988), *Medieval Theory of Authorship* (2nd edn, Aldershot: Scolar).
Minnis, A. and Scott, A. B. (1991), *Medieval Literary Theory and Criticism c.1100–c.1375: The Commentary Tradition* (rev. edn, Oxford: Clarendon Press).
Moleta, V. (1983), *From St Francis to Giotto: The Influence of St Francis on Early Italian Art and Literature* (Chicago: Franciscan Herald Press).

Mollat, G. (1926), *Manuel de l'Inquisiteur* (2 vols.) (Paris: Champion).
Mollat, G. (1949), *Les Papes d'Avignon (1305–1378)* (Paris: Letouzey & Ané).
Mollat, M. (1974), *Etudes sur l'histoire de la pauvreté jusqu'au XVIe siècle* (Paris: Sorbonne).
Mollat, M. (tr. A. Goldhammer) (1986), *The Poor in the Middle Ages* (New Haven and London: Yale University Press).
Moorman, J. R. H. (1968), *A History of the Franciscan Order from its Origins to the Year 1517* (Oxford: Clarendon Press).
Moynihan, A. P. (1974): *see* John of Paris.
Müller, E. (1934), *Das Konzil von Vienne 1311–1312: seine Quellen und seine Geschichte* (Münster i. Westf.: Aschendorffsche Verlagsbuchhandlung).
Murray, Alexander (1982), 'Piety and Impiety in Thirteenth-Century Italy', *SCH* 8, 83–106
Musa, M. (1974), *Advent at the Gates: Dante's 'Comedy'* (Bloomington, Indiana: Indiana University Press).
Nardi, B. (1944), 'La "Donatio Constantini" e Dante' in *idem, Nel Mondo di Dante* (Rome: Edizioni di storia e letteratura).
Newhauser, R. (2000), *The Early History of Greed* (Cambridge University Press).
Newman, J. H. (1997), *Catena aurea: Commentary on the Four Gospels . . . by St Thomas Aquinas* (4 vols.) (Southampton: St Austin Press).
Nimmo, D. (1987), *Reform and Division in the Franciscan Order, 1226–1538* (Rome: Capuchin Historical Institute).
O'Byrne, S. (1965), 'Dante and Franciscanism', in *An Irish Tribute to Dante*, ed. G. Bistolfi (Dublin: Istituto Italiano di Cultura), pp. 111–28.
Ockham, William of (ed. A. S. McGrade) (1992), *A Short Treatise on Tyrannical Government* (Cambridge University Press).
Ockham, William of (ed. A. S. McGrade and J. Kilcullen) (1995), *A Letter to the Friars Minor and Other Writings* (Cambridge University Press).
Oliger, L. (1911), 'Documenta inedita ad historiam Fraticellorum spectantia', *AFH* 4, 688–712.
Oliger, L. (1912), 'Documenta inedita ad historiam Frabicellorum spectantia', *AFH* 5, pp. 74–84.
Oliger, L. (1918), 'Petri Iohannis Olivi de renunciatione papae Coelestini quaestio et epistola', *AFH* 11, 309–73.
Oliger, L. (1924), 'Servasanto da Faenza O. F. M. e il suo *Liber de virtutibus et vitiis*', in *Miscellanea F. Ehrle* (Rome: Biblioteca Apostolica Vaticana) 1, pp. 148–89.
Oliger, L. (1950), *Expositio quatuor magistrorum super Regulam Fratrum Minorum (1241–1242)* (Rome: Edizioni di storia e letteratura).
Olivi, Petrus Iohannis: *see* Lewis, W. Burr, D. and Note on Citations, Translations and Manuscript Sources, p. xiii
Olsen, G. (1969), 'The idea of the *Ecclesiastica Primitiva* in the Writings of the Twelfth-Century Canonists', *Traditio* 25, pp. 61–86.
Paatz, W. and Paatz, E. (1952), *Die Kirchen von Florenz: Ein Kunstgeschichtliches Handbuch*, vol. 1 (Frankfurt am Main: Klostermann).

Panella, E. (1979), *Per lo studio di fra Remigio dei Girolami (+ 1319), Memorie domenicane* 10.1.

Paparelli, G. (1967), 'Il canto XIX del *Purgatorio*', in *Lectura dantis Scaligera* (Florence: Le Monnier), pp. 693–755.

Paparelli, G. (1975), *Ideologia e poesia di Dante* (Florence: Olschki).

Papi, A. B. (1996), 'Mendicant Friars and Female *Pinzochere* in Tuscany: From Social Marginality to Models of Sanctity', in Bornstein and Rusconi (1996), pp. 84–103.

Park, D. G. (1970), 'Dante as Reformer' (PhD dissertation, Tulane University).

Pásztor, E. (1958), 'Le polemiche sulla "Lectura super Apocalipsim" di Pietro di Giovanni Olivi fino alla sua condanna', *Bullettino dell' Istituto Storico Italiano per il Medio Evo e Archivio Muratoriano* 70, pp. 365–424.

Pásztor, E. (1970), 'Giovanni XXII e il gioachinisno di Pietro di Giovanni Olivi', *Bullettino dell' istituto storico italiano per il medio evo* 82, 81–111.

Péano, P. (1975), 'Ministres provinciaux de Provence et Spirituels', *Cahiers de Fanjeaux* 10, 41–65.

Peck, G. T. (1980), *The Fool of God: Jacopone da Todi* (Tuscaloosa: University of Alabama Press)

Peters, E. (1980), *Heresy and Authority in Medieval Europe: Documents in Translation* (Philadelphia: University of Pennsylvania Press).

Petrocchi, G. (1957), 'Intorno alla pubblicazione dell'*Inferno* e del *Purgatorio*', *Convivium* (n.s.) 25, 652–69.

Petrocchi, G. (1967), 'Dante and Thirteenth-Century Asceticism', in *From Time to Eternity: Essays on Dante's 'Divine Comedy'*, ed. T. G. Bergin (New Haven and London: Yale University Press).

Petrocchi, G. (ed. C. Ossola) (1994), *Itinerari danteschi* (rev. edn, Milan: Franco Angeli).

Piaia, G. (1977), *Marsiglio da Padova nella riforma e nella controriforma: Fortuna ed interpretazione* (Padua: Antenore).

Piccard, G. (1978), *Wasserzeichen: Anker* (Stuttgart: Kohlhammer).

Pope-Hennessy, J. W. (1938), *Giovanni di Paolo, 1403–1483*. (New York: Oxford University Press).

Pope-Hennessy, J. W. (1993), '*Paradiso*': *The Illuminations to Dante's 'Divine Comedy' by Giovanni di Paolo* (London: Thames & Hudson).

Porena, M. (1947), *see* Dante Alighieri.

Potestà, G. L. (1980), *Storia e eschatologia in Ubertino da Casale* (Milan: Pubblicazioni della Università Cattolica).

Potestà, G. L. (1989), 'Ideali di santità secondo Ubertino da Casale ed Angelo Clareno', in *Santi e santità nel secolo xiv: Atti del convegno internazionale, società internazionale di studi francescani* (Assisi: Centro di studi francescani), pp. 103–37.

Potestà, G. L. (1990), *Angelo Clareno dai Poveri Eremiti ai Fraticelli* (Rome: Istituto storico italiano per il medioevo).

Ptolemy of Lucca (ed. and tr. J. Blythe) (1997), *On the Government of Rulers (De Regimine Principum): Ptolemy of Lucca, with Portions Attributed to Thomas Aquinas* (Philadelphia: University of Pennsylvania Press).

Pullan, B. (1973), *A History of Early Renaissance Italy, from the Mid-Thirteenth to the Mid-Fifteenth Century* (London: Allen Lane).
Raimondi, E. (1971), 'Canto I', in *Lectura Dantis Scaligera: Purgatorio*, ed. S. Paquazi (Florence: Le Monnier), pp. 1–42.
Rand, E. K. (1929), 'The Classics in the Thirteenth Century', *Speculum* 4, 249–69.
Reeves, M. (1969), *The Influence of Prophecy in the Later Middle Ages: A Study in Joachimism* (Oxford: Clarendon Press).
Reeves, M. (1992), 'The *Vaticinia de Summis Pontificibus*: A Question of Author[ship]', in *Intellectual Life in the Middle Ages*, ed. L. Smith and B. Ward (London and Ronceverte, WV: Hambledon Press), pp. 145–56.
Renier, R. (1883), *Liriche edite ed inedite di Fazio degli Uberti: testo critico* (Florence: Sansoni).
Renouard, Y. (1941), *Les relations des papes d'Avignon et des compagnies commerciales et bancaires de 1316 á 1378* (Paris: De Boccard).
Renouard, Y. (tr. D. Bethell) (1970), *The Avignon Papacy, 1305–1403* (Hamden, Ct: Archon).
Renucci, P. (1954), *Dante disciple et juge du monde gréco-latin* (Paris: Les Belles Lettres)
Renucci, P. (1965) 'Dante et les mythes du *Millennium*', *Revue des Études italiennes* 11, pp. 393–421.
Roddewig, M. (1970), 'Franz von Assisi in der *Göttlichen Komödie*', *DDJb* 46, 132–60.
Roddewig, M. (1991), 'Lectura Dantis: *Paradiso* XI', *DDJb* 66, pp. 81–105.
Roest, B. (1994), 'Franciscan Commentaries on the Apocalypse', *SCH subsidia* 10, 29–37.
Rossi, L. (1996): *see* Dante Alighieri.
Sabatier, P. (1898): *see* '*Speculum perfectionis*'.
Sacrum commercium Beati Francisci cum Domina Paupertate, ed. S. Brufani (1990) (S. Maria degli Angeli: Edizioni Porziuncola).
Salinbene: *see* Holder-Egger, O.
Sanguineti, E. (1961), *Interpretazione di Malebolge* (Florence: Olschki).
Sapegno, N. (1926), *Frate Jacopone* (Turin: Baretti).
Sapegno, N. (1952), *Poeti minori del Trecento* (Milan and Naples: Ricciardi).
Saward, J. (1980), *Perfect Fools: Folly for Christ's Sake in Catholic and Orthodox Spirituality* (Oxford, New York, Toronto and Melbourne: Oxford University Press).
Scase, W. (1989), '*Piers Plowman' and the New Anticlericalism* (Cambridge University Press).
Scott, J. A. (1970), 'The Rock of Peter and *Inferno* XIX', *Romance Philology* 23, 462–79.
Scott, J. A. (1996), *Dante's Political Purgatory* (Philadelphia: University of Pennsylvania Press).
Scrivano, R. (1989), '*Paradiso* 28', *Quaderni d'Italianistica* 10, 269–85.
Serravalle, Giovanni da (ed. M. da Civezza and T. Domenichelli) (1891), *Fratris Iohannis de Serravalle: Translatio et comentum totius libri Dantis Aldigherii* (Prato: Giachetti).
Shaw, P. (1996): *see* Dante Alighieri.
Silverstein, T. (1938), 'On the Genesis of *De Monarchia* II,v', *Speculum* 13, 326–49.

Sisto, A. (1971), *Figure del primo francescanesimo in Provenza: Ugo et Douceline de Digne* (Florence: Olschki).

Soave Bowe, C. (1987), '*Purgatorio* 19: Adrian V', in *Dante Readings*, ed. E. Haywood (Dublin: Irish Academic Press), pp. 123–42.

Sorrell, R. D. (1988), *St Francis of Assisi and Nature: Tradition and Innovation in Western Christian Attitudes toward the Environment* (New York and Oxford: Oxford University Press).

Southern, R. W. (1970), *Western Society and the Church in the Middle Ages, Pelican History of the Church*, vol. 2 (Harmondsworth: Penguin Books).

Speculum perfectionis seu S. Francisci Assisiensis Legenda Antiquissima, ed. P. Sabatier (1898) (Paris: Fischbacher).

Stäuble, A. (1995), 'La tenzone di Dante con Forese Donati', *Letture classense* 24, 151–70.

Stein, J. (1976), 'Dating the Bardi St Francis Master Dossal: Text and Image', *Franciscan Studies* 36, 271–95.

Stephens, J. N. (1972), 'Heresy in Medieval and Renaissance Florence', *Past and Present* 54, 25–60.

Sternfeld, R. (1905), 'Der Kardinal Johann Gaetan Orsini', in *Historische Studien* 52 (Berlin: Ebering).

Sticca, S. (1991), 'Italy: Liturgy and Christocentric Spirituality', in *The Theatre of Medieval Europe: New Research in Early Drama*, ed. E. Simon (Cambridge University Press), pp. 169–88.

Stubblebine, J. H. (1985), *Assisi and the Rise of Vernacular Art* (New York: Harper & Row).

Swanson, R. N. (1995), *Religion and Devotion in Europe, c.1215–c.1515* (Cambridge University Press).

Szittya, P. R. (1986), *The Antifraternal Tradition in Medieval Literature* (Princeton, N.J. Princeton University Press).

Thomson, W. R. (1972), 'The Earliest Cardinal-Protectors of the Franciscan Order', *Studies in Medieval and Renaissance History* 9.

Tierney, B. (1980), *The Crisis of Church and State 1050–1300* (New York: Simon and Schuster; repr. Toronto: University of Toronto Press, 1988).

Tierney, B. (1988), *Origins of Papal Infallibility 1150–1350: A Study on the Concepts of Infallibility, Sovereignty and Tradition in the Middle Ages* (Leiden: Brill).

Tocco, F. (1902), *Lectura Dantis Orsanmichele: Il canto xxxii del 'Purgatorio'* (Florence: Sansoni).

Tocco, F. (1903), 'I primordi francescani nella *Divina Commedia*', *Giornale dantesco* 11, 162–70.

Tocco, F. (1910), *La questione della povertà nel secolo xiv* (Naples: Perrella).

Torri, A. (1892), *see* Lancia, Andrea.

Toynbee, P. J. (1921), *Dante Studies* (Oxford: Clarendon Press).

Toynbee, P. J. (1966), *see* Dante Alighieri.

Turley, T. (1989), 'John XXII and the Franciscans: A Reappraisal', in *Popes, Teachers and Canon Law in the Middle Ages*, ed. J. R. Sweeney and S. Chodorow (Ithaca, New York: Cornell University Press), pp. 74–88.

Ubertino da Casale (1485, repr. 1961), *Arbor vitae crucifixae* (Turin: Bottega d'Erasmo).
Ubertino da Casale (ed. F. Ehrle) (1886), *Sanctitati apostolicae* (1311), *ALKG* 2, 374–416.
Ubertino da Casale (ed. F. Ehrle) (1887), *Sanctitas vestra* (1310), *ALKG* 3, 48–89.
Ubertino da Casale (ed. F. Ehrle) (1887), *Rotulus iste* (1310), *ALKG* 3, 89–130.
Ubertino da Casale (ed. F. Ehrle) (1887), *Decretalis etiam* (1310), *ALKG* 3, 130–5.
Ubertino da Casale (ed. F. Ehrle) (1887), *Declaratio fratris Ubertini de Casali et sociorum eius contra falsitates* (1311), *ALKG* 3, 160–95.
Ubertino da Casale (ed. A. Heysse) (1917), *Super tribus sceleribus* (1311), *AFH* 10, 103–74.
Ullmann, W. (1974), *A Short History of the Papacy in the Middle Ages* (London: Methuen).
Vallone, A. (1965), *Studi sulla 'Divina Commedia'* (Florence: Olschki).
Vallone, A. (1988), *Antidantismo politico e dantismo letterario* (Rome: Bonacci).
Vallone, A. and Scorrano, L.: *see* Dante Alighieri.
Vasina, A. (1982), 'Dante di fronte ad Avignone', *Letture classensi* 9/10, pp. 173–89.
Villani, Giovanni (ed. G. Aquilecchia) (1979), *Cronica, con le continuazioni di Matteo e Filippo (scelta)* (Turin: Einaudi).
Villani, Giovanni (ed. G. Porta) (1990–1), *Nuova Cronica* (3 vols.) (Parma: Guanda).
Vinay, G. (ed.) (1950): *see* Dante Alighieri.
Watt, J. A. (1964), 'The Theory of Papal Monarchy in the Thirteenth Century', *Traditio* 20, 179–317.
Wenzel, S. (1982), 'The Wisdom of the Fool', in *The Wisdom of Poetry*, ed. L. D. Benson and S. Wenzel (Kalamazoo, Michigan: Medieval Institute)
Wieruszowski H. (1971), *Politics and Culture in Medieval Spain and Italy* (Rome: Edizioni di Storia e Letteratura).
Willemsen, C. A. (1927), *Kardinal Napoleon Orsini (1263–1342), Historische Studien* 172.
Wolf, K. B. (2003), *The Poverty of Riches: St Francis of Assisi Reconsidered* (Oxford and New York: Oxford University Press).
Zambrini, F. S. (1865), *Scelta di curiosità letterarie inedite o rare dal secolo xii al xvii* (Bologna: n.p.).

Index

CAMBRIDGE STUDIES IN MEDIEVAL LITERATURE

1 Robin Kirkpatrick *Dante's Inferno: Difficulty and Dead Poetry*
2 Jeremy Tambling *Dante and Difference: Writing in the "Commedia"*
3 Simon Gaunt *Troubadours and Irony*
4 Wendy Scase *"Piers Plowman" and the New Anticlericalism*
5 Joseph Duggan *The "Cantar De Mio Cid": Poetic Creation in its Economic and Social Contexts*
6 Roderick Beaton *The Medieval Greek Romance*
7 Kathryn Kerby-Fulton *Reformist Apocalypticism and "Piers Plowman"*
8 Alison Morgan *Dante & the Medieval Other World*
9 Eckehard Simon (ed.) *The Theatre of Medieval Europe: New Research in Early Drama*
10 Mary Carruthers *The Book of Memory: a Study of Memory in Medieval Culture*
11 Rita Copeland *Rhetoric, Hermeneutics and Translation in the Middle Ages: Academic Traditions and Vernacular Texts*
12 Donald Maddox *The Arthurian Romances of Chrétien de Troyes: Once and Future Fictions*
13 Nicholas Watson *Richard Rolle and the Invention of Authority*
14 Steven F. Kruger *Dreaming in the Middle Ages*
15 Barbara Nolan *Chaucer and the Tradition of the "Roman Antique"*
16 Sylvia Huot *The "Romance of the Rose" and its Medieval Readers: Interpretations, Reception, Manuscript Transmission*
17 Carol M. Meale (ed.) *Women and Literature in Britain, 1150–1500*
18 Henry Ansgar Kelly *Ideas and Forms of Tragedy from Aristotle to the Middle Ages*
19 Martin Irvine *The Making of Textual Culture: Grammatica and Literary Theory, 350–1100*
20 Larry Scanlon *Narrative, Authority and Power: the Medieval Exemplum and the Chaucerian Tradition*
21 Erik Kooper *Medieval Dutch Literature in its European Context*
22 Steven Botterill *Dante and the Mystical Tradition: Bernard of Clairvaux in the "Commedia"*
23 Peter Biller and Anne Hudson (eds.) *Heresy and Literacy, 1000–1530*
24 Christopher Baswell *Virgil in Medieval England: Figuring the "Aeneid" from the Twelfth Century to Chaucer*
25 James Simpson *Sciences and Self in Medieval Poetry: Alan of Lille's "Anticlaudianus" and John Gower's "Confessio Amantis"*
26 Joyce Coleman *Public Reading and the Reading Public in Late Medieval England and France*
27 Suzanne Reynolds *Medieval Reading: Grammar, Rhetoric and the Classical Text*
28 Charlotte Brewer *Editing "Piers Plowman": the Evolution of the Text*
29 Walter Haug *Vernacular Literary Theory in the Middle Ages: The German Tradition in its European Context*

30 Sarah Spence *Texts and the Self in the Twelfth Century*
31 Edwin Craun *Lies, Slander and Obscenity in Medieval English Literature: Pastoral Rhetoric and the Deviant Speaker*
32 Patricia E. Grieve *"Floire and Blancheflor" and the European Romance*
33 Huw Pryce (ed.) *Literacy in Medieval Celtic Societies*
34 Mary Carruthers *The Craft of Thought: Meditation, Rhetoric, and the Making of Images, 400–1200*
35 Beate Schmolke-Hasselman *The Evolution of Arthurian Romance: The Verse Tradition from Chrétien to Froissart*
36 Siân Echard *Arthurian Narrative in the Latin Tradition*
37 Fiona Somerset *Clerical Discourse and Lay Audience in Late Medieval England*
38 Florence Percival *Chaucer's Legendary Good Women*
39 Christopher Cannon *The Making of Chaucer's English: a Study of Words*
40 Rosalind Brown-Grant *Christine de Pizan and the Moral Defence of Women: Reading Beyond Gender*
41 Richard Newhauser *The Early History of Greed: the Sin of Avarice in Early Medieval Thought and Literature*
42 Margaret Clunies Ross *Old Icelandic Literature and Society*
43 Donald Maddox *Fictions of Identity in Medieval France*
44 Rita Copeland *Pedagogy, Intellectuals, and Dissent in the Later Middle Ages: Lollardy and Ideas of Learning*
45 Kantik Ghosh *The Wycliffite Heresy: Authority and the Interpretation of Texts*
46 Mary C. Erler *Women, Reading, and Piety in Late Medieval England*
47 D. H. Green *The Beginnings of Medieval Romance: Fact and Fiction 1150–1220*
48 J. A. Burrow *Gestures and Looks in Medieval Narrative*
49 Ardis Butterfield *Poetry and Music in Medieval France: From Jean Renart to Guillaume de Machaut*
50 Emily Steiner *Documentary Culture and the Making of Medieval English Literature*
51 William Burgwinkle *Sodomy, Masculinity and Law in Medieval Literature*

Lightning Source UK Ltd.
Milton Keynes UK
UKHW012241221220
375475UK00009B/208

9 780521 099042